"In *Home Boys*, Anthony DiMatteo—accomplished poet, classicist, translator and Shakespearean—takes us into a troubled world of homeless children in New York City during the late seventies and early eighties. This is a very sad time for lost children and for those in-house counselors who, like DiMatteo, attempt to rescue them from abandonment, drugs, sex-trafficking and hopelessness. To be sure, there is much to rue in this book. But all is not lost. Almost miraculously, *Home Boys* leaves us not with despair but with redemption, borne of the author's decade-long commitment to the challenges of the work and, especially, his rare talent at writing a compelling and deeply moving narrative."

— Marvin W. Hunt, author of *Among the Children of the Sun* and *Looking for Hamlet*

"In his deeply resonant memoir, Anthony DiMatteo investigates what the endeavor to help others entails. While working for more than a decade as a live-in supervisor of a boys group home in New York City (and teaching literature classes in prison for a public college), he discovers the vast gap between the desire to support disadvantaged children and the reality of doing so, marked by compromise and confrontation. As pressures mount, he struggles to maintain his marriage and honor his path as a scholar while offering the boys the sort of kindness and support they would not receive elsewhere. *Home Boys* is a thoughtful and humanist book that will stir readers to reflect on our common values and lives."

— Anatoly Molotkov, author of *A Broken Russia Inside Me* and numerous poetry collections

Home Boys

Home Boys

Anthony DiMatteo

First Edition

Library of Congress Control Number: 2025948854

Casebound ISBN: 978-1-62720-629-7
Paperback ISBN: 978-1-62720-630-3
Ebook ISBN: 978-1-62720-631-0

Design by Leo Arcelay-Christiano
Editorial Development by Colleen Bayley
Promotional Development by Colleen Bayley

Cover painting: *Empathy*, with the generous permission of the artist, Gérard DuBois

Published by Apprentice House Press

Loyola University Maryland
4501 N. Charles Street, Baltimore, MD 21210
410.617.5265
www.ApprenticeHouse.com
info@ApprenticeHouse.com

This book is dedicated to the more than 30,000 children who received preventive services in 2024 according to NYC.gov

Contents

Foreword

For all their help in the writing of this book, I'd like to thank Manuel Andújar, Robert Guidice, Lucy Panepinto, Andrea Doelger, Al Coleman, Thad Cook, Sebastian Restifo, Laury Magnus, Amanda Golden, Elaine Brown, Luis Navia and Marvin Hunt. Without these people, there'd likely be no *Home Boys.* Some in that list might be surprised to find themselves named here at the very beginning of this book (this is no place to puzzle the question of beginnings since I am writing this foreword last). But all provided me with different motives for writing *Home Boys*. That took me more than twenty years to do so patience has been crucial. This virtue among many others has been especially shown by my wife Kathleen O'Sullivan who has heard over and over many of the stories told in the pages ahead. Her belief in the book was often greater than I could summon. She kept me going.

What hampered me most was figuring out how to respect the privacy of the more than hundred boys who lived with me in the group home or came under my supervision over the course of ten years. And what of the members of the staff and my own family? And what of the narrator, my persona? How little did I know of him then when I lived through events that he tells a version of here.

To give some due to the different realities of so many life stories, I transposed and telescoped things that happened over many years in some cases and with different details than given here. If people only half-recognize themselves in their recall of how things happened, I have succeeded. I loosely drew upon my experiences and that of the boys'. However, I think all that is told in *Home Boys* could have happened given what did happen. Being scrupulous in that regard was the hardest of challenges. For how well the book meets it, I bow to the discretion of my readers.

The overwhelming reality - the suffering of children - remains. All children need the greatest support that we can muster. Success in that regard is the ultimate measure of who we are as people. I hope this book moves us to make the future brighter for the children in our own lives, our communities and our cities.

Chapter 1

Dream Pieces

Some nights the faces will not stop. The boys invade my own childhood. They appear in the hallway outside my bedroom, waking me, telling me to clear the room, get ready for some fun. I can barely recall the house I grew up in without seeing them there too, hanging onto banisters, rummaging through the attic, bouncing spaldeens off the brick wall. Yet how different the places of our childhoods, mine, a maple-lined section of the north Bronx, theirs mostly scattered along the Northeast coast off strip malls or in public housing or temporary dwellings. I entered their lives as their group home supervisor. How little did I realize then that they would change my life and my whole view of the world. Where to begin? How to tell another person's life story?

One sixteen-year-old boy who came to the home claimed to have been picking cotton for a couple of years in different places down South. "I put to work real good." When eight years old, he had been thrown out of his house in Georgia by his alcoholic father, his mother long dead, and became attached to migrant farm workers. It's hard to believe a child can live this way.

Dion challenged understanding in other ways. Having lived outside for so long, he had taken up a lifestyle that included mistrust of bathrooms. He would defecate in our plants, especially the large rubber plant, burying until the ample pot soil could no longer cover the smell. He was found out as I returned to the home late one rainy night. "Don't like the water rolling like that," he told me. This child needed a "more secure environment" as the Bureau of Child Welfare termed it then. He was sixteen going on four in some obvious ways, but also on fifty, with a bad back and knees and a life-experience far beyond his years. He'd humbly wait until everyone's dinner plate was full before he'd take his, mostly with his hands. How could I help him? His needs were too great for our home. At my request, the agency social worker transferred him after three weeks to an upstate facility for the mentally impaired. I never heard what happened to him. Where is he now?

Dion's is one of many voices in my dreams. I moved out of the home more than a decade ago. It still breathes inside me.

Twelve-year-old Pedro I recall again and again even though he too lived with us for only a few weeks. The BB, some gang in upper Manhattan, had claimed him as their own. At nine, the boy's mother died of cirrhosis and his alcoholic father constantly beat him up, his way of driving the boy out of their small apartment on 114th Street. I imagine Pedro leaving home for the last time.

"So that's it, old beanbag, I'm outta here, my boys gonna size me up."

"What did you say to me, you loco piece of shit?"

But Pedro would not answer his father, already past the hallway with the common bathroom and its missing outside wall, down a dark staircase and over the crumbling brick stoop. He ran off victorious, defiant, his father's cash now in his pocket, in the other pocket, a dozen or so vials of crack he had managed to pilfer over the last few weeks running errands for the Bling Boys or whatever they call themselves. Crack was fairly new then, selling in tons through little carriers and little vials. It cracked lives, young and old.

The boy's dream of independence fell apart a year later. He was found shivering on the street from December cold by a social worker. The nice old woman down the street who had often taken Pedro in had died, and the gang he worked for was after him for skimming and some "moonlighting" work he had done for a rival group. Alone, cold and starving, Pedro gave in to the social worker and was placed in my group home.

I recall how nervous he was in the required "new arrival interview," sitting with me one Tuesday night in the counselor's room in the basement, smiling wildly from across my desk.

"Mr. D, I love it here. The guys are down and the rooms tight. O my God, the food. You be living it here."

He told me he had never done crack, only ran errands for the guys who sold it to survive the streets. Crack was something I had read of in the papers (this was 1984) but had yet to connect it to twelve-year olds with big puppy dog eyes like Pedro had. "I want to stay here real bad, Mr. D." So I read him the rules, about having to go to school, and do homework, at least one daily chore in the house and his own laundry. "Don't worry, we'll show you how," I assured him, seeing his look of panic he made when he glanced over at the large washer machine and dryer in the corner. I told him he had to come home every day directly after school, no hanging out. Pedro sheepishly grinned as if I saw right through him. He had to come to dinner with everyone else at 6:00 and be in bed by 9:30. I was his supervisor, living there all the time, and our four counselors were also there off and on all week to help him make our home his.

"We're kind of like a family here, Pedro. I've lived with most of the boys here for years, and we've seen lots of other kids come and go. You make it here by following a few simple rules and doing your best to get along with everyone. If it doesn't work out for you here, then we'll have to ask the Bureau people who may not have such luck finding you a place like this. Give us a chance, Pedro. I think you'll like it here."

This was my standard speech to new arrivals who would either end up fitting in with the six boys already in our home on a long-term basis or end up part of the transient population numbering almost a hundred over the course of my ten years of living there. The hardest part of my life, besides being on call seven days a week, was telling a child he needed more help than we could give. And there was pressure from above to keep a full house. "You've got 10 beds to fill, Tony," my agency director would tell me over and over. "You're at 8.6 per diem so far this year. We need to do a bit better to stay open." Calling in the count five mornings a week was to be placed at the top of our list of things to do "in the field" as if we were sizing up livestock or counting poppy heads.

As for this count, my home was always compared to the boys group home right next door to us. Which home had a higher rate of occupancy? It was like an endless horse race. In terms of population and architecture, the two homes were mirror-images of each other, occupying the same two-story rectangular brick structure divided by an inner wall, semi-attached as it were, a double-two family side by side. On my side of the brick block were five bedrooms for the boys, three on the first floor and two on the second. On the first floor was also a kitchen, living and dining room, and a bath and a half. The supervisor's separate apartment was on the second floor, at the head of the front entry stairwell. A finished basement had a laundry, tv and counselor rooms.

I recall the first day my family and I moved into the home. My wife Lisa liked the clean, spacious apartment and felt relieved the boys were so polite. Ariana, our three-year old, was thrilled.

"Boys stay with us, mommy?"

"Yes, in the same house...but not here inside with us."

Ariana pinched her brows together. Lisa tried again.

"They're not part of our family where you, me and Daddy live."

Lisa and I grimaced. First thing we did was install a childproof lock on the inside of our front door to keep Ariana from wandering. This was a constant worry. But things went well those first weeks. The boys were respectful and thoughtful, trying to make sure we liked it there. Fernando and John set the tone.

"How are you today, Miss Lisa? You need help with those packages?"

"Mister D, want me to peel those potatoes?"

Lisa soon found full-time work as a librarian in a nearby hospital. When I couldn't be home with Ariana, I'd leave her with the wife of another group home supervisor, a babysitting service she provided through the agency. The boys and I hit it off right away. We'd knock heads playing sports up the block in a schoolyard, and they loved my Italian cooking. We were tapping each other up in the hallways.

"Yo Mr. D, what up?"

"We good," I'd say. "Tap."

I thought I knew the score. The supervisor I replaced had burned out, but what has been need not set in stone what might be. Or so I thought, mangling a poem by Lao-Tze. The past weighs. How much? Our make-shift family lived in the once prosperous village of Port Richmond on Staten Island. On the map, the village mimics the whelk shape of the whole island as if it too were formed by the sea.

The home was on a corner a couple of blocks from Richmond Avenue at the village's tail end, close to the highway. Once a thriving dock and rail hub in the region, the namesake port at the head of the whelk had long since fallen into disuse.Cargo ships and freighters lay rotting in the horribly polluted Kill Van Kull which separates Staten Island from Port Elizabeth, New Jersey, at the southern end of Newark Bay. Houses fan out south of the port in rectilinear plots of land stretching west to the expressway that leads to the Bayonne Bridge and the oil refineries that surround it, smelling up our air if the wind blew the fumes our way. The largely blue-collar population of the neighborhood lived in modest one- and two-family homes on small lots close together with a bit of backyard. Whites and Hispanics, mostly Mexican, made up eighty percent of the population, two bodegas for every one supermarket. Segregation was *de facto,* mostly white in the more affluent southern half of Port Richmond, mostly Latino and black along the Richmond Terrace area along the dilapidated shoreline. The weight of the past could be seen on every street.

The two group homes side by side on the corner were like a miniature version of the neighborhood in this regard. The staff were mostly white, the residents mostly Hispanic.

Our new placement Pedro fit in very nicely at first, too nicely as I was to find out. Two of the long-term boys, Jimmy and Juan, told me he was "OK. Just another amigo lookin' for help." "He even likes Devon." Devon was a fourteen-year-old who had come from Brooklyn Family Court. He stuttered and twitched a lot, and the other boys made fun of him. Pedro seemed to enjoy getting him to laugh.

"So Dev, where you from yo?"

"Ain't nowhere really, ain't no place you'd know."

"I'm from the city streets. Yeah, like, no peace."

"Mr. Kevin says you been sleepin' in the street."

"Yeah, my aunt died and I had to hide out and stuff."

"Why'd you have to hide? Why she die? She killed?"

"No, dude, she was takin' care of me and, like, the cops knew who I was workin' for. But what do you mean nowhere. I bet I heard where you from."

"Olive, Texas."

"There ain't no olive in Texas."

"So I don't know where I lived?"

"You couldn't fit in no olive, Devie, your eyes too droopy but I like you anyway."

Pedro pulled Devon's hat over his face and ran out the door into the new snow. The chase was on. Devon lit up with glee from all the attention, and Pedro's bolting outside at 9pm was sign of a new kind of play in the house that Devon was finally let in on. The brothers Fernando and José came up onto the landing just as the two were hitting the door.

"Yo, guys, watch where you runnin."

"I knew it, these two right away. Now Devil-D gonna go off."

"What the hell's going on out there?" the counselor yelled out from the kitchen.

"See now Mr. K's gonna get loud. Don't mess around with his Friday night, D-D man."

But Fernando had called out to the two already disappearing round the house into the night.

"Mr. K," José dutifully informed, "the new kid and Devie be gone."

"Yeah well, they better not get lost. I don't feel like making any big reports."

"Mr. D coming back tonight?"

"No, they're gone for the weekend."

"He didn't give me allowance."

"José, stop whining, OK, I'll take care of you tomorrow when I get change. Do the stairs, OK? Don't put it off like last weekend."

"Yeah but with all the snow all the guys gonna track it up so I should wait till later."

Fernando went down the hall into his very neat room to leave all the typical confusion behind. Friday nights were always a little crazy, especially now that everyone would know the supervisor was gone. Kevin was a flexible guy who always had the house under control when I came back on Sundays, those few weekends we could get away. The boys had figured him out. Just avoid making a lot of noise when his girlfriend was there and Friday nights could really swing. But by Sunday, get your shit together. Fernando loved to play all kinds of music in his room when he could just close the door, be alone and organize his room to the rhythm. His brother José, actually his half-brother, was more into a little mischief on Fridays, getting on the counselor's nerves with Mr. D away as if he craved a man's attention. The pranks and tough-guy posing were José's modest way of living it up.

The new boys Charlie, Robby and Stephen were already deep into their Friday-night routine. Charlie was in his room listening to Kiss, a little stoned, and drifting into fantasies about little girls on buses as we were to find out. Robby and Stephen were off in the woods a few blocks away, a tangle of overgrowth in a large vacant lot surrounded by abandoned houses on the Port Richmond shore. They were sucking down marijuana smoke, exhilarated by their crazy prospects of adventures that would never happen.

"I'm heading down south again, gonna get me a job and just live a gypsy again. You know, a gypsy like Hendrix.

"More like dummy Dion. Yo, Steppie," Robby taunted, "you want that road freedom but you like food, remember?"

"Fuck food. I'm as good a thief as anyone. I can outslick the slickest."

Sixteen-year-old Stephen after he left his uncle's care had wandered up and down the east coast as a male prostitute, shoplifter, and then errand boy for a drug group in Baltimore, whatever "work" he could get that didn't involve staying put in one place. Both parents had died when he was five in a car accident. The car had flipped into a ditch and took down a telephone pole. They died the way they lived - apparently loving to destroy each other, from what I could make out from the case record about them, with drug abuse involved. Stephen ended up in an uncle's house in Florida that burned down one night from a torch dropped on the floor during a party. His uncle was severely burned and had to be hospitalized. Stephen, ten years old then, decided to try a life on his own. He knew two older boys living in a cabin in the middle of nowhere and he decided to join them. So began a five-year life of vagrancy and entanglements with all kinds of people usually met on the side of a road or in gas stations. He had survived all this until in Newark, New Jersey, he had been tied up by a john and beaten into a coma. His story made the back pages of the *Staten Island Advance* because a Family Court judge had gotten involved, answering the appeal of the doctor who was treating him in the hospital. The "lost teen" as the paper called him ended up in the judge's court and was placed in our home at the explicit designation of his honor. Now Stephen felt immune to the rules of the home, having a judge in his pocket as he thought.

Robert or Robby as he called himself was another story altogether. He had lived on Staten Island his whole life. His parents hadn't been together for long. At first he lived with his mother who had many boyfriends. Some would stay for a month, some for a year. All of them had become his father for those periods of time.

His mother worked several part time jobs and was hardly ever home. Robby was basically raised by his maternal grandmother, and when his mother disappeared one day, he moved into his grandmother's house for good. She eventually realized she could not deal with his constant hanging out and his two to three-day disappearances. Finally, she took out a petition at the Family Court, and the same Judge Gedy who had Stephen placed designated my home for Robby. For some reason, the Judge loved my home. Both boys were tall, blonde haired, blue eyed and Irish, perhaps the reason motivating his honor's personal involvement. The judge called my home regularly to speak to both boys and me or my counselors to check on their progress. One time he just walked into the home to see for himself. Coming down the stairs to the front hall, I was shocked to see him there unannounced and so early in the morning. I was still in my bathrobe, sipping coffee.

"Just thought I'd drop in to see how the boys are doing."

"Excuse me, your honor, I wasn't expecting you."

He looked at my outfit.

"As you can see, Judge, in this house, I wear the robes."

The words were no sooner out of my mouth when the two boys bolted out the door.

"Why aren't Stephen and Robert in school?"

"They're late for school again, hanging out in the house. Thanks for the help busting them, your honorable."

This one Friday night was moving fast, all the boys doing their thing with the arrival of Kevin's girlfriend Sandy. She admired Kevin for his work with children, and as all the guys knew, was given to showing her love for him openly while he was on duty. The two had already settled down to watch television in the basement lounge room when Pedro and Devon returned at 10pm.

"Yo, check this out," Devon directed Pedro, "follow me."

The two left the house again to swing round the back into a dark driveway. Quietly moving garbage cans out of the way, Devon crouched down to look through a small basement window.

Giggling behind his hand, he whispered, "Check this out, P, check it, check it." Pedro knelt down into the darkness and saw Kevin and Sandy begin petting. She was sitting next to him on the couch, his hand on her thigh, hers on his, and they were kissing now and then as they "watched" TV.

"Yo man, are they gettin hot yet?"

"You crazy, man, doing this stuff, we're gonna get caught. Mr. K get pissed."

"Yeah but c'mon, she's got titties. Be cool man. Watch. Like no one supposed to know she's taken it off under her blouse."

"Oh dang, he lickin her neck now."

"See man I knew you'd get into it. Let me see."

Moving Pedro out of the way, Devon knocked a garbage can lid on the cement. Kevin shot to his feet and ran up the basement stairs. Pedro was about to bolt down the street but Devon grabbed him, making him follow him up and over the first floor terrace above them and into the living room. By the time Kevin returned from round the house, the two were already in front of the first floor TV, drinking lemonade.

"What the hell was that noise?"

"Must be that raccoon again, Mr. K, messin with the cans."

"I don't want you guys outside anymore tonight, OK? And stay here or in your room, don't come downstairs. If you need something, call down, OK? Any bullshit from you two, and you're in your room tomorrow."

Kevin made a quick tour of the house, looking in on Charlie and Fernando. Not finding José, he went back into the living room where José had suddenly appeared. Satisfied all was quiet on the front, Kevin went downstairs.

"Yo Devie, Mr. KK's all red face again."

"That's right, José, they're smootchin it up."

"Yo Pedro, do my stairway for me? Maybe you can catch a peek at her on the bottom stairs - just look through the crack in the door."

"I ain't into that stuff, I got my own girl in the city, but I'll do the stairs for you if you want. I owe you, right?"

"Oh yeah, you owe me big time. Mr. D sure as hell put you out if he knew."

And so another weekend rolled on in teen city. My own family of three had escaped to the country of the seven-lakes region in Rockland County. The hordes of city kids that descended on the woods and lakes reminded me that there was no escape from our escape.

"The world's become a playground with supermarkets. Or maybe it's one big parking lot with mobile homes and tent sites, a detention camp, a global reformatory. I forget which one. I've got to read the papers more."

Half-listening to me, my wife Lisa settled a little deeper into her novel at the lakeside. She anticipated the cavalcade of droll remarks that were usually sure to follow a cynical lament. But I spared her this time, wandering off a mile into the woods along the shore, disturbing the geese who had found their weekend refuge there, driven off by all the Frisbees and yelping kids. Among green moss and copious geese remains, I sat on a lichen-covered rock, cleaning my bespattered sneakers under tangled spruce and fir, the noise at the beach barely audible.

The distant activity seemed another version of the way water moves or the wind whips. My self-talk always went from idealism to skepticism.

"I guess working at the home is as serious a job as can be.

So pin a medal on yourself. Tag. You're it. Someone's got to account for our human remains. If you've got a whole lot of cars, someone's got to pump the gas. If you've got a whole lot of abandoned kids, well, there you go."

The dissertation I was writing on ancient myth seemed plausible in this light too.

"If there's so many things believed in, well, there's got to be a real story why behind some of them you would think. We can't be duped into foolishness all the time. On the other hand, it's harder to convince a fool he's been fooled than for him to be fooled or something like that. Was it Twain or Brecht who turned the phrase?"

I shook my head. I lost track of why I went off to join the geese, but had ended up growing a little hopeful, thus storing up more reason to be idealistic, briefly followed by drollery. Cycles.

"We're a mote in the eye of God. Or perhaps lower down the sacred body. We're a single strand of hair on his shoe or maybe a kind of ballcap the gods used to wear until we were discarded into the foul ashbin of progress like the Mets."

There was a faint light in deep shadow below the trees where the shoreline turned rocky and high across the way. The sun could not penetrate my overhung spot. The soft haze of light and dark momentarily squelched my melancholic need to explain things to myself. I wandered back among squawking geese regathering behind me. The whole group home thing was driving me further into cynicism and sadness than I knew was good for my sanity or my marriage. It was a crazy life for the best cause. I felt I was beginning to drown.

We drove back in worried silence. This would prove a typical frame of mind whenever we returned to the home after a brief respite. My wife had bravely gone from altar to group home, as if marrying me had meant placement with our daughter. The anxieties I would feel for the three of us every Sunday night made me jittery at the wheel as I wondered what had gone on in the home. But I refused to be on call seven days a week unless there was some urgent issue. Though I would phone the counselor once a day any weekend spent away, we had to reconcile ourselves to surprise or even shock upon returning. I recall one Sunday night we entered a dark restful home. I thanked the counselor who told me all was ok, all the kids in home and in bed. He handed me the keys and left. I quickly read his entry in the logbook we were mandated to keep and opened a light in the kitchen. It sparkled as did the floor and stairwell. Before I went into my separate apartment, I opened the upstairs bedroom door right next to it and found an older boy Juan gingerly sodomizing another. The younger boy seemed not to have the foggiest idea of what was going on while the other boy ran behind the opened door pretending to be rearranging his bathrobe. This was before AIDS was known. I was at a loss about what to do other than have both seen the next day by a doctor, but the medical check-up would have to wait at least until my visit to the Board of Education to get one of the other kids into Special Education. Missing that appointment meant waiting who knows how long. I remember saying blandly to the two boys who shared the room,

"No more dancing tonight, guys, get to bed. If I hear anything in here you're both grounded for a week."

But I planned a long talk with Juan the next day and many there after besides the immediate trip to the doctor for both. I also had to move Sammie out of Juan's room. I knew I might as well tell flies not to bite as tell Juan not to frolic. Though I'd speak to little Sammie, he was probably going to suffer such dances all his life in institutions. He was "borderline retarded" the agency psychologist told me, using a label that even by the 1980's had gone out of favor. Sammie went along blithely with any activity, never responded to insult, and loved to laugh somehow at the right time, a real social power to incite general mirth whatever the psychologist's label implied. We were a make-shift family of jokers, jocks, lunatics and lovers, and Sammie had made his stand despite the horrific odds against him. His hillbilly father had once called me frantically at 2AM in the morning to tell me to leave ten thousand dollars in the Holland Tunnel by noon or he would blow up my apartment. I sleepily said "OK" and hung up the phone. I dreamt of the figure. Ten thousand? Why not charge a hundred? Is he going on vacation? Shouldn't I take one? Should I make a home visit? And why not the Lincoln Tunnel or a pizza store? In the morning, I felt both amused and outraged. When I told Jimmy, Sammie's older brother, what his father had said, he looked down at the floor and smirked.

"Ten thousand all he thinks we're worth? Dream on, Pops. I like it right here. Tell that to the judge next week, Mr. D. I ain't goin home."

To me, family court seemed a dream land, a smashed dream land, hushed voices speaking in codes, shifting, standing about, the endless dictation in sobbing rooms presided over by large portraits, dusty flags, a muted sun, a white man in robes. I had been to all the family courts in New York City, one in each borough, witness to the misery and innocence of girls and boys, as if I were a stranger, surrogate parent, mother goose and father time wrapped in one. Bound by the soft chains of my idealism, I had arrived at the hinterlands of the American family, its abandoned or tortured children like products from a dysfunctional factory, aberrant discharges from the nuclear unit of society, very uncelebrated people never made mention of in a newspaper much less appearing on the cover of *Time* or *Vogue*. Bound by one's own life and issues, it's easy to forget how we all walk in circles together, with each child's story a revelation of who we are, worth more than the Bible or the Constitution in terms of what it tells us about our actual values.

At the end of this one weekend, as I opened the door to Juan's sexual limbo, my wife dashed into our apartment behind me, Ariana in hand. "Come right in now, leave it for tomorrow as you promised," she reminded me. It was late, the house silent, and my wife had to scramble to bed for work tomorrow at the hospital. After making sure Sammie and Juan got back into their bunk beds, I sat for a while on the stairs, listening into the darkness, refusing to open any other doors in the maze of hallways. I vowed not to mention it to my wife who was very fond of Juan as I was too. He was always helpful and good humored. Now this. I was shaking. I checked into their room a few times that night, telling my wife I had a headache or had to pee.

At 7AM Fernando knocked on my apartment.

"Mr. D, sorry to bother you but you better come."

"What is it?"

"Devie's freaking out in the bathroom and Pedro's in there telling him to be quiet. They won't open the door."

I grabbed a butter knife, slipped it into the catch, and found Pedro holding Devie's head under cold water in the tub crying.

"I don't know, Mr. D, what's wrong with him. Help me."

Devie's eyes were spinning in his head and his knees were shaking.

"Yo Mr. D, look at this, look," Fernando called out from an adjacent bedroom. I went in to see on the floor some empty vials of crack that had tumbled out of a concealed spot in Pedro's suitcase. Devie had gotten high with Pedro. Within minutes, Pedro told me the sorry story that the city caseworker had yet to catch up with when he was placed in my home.

"I had them in my case 'cause of my old job, Mr. D. I ain't selling or using anything anymore, I ain't, Mr. D."

With no counselor set to arrive until 3pm, I waited for all the other boys to leave for school down the block and locked the house, taking Devon, Pedro and my daughter to the hospital so Devon could be examined in the emergency room. He was sedated and admitted for observation. I had to call his mother to let her know, but fortunately the medical authorization form I had had her sign was enough clearance for the doctors to medicate Devon. Devon's alcoholic mom was difficult to locate in the building complex where she lived and worked, ironically enough, in various apartments as a baby-sitter.

Pedro needed a more secure environment, probably detoxing and drug rehab. I couldn't afford to have him stoning out the house. Making the necessary phone calls to the Bureau of Child Welfare, I tried to explain to a desperate Pedro why I was driving him back to Lafayette Place in Manhattan.

"You need counseling, Pedro. That way you lived for so long has a hold on you, and you need to get clean of the drugs and the gang thinking. We'll take you back once I get the OK you're clean. It's just temporary, and we'll take you back when you're clean of the drug."

Of course, Pedro suspected we wouldn't.

"Please, Mr. D, I told Devie he shouldn't try that stuff. I only had a little piece left anyway and I didn't want to throw it out. I'm sorry. I smoke once in a while but I ain't cranked, Mr. D. You'll see. I won't do that stuff anymore. It's just the way I had to live. No more now, Mr. D, no more, I promise. Please, Mr. D, please, don't send me away."

My daughter in the backseat of the agency van just looked wide-eyed at the two of us, at my denial of Pedro's sobs and pleas to turn around, my staunch calm, and his total misery. For the first time in her life she was dumbstruck by sheer human suffering.

I managed to get Pedro into the elevator to the agency office by promising him he might not be away longer than a month depending on his success getting clean.

"Then you'll take back most of my bags, Mr. D, OK? I'll only need my backpack and a few clothes, right? Some of my things were stolen last time I was here. And you bought me all this nice stuff."

We shuffled in to see a social worker. We passed a few kids lying down on the floor in cots.

"See what I mean, Mr. D. Nothing's safe here. It's crazy."

Another social worker brought my daughter and me into a separate room, and I told her the story of Pedro's addiction, handing her my report.

"You have to realize I can't deal with it in a group home. Who knows how long he's been using or how much. He'll need to find access again to the stuff and I'm afraid of him or another child overdosing or freaking out. I feel horrible. He's a nice kid, but we can't risk the chance of his withdrawal on his own."

"Mr. Danilo, you see all the kids here - there's no place for them to go. No place. Since this crack hit the streets, I've never seen such devastation. As if things weren't bad enough. But OK, Mr. Danilo. I understand why Pedro needs a more secure setting. We'll do our best."

"I'm sure I'll get a new placement by the end of the week. There's a lot of kids out there my home can help. Pedro would just take too much of my staff's time from the other boys, and besides, the kid's probably got a full blown jones, and you know what that means."

She assured me she did. I felt a bit absolved but mostly sad and cruel. It looked like a lose, lose situation. Poor kid.

As my daughter and I headed to the elevator, the door to the office where Pedro was being interviewed opened. He saw me, not carrying out any of his baggage. He realized what was happening.

"Mr. D, no, no, don't leave, don't leave me here!"

He tried to scramble out of the office but the social worker restrained him. He was trying to hold onto the door as she pulled him back into the room. The elevator doors opened and closed, silencing his cry. I was stifling tears.

"Daddy, why are we leaving Pedro? He wants to come home with us. Why can't he, Daddy? I know you don't want to leave him here. Take him home, Daddy. Don't cry."

I cried a bit all the way down the street. Heads turned to watch the weeping adult led by a child.

Pedro will never fade from my mind. No hallway or lifetime could be long enough to still his plea. One long, strange day I would find out what happened to him, but for now my attention turned to another boy quickly placed in my home by week's end. I felt I had played God again with a child's life. All felt in ruins.

Chapter 2

The Willies

Sometimes hurricanes don't end. They show up at your door, bringing people who stay inside you all your life. Such was Willie, a Suma-wrestler of a child at twelve, 4 foot 3 tall, 140 lbs. Having been raised in a brothel in Georgia run by an aunt, Willie Moncado had seen quite a few things already. Right from the start his grin was infectious enough to take over the house, and his will to do what he wanted was strong enough to dent a wall, which he in fact did a few times in different rooms. Willie was large, willing, and able to drive whoever would be his master crazy and he was heading straight at me.

One of my counselors, Mr. Will, a huge green-eyed man from New Orleans who worked every other weekend, saw the signals right away as soon as Willie first arrived late Friday evening after I had already left for the weekend. He put Willie in Fernando's room where there was an empty bed. Mr. Will at my explanation also put a third bed in Tony and José's room where Sammie would sleep far away from Juan.

"Fernando, you keep an eye on Willie here and make him feel at home a little," Mr. Will said.

Mr. Will winked at Willie who laughed.

"Yes, I think you're going to like it here, maybe a little too much. We have really nice food here all the time. Just put your stuff on the bed for now. We'll sort that out later, but right now it's dinner time. Come get some of my down-home cooking."

He brought Willie down the hall. The house was already beginning to jump.

"Yo, you see the new kid. He's big enough to get stuck in a refrigerator."

"Think so? Well, Mr. Will makes him look like a jellybean. Mr. Will's a whole bag of `em."

"Man, those two get going ain't gonna be no food left."

Willie loved the place. He was laughing at all the food in the fridge as Will pointed it out. "All this for the weekend but you got to behave. If you do, you'll have a good time. You'll see."

"Who lives upstairs?" Willie asked, already having cased the joint.

"Oh, that's Mr. D's place, the supervisor. He's gonna give you a talk when he gets back Sunday. Heh, Jimbo, set the table for six."

Some of the boys had left for weekend visits home. I had told Will to keep an eye out on Jimmy and his brother Sammie. Jimmy's father, the same man who had called me about leaving money in the Holland Tunnel, had been seen driving around the neighborhood in an old Chevy Malibu waving a handgun. The two boys had to stay in the house so his father wouldn't abduct them. As I had asked him to, Will had called the police.

"That man's one crazy cowboy. Lord have mercy," he told the cop who came to take the report. It was just another weekend waiting to go off.

Willie dug into the spaghetti, piling it into his plate. He looked around sheepishly.

"What's wrong, boy? Go ahead. Eat up," Will told him. "You must be hungry after your long ride."

"Got some American cheese slices?" Willie asked.

"What you gonna do with slices, boy? This here is spaghetti sauce and you put grated cheese in it."

Willie got really quiet and looked down at the floor. Nicky said, "Oh I'll get him some."

Seventeen-year-old Nicky, though only a few months into his residency with us, had become like a lawyer for the boys. He was the bargainer who spoke from the side of his mouth. The boys called him "the sidewinder" after I had called him this when he knocked at my door to complain that the curfews were too early for Tony and Jimmy.

"What's this to you, Nick?"

"It's just, you know, kids need some fun at their age and I was hearing all the trouble about this..."

"Nick, are you supposed to be their Philadelphia lawyer, their main man with the boss man or something? I don't think so, Mr. Nicholas, Esquire. Stop the sidewinding. Mind your own p's and q's."

And so the name caught on. Nicky made subtle trouble always. He would become Willie's Defense Minister.

The assaults started at night. There were strange noises that would wake me up, the sound of something being grated, or a pipe being tapped, or a scratching noise. They seemed to come from different windows or under the floor, or even on the roof above my bedroom. My wife and I couldn't quite make them out. Once we thought we heard in the driveway something that sounded like sheets of rain. Then there was the invasion.

"Something's in the bed," Lisa said in the middle of the night.

"Please, you must be dreaming. Everything's OK."

"No, I felt something crawling."

"Come on, you're just...my God, you're right. There is something."

Lisa shot up like a rocket to jump on the bed.

"Hay, haay, get it out of here. Get it out."

A leg of the bed gave way and the mattress violently heaved down into the dresser, taking my wife with it like a landslide. I shot out of the bed to catch after a shadow that had run for the corner and grabbed it before it got into the closet. It was Fernando's hamster. I got the point immediately. I saw the door to my apartment had been opened, the chain lock still on, and the little demon had been let in. Hamster in hand, I walked downstairs into Fernando's room.

"What's up with this, Fernando?" I said as I opened the light and put the hamster directly in front of his sleeping nose.

"Mr. D, I told Willie to put it back. He didn't listen and I just fell asleep."

Willie was beneath blankets, suppressing laughter. He had gotten to me. The next day a search revealed instruments of agitation hidden behind the basement stairs, a wrench, a cheese grater, a hollow pipe, a sheet of tin, noisemakers for the midnight rambler Willie.

Despite the warnings issued to him, Willie persisted in after-hour pranks that quickly elevated into crime. Once he entered the high school down the block, he hooked up with some local kids to get a market of stolen goods together. Nothing serious at first, just the usual pilfering of student lockers, tape players, jackets, gloves, whatever. That was going on already and Willie somehow got into the middle of. The stuff started circulating in the house when Willie would wait for Fernando to fall asleep, creep out a window and pick up his loot out of the garbage bin where he kept it in a laundry bag. For his size, he was more nimble than Santa, jumping in and out of windows the way he would negotiate plate shuffling at dinner. He was taking it all in and sizing it up, all in a spirit of laughter and shenanigans. He was storing longer term wares in a basement closet.

Soon Willie decided to make the place really feel like home. After just three months in the neighborhood, he had made contacts. He managed to start sneaking meals out to a mentally challenged twenty-eight-year-old woman who lived down the block. Eventually, he convinced her to leave her house every other weekend when Mr. K. was preoccupied with his girlfriend, and sleep in the basement of the home where the guys would visit her at a price Willie negotiated. The basement was now a black market and bordello. I ran into the woman one drowsy Monday morning when I returned from a weekend escape a little earlier than planned. She was walking out the door as I entered. Eddie, Willie's begrudging lieutenant, immediately told me "Elvie" was there to visit Jimmy and was a friend of his father. Eddie had wanted to be the boss man of the home all along, but when Willie came on the scene, he had to relinquish any hopes to be chief cock of the walk in face of the obvious talents and know-how of the whirlwind child from Georgia. I woke up the sleeping counselor, still groggy from a night of petting, and asked him what he knew of this "Elvie" woman. "What do you mean? Who's that?" he asked. My search of the basement uncovered some blankets, a pillow, crusted plates of food in a closet, and a very used condom. My confronting the boys later that night met with a stony silence. Even Fernando knew nothing, he rightly claimed. Jimmy had never heard of any "Elvie." Finally, José told me she lived a couple of blocks away and visited Tony regularly. Tony denied he wanted her to visit him, laughing.

"Tee hee, tee hee, she's just hangin on me, Mr. D."

Willie sat with arms folded on the couch, waiting for the TV to be turned back on. I did not suspect his masterminding anything. I was gullible.

Eventually the story came out as did Willie's case-history, assembled together from a horde of social worker reports and court documents from several states.

Willie's parents were at times itinerant actors, circus performers or gypsies, wandering through the South, piecing together a living from performances of some kind and no doubt from petty larcenies of all types. They were road junkies trailing around their rapidly growing son. From what I could piece together, the father overdosed, and then the mother died in prison after her arrest for soliciting. Willie bounced around a bit, living with someone who called himself Uncle Maxie. The record was spotty, a home visit reported by a social worker responding to a truancy notice from a school in Georgia, a Court paper, an obituary, some letters. An aunt had written letters to various agencies begging for help. She worked hard, she wrote, too hard to care properly for him. He had been dropped off by Uncle Maxie for a visit with her and Maxie never came back. She was also rehabilitating herself and couldn't deal with a child. Meanwhile, over the months, Willie would say cryptic things to me that would eventually clarify as I came to understand him.

"I know how to honk the goose," he'd say, "from my aunt."

This meant, in his mind, how to find out what people really wanted from you. His aunt would probably say this whenever she finally got her boyfriends to pay her or support her habit. That she lived in a flophouse or brothel - I guess there is some difference - I found out when I called Atlanta to speak with a previous caseworker. Willie too told me of an endless parade of guys coming and going, some staying a couple of days, some just going from woman to woman, living there a month or so.

" 'Bout five or six ladies there, my aunt's friends, one of 'em she called sister."

He'd always be sent on errands. One time he hauled cages of chickens into the house that a john brought with him in a pick-up truck. Another time he kept a mule as a pet that some lover had hitched up to the backyard fence in the small town a few miles outside Atlanta where all this traffic in bodies and goods took place.

"Just one thing and another, always somethin" Willie told me raising, then dropping his arms. "The way things be."

Attempts had been made on Willie's life, I found out from the letters and the case-worker. One john had tried to drown the boy in the bathtub, a trauma that would come home to roost again in his life and in my life for reasons I will tell. Another customer tried to run him and his aunt down by driving a jeep onto the front porch where they were sitting. The aunt had called the guy's wife and complained about his sexual freeloading and beating her, and then running home to his family in time for dinner. I imagine aunt Rosy and Willie there, she waiting for some relief or justice to come, legs crossed, blowing the smoke of her cigarette nervously into a hot summer, seated one step higher than the nine-year-old under her hand, the child already strong enough to haul anything in or out, whatever it took to bring the day to an end, the jeep's race down the street attempting to launch them into the magnolia tree just another obstacle coming at him he had to get by. "No biggie," he'd say to me no matter what I caught him doing.

So with Elvie. "She was all alone, Mr. D., and I figured she needed to eat and have some friends. No harm done." Willie had simply invited her, the bought sex part of any normal home life to him, being nice to get nice.

The best talk Willie saved for Mr. Will who always brought out the stomach laughs in Willie. Their banter jolted into jolliness all in earshot for a moment no matter the mischief about.

"Man, Willie boy, you some kind of crazy bringing a woman here."

"Wouldn't do it to you, Mr. Will."

"No because you know I'd smell you and her out the door. Lord have mercy. You testing Mr. D's patience and there's no telling where you gonna end up if he send you away."

"As long as there's you Mr. Will, I'll be eatin my fill."

Sammie, Eddie, Nick and Tony were snickering at this, admiring Willie's confidence and Mr. Will's wide-eyed disbelief at the boy

"Sounds like you're too sure of yourself, Willie. Stop talking bull. And quit trying to get on my good side. I have none."

"But you sure got sides like me, Mr. Will."

Then even Mr. Will would cry out, "Good God almighty, Willie boy, you lunchin' with the devil now," and send him to his room for an "over and out" hour. "You can't talk right, you'll have to learn how to sit tight. Get a book there and go read it." Then with a sweep of his huge arm, he'd "x" the behavior chart on the fridge door next to Willie's name under the category "nastiness." Each mark meant reward or punishment although Willie seemed to confuse the two.

Nastiness applied to both verbal and health-related things, from funky feet to funky remarks. The boys thought the category funny but too subjective.

"I like my funkies, they're just me, Miss Sheila, so what's Mr. D. gonna tell me to brush for."

"'Cause next time he doesn't want the dentist to have to sandblast the petrified moss off your teeth, OK, John? Nasty is just common sense, and when the counselors or Mr. D. say it, it's nasty, plain and simple, an X. You guys just got to wash and speak clean with us, that's all."

John was a suspiciously friendly teen. In other words, he'd make people stand back from his long intimate stories which he would tell strangers as he stood there like a buoy rocking east to west, slightly shifting his weight to each foot. As the story would get to his favorite part, usually about something weird he noticed about his body, John would look up back and forth, side to side, at the ceiling directly above the person he was speaking to, sometimes making the person turn to look up, saying something like, "the back of my ears smells like the stuff between my toes." Ms. Sheila was a hefty no-nonsense woman of large capacities, humorous and vulgar in the better sense of the word. She spoke street wisdom to the kids and they respected her for it. While she was on duty 9 to 5, Monday through Friday, there was a heavy serenity in the house. She had clever eyes that would watch your mouth speak, and when you said something she thought funny, she'd turn her gaze to your eyes and say, "You got that right, ahunnn, ahunnn, you got that," shaking her head side to side as if she were in a Baptist church. She knew how to have fun with the boys and yet remain firm in her discipline of them. I don't know how she did it but her girth and merry intensity certainly helped to hold the guys in peaceful check.

One time I recall telling Sheila about John's trip to the doctor. John, despite or because of his bad hygiene, loved going to dentists, doctors, psychiatrists, anyone willing to pay him close mind. He had expressed this fondness once far too eagerly when I had brought him for a physical to our local doctor, Dr. Lina Guerino. She was a matronly woman from a family with political connections. She told me she was doing "a favor to God" by seeing the home kids, and she saw them in droves, both boys and girls, storing up the indulgences, I guess, for the privileged involvements of her family. Still, it was an act of kindness on her part whatever her motivation. Our agency had eight homes on the island. "Somebody has to see these poor children. Bring the big baby in here now," she told me, referring to John, without a change in her stiff tone or mood. She was always above board, the "big baby" just a description of John's hypochondria she was only too familiar with.

And so this particular examination proceeded at a brisk pace, with John standing, rocking, looking up, as she had him unbutton his shirt and drop his drawers. John complained of a "pain inside my ass full of constipation." This sent the doctor scurrying for her gloves, chalking up her droll fate to a need to do good works. "Come on, John, drop the underwear too." But John's briefs were too propped up for this and he looked at me with a big grin before his eyes shot to the ceiling above the doctor. She yanked the briefs off briskly and with a quick snap of a gloved finger struck down his rowdy membrum, disenchanting John. "Owww," John said, "that hurt." "Having to do it hurts even more. Just bend over and let me see." I took all this in, too dumbstruck to laugh. It was another John Manning story. Ms. Sheila heard it slapping her hands together.

"Man oh man, that boy John. You never know which way that kid's going to point, do you? Shoot. Just try something stupid like that with me and it's off into the meat sauce with him."

Fernando and I heard this and bent over sideways with laughter. John loved any story told about him, especially this one. He'd bob and weave with glee. I made sure to record the doctor visit into the mandatory daily log, for the sake of legal necessity and humor, an unlikely pair.

The arrival of Marcos into the same house with Willie was a turning point in my state of mind for the next twenty years. The bed became available when Eddie left to live with his aunt. The father had wanted Eddie back and the child wanted to return to their 123rd Street apartment in Manhattan, but my home visit there showed it was not possible. The alcoholic father had taken up residence on a bed in front of the kitchen sink while three children lived in two small bedrooms. There was only one large pot to cook in. The dog ate from it too whatever was left over. There was a bathroom in the corridor shared with two other apartments on the same floor. The bathroom's wall facing the open interior courtyard was half missing, making for a perilous and windy view of things, giving a twist to the idea of heeding nature's call. Eddie wanted to go back to this place but wasn't allowed. This is when an aunt luckily came forward for the boy. When his bed opened, Marcos arrived. Willie lost his part of his Defense Ministry and gained a loose cannon. Interconnected lives.

The one-man Mardi Gras was soon to swell. The rough night music continued in the alleyway, despite the confiscation of the noisemakers. Marcos became a slave of mayhem, performing Willie's commands. One night Lisa and I awoke to a cat's yelp in a clang of garbage pails. Somehow the lid of the can fell on the pail and trapped the cat inside. As I looked down from my window, I stupidly only half-suspected foul-play. Then there was the knocking one sleepy Saturday night beneath our bedroom, a few single hard knocks that went on and on minutes apart. It sounded like a broomstick poked into the ceiling below. I flew downstairs into José and Tony's room who had been roommates for two years and were somewhat responsible older teens, Tony more so compared to José who would soon call himself "Doctor Drop," planning to enter the Gold Glove Competition and practicing his air jab on anyone at any time. But that hadn't happened yet. Tony and José woke up from their drunken sleep startled into semi-awareness by the same thud that shook my wife and me. Willie, of course, was knocked out in a knot of blankets while his roomie, the oldest home boy Fernando, slept beneath neatly folded sheets. The new cherub Marcos was also asleep in a three-boy bedroom. So what does one do? Wake up eight boys at 3AM and start the inquiry? The counselor was sure to be passed out on the basement couch or in his room. Returning to my bed in this state - downcast head, the silly sense of one's sleep-induced dishevelment marching up the stairs, past the thriving rubber plant Dion had once defiled - made for a feeling of defeat. I stopped blankly to sit down at the top of the stairs. Who could even keep track of who was whom, the mind-blowing case-histories? So many had come and gone. At least, five boys who stayed for years thankfully had taken root, a blessing to us all. As I mused, I noticed the two amber-colored, rose-patterned windows of the large stairwell, and how they provided a soft moonlit backdrop for this moment of respite, a pretty picture in what now felt like some hovel in hell. Who has not known these places where one comes to hide for a minute from the line of duty if not from despair? A few dandelions in an alleyway behind a factory. A bird's nest high above a parking lot next to an office building. Such are a worker's brief reprieve.

I thought of my own dark cubicle in Manhattan at the agency's headquarters shared with seven other Staten Island group home supervisors. It seemed the further you were away from actual contact with the children, the higher your salary and the more space awarded for your office with windows facing out to 1st Avenue below, some daylight, some clouds. I recalled the voice and face of a woman at her surprise retirement party I had attended. She rose from the desk she had sat at for decades to thank everyone for their support, an assistant librarian for thirty-eight years at my wife's hospital and the mother of three and grandmother of four, her "other line of work," she proudly said. One could see the toll her job and life had taken, the slight haunch to her frame, her nervous attention to detail, the corsage given to her fiddled with until it sat exactly at the angle she wanted on her lapel. It wouldn't stay. I thought of her dusting all those bookshelves, her small frame going up and down, backwards and forwards, the ladder and table of books rolling, the hard-edged doctors standing over her, their operations of life and death looming, Mrs. Kutcheon's assistance meaningful only insofar as it forwarded their mission. All those male commands directed her way and her anxious replies. "OK, Dr. Answar." "Of course, Dr. Stends, give me a moment please."

To fall back asleep that night of the broomstick, I thought of the many people I knew who worked in some kind of institutional setting, counting them instead of sheep at 4AM in the morning. Like vines up a tree, wrinkles took over their youthful flesh turning it into corduroy. I dreamed of a clock's hands moving through dust like wind over sand, swirling it into a dark shadow. I watched myself turn into one hand, my wife the other. When the hands joined, they formed an opening into a warehouse storing a huge colorful hodgepodge of debris where children played. We clung together to the hands of the clock doing a slow dance to prevent losing ourselves in the warehouse we were in danger of dropping into. But we were both fascinated by the warehouse beneath us, and when I bent the hand of the clock my body had become to look into the hole where we were joined, I saw amidst the endless boxes neatly shelved and piled high above the drone-like workers on the floor, the home boys' bodies piled up on a special frame built to hold human packages. In the ceaseless cycle of production, the kids were being churned out like so much merchandise waiting for an order to come in. Then there were two loud knocks that I thought were ticks of the clock being shot off like grenades sending all the shelves and workers flying. I awoke to the dismal knowledge that the hazing beneath us continued. Such was one of our many broken nights.

The invasion of our bridal chamber would not stop. There would be more "tick-tocks" to the floor of my apartment, sometimes near the hallway door outside my bedroom, sometimes to the bathroom next to the bedroom, sometimes a Louis the Fourteenth shot directly beneath our bed. These would come in rapid succession or delayed by an hour or so, three to four nights a week. The full staff meeting with the boys confirmed mostly everyone had heard the knocks, except for the four boys who slept upstairs. One of the four, fourteen-year-old Juan was probably the sharpest kid in the house but was the frequent target of insult by the other boys. He was effeminate to their standards of macho maleness, the nylon doo-rag and white cream on his lips he put on as his routine preparation for bed not helping his male image in their eyes. Juan's love-making to the mentally challenged Sammie which I walked in on two years later when Juan was a slender hipped 16-year-old confirmed what Juan had denied since he had reached puberty. "It's OK to be different from some of the other boys," I told him. "Sports ain't your thing but you enjoy dancing, don't you? And you love art and music. Acting too, no?"

"But Mr. D., I'm not frigging gay like they say I am. I'm just more sensitive."

The culprits who really attacked Juan were usually new placements into the home although the friendlier teasing of the regulars was constant. Calling him by his nickname "Mr. Blackie Gays" made the staff mark up the nastiness column every week for everyone except Fernando who just rolled his eyes over the whole affair.

One day Juan told me he had seen Marcos scurrying about in the middle of the night when Juan got up to go to the bathroom downstairs. The bathrooms were a constant problem in the house.

My upstairs apartment had a full and a half bath, while downstairs, there was one and a half, the only ones accessible to the staff and "homies." This bad design privileged the supervisor's family and caused a log jam when it came to take showers especially when the home reached its capacity of ten boys. To change the arrangement meant losing the privacy of the supervisor's separate apartment. Might as well adopt all ten kids then and create our own tribe. Tribal rites certainly were in full swing anyway. Who could drive the supervisor and his wife nuts first appeared the mark of warriorship. In retrospect now, given the stress for my wife and me, we were both getting "willied" with dancing night-stalking boys instead of the classic wilis - as in the Slavic myth of dead unrequited maidens dancing male victims to death who stumble into their night-blackened graveyards. I would be even more willied out of my mind soon.

The claps and thuds suddenly stopped for several nights in a row. "I guess the ghost hasn't been walking," Lisa observed.

I said, "Maybe they're getting bored and tired having to wake up like that and thump around."

"You make it sound like a duty."

"Oh absolutely. It might be the norm for some of these guys to hear banging and slams or they can't sleep. I know Marcos is probably doing it at Willie's command. But what is Willie doing for him? And why does Willie want it done? Well, we're back to the therapists with this one."

Lisa was trying to shrug things off lightly again, but I could see she was beginning to realize that moving into a group home made her something like a pioneer's wife, born into the city and then hauled off to the outer frontier of the empire, so to speak. I loved her for being willing to do this and for the composure with which she would do things, like calmly returning to our bed that night when its hamster-induced structural failure occurred. She was living my job for love of me, and I felt heavily bound and grateful to her, and more than a bit ashamed for asking her to do it. It's one thing to be married to someone you work with; it's another altogether when you have to live, raise your children and sleep at the place of your spouse's job. That became a big part of her life no matter how I worked to shield her from the stress. But the fact was she was the only woman living in the house every day. The rough bridal music was inevitable, I guess, given the male teenage hormones raging on all sides of the home.

After the ceasing of the thuds came a swirling sound beneath our apartment at night. It sounded like someone scraping the ceiling with a trowel. This happened a couple of nights in a row, stopped, and then continued for a week, lasting always about twenty loud seconds. Finally, I decided to play scout. With José visiting a friend and Tony working nights late at the supermarket, their room beneath my bedroom was usually empty until Tony came home at midnight and went heavily to sleep. I decided to plant myself in José's closet one night with the door slightly ajar. It might take an hour, it might take four. At 11:45 pm I started my wilderness watch, a couple of pillows behind me, seated on the closet floor, waiting like a panther for movement. Tony came home and fell into his bottom bunk bed. At 1am, the moment arrived. Out of the utter quiet of a house-full of people sleeping came the slow creek of a door down the hall, the little sound of bare feet on a carpet so slowly coming closer, the creak of the hallway floor right outside the overworked bathroom, then the opening of the bedroom's half-closed door. I watched the human form climb up the bunks' ladder, take a large object, place it beneath the ceiling directly beneath my bed upstairs, and then pressing his head against the object, begin to listen. This went on for about five minutes in dead silence. Our bed above was under surveillance. Then positioning himself on the ladder to ready an escape, the figure swirled the big glass cup against the ceiling and lit out of the room. I caught up with him in the dark hallway and put on the light. It was Marcos looking a bit delirious.

"I was just getting a drink, Mr. D."

"From the ceiling?" I said.

I took the cup and sent the boy to bed, leading him hard by the arm and slamming the door to his room behind him. I was upset more by the prospect of telling Lisa what was up than by the deed itself. It wasn't enough to wake us up. We were being voyeured too. I found out the next day from a shaken Marcos that Willie had put him up to it, on some nights, when Fernando wasn't around, getting other boys to wait for a listen in on the cup. It was ludicrous, desperate and humiliating. The human comedy of it all was apparent too, but Lisa and I hurt when we laughed about it. But what was Willie doing for Marcos that he would risk such behavior? Willie wouldn't budge from his story, that yes, he had thought of spying "just to have a little fun, Mr. D., sorry" but that Marcos had been fool and horny enough to start it.

I imagined that the conversation around the dinner table that Saturday must have been ripe as Mr. Will lashed into Willie and Marcos.

"What's this I hear you two been doing? Why not just burn your own shoes or throw your own dinner out. Don't you know even a dog knows not to bite its master? What the hell is wrong with you boys? Lord have mercy, peeping on Mr and Mrs. D. You're lucky we don't strap your butts to your bed as if you were in a lock-up which is exactly where you going if you keep this bullshit up."

"Mr. D. likes to snore it up, Mr. Will, unless that's his wife making all the wind."

"Take your tongue out of your pants, Willie, you're playing with fire there getting Mr. and Mrs. D. all worked up."

"You're right, Mr. Will. Mr. D don't need no help in getting all worked up."

"Willie, you've got two X's coming your way, just keep up the smart remarks. And Marcos, what about you, you been watching that fly buzzing around your head too long. Don't latch onto this bully boy here because he'd lead you to hell and slam the door for a laugh. Good God almighty, you're fool enough to polish the doorknob for the devil too. I don't want any of that stuff no way, no wise this weekend. You'll be sitting a long time if you do."

"As long as you're not on top of me," Willie whispered under his breath, inciting a roar of laughter, with Mr. Will jerking to his mountainous legs and pulling Willie from his seat right to the stairs.

"Now you can do José's chore and Fernando's too. No more bullshit from you, bully boy."

But Willie would do anything to get a laugh, anything to secure his rising position as the jester in this kingdom of orphans and lunacy. Willie's sense of a good laugh was a riot in a bar or a fire in a brothel. Half Mexican, half Cherokee, Willie had received the complete American upbringing, with full exposure to prejudice, but he would not be kept down. His family featured lots of drug addiction, constant mobility, and endlessly crooked forms of employ. He had to be ready to live without food somedays so that he gorged himself whenever he could. He had to be the main man whatever the situation, the center of attraction because he felt he always was about to drop out of sight. He had to leave some kind of legacy behind. Getting people to talk about him was his only way to establish his worth. Mischief was his direction, laughter the tiller.

Marcos was without direction. His Hispanic father had disappeared one day when he was four. His frail Russian mother Tatiana was always emotionally wound up to the point where she would garble her words, each one a weight she had to pull out of her. She had come from a very poor family of seven children who one by one fled from the tenements they had wandered into all around the New York City area, with the south Bronx always returned to and then left behind. Tatiana, the last child, had overstayed her time, a frazzled teen alone with her parents who ran some kind of grocery store twenty-four-seven, and when together, would drink into semi-oblivion to prepare for the next day's onslaught. Her father would pull up roots usually because of pregnant girlfriends and their outraged families or husbands. So the mother whom her son Marcos called "Titi," knew all her life battering work and adultery, the former a horrible drudgery, the latter her father's way of escaping it. Finally, she made her own way out by getting pregnant and latching on to her lover. Off to the Mariners Harbor tenements in Staten Island she went, the only borough her family had not lived in. Marcos's father Luis at first was proud of his son and common law wife. The problem was that he was married to a woman in Puerto Rico and had three daughters there. Eventually, he would send for them, he told them, once he made connections in New York. But he never really intended to, and when he met Titi, frail and desperate, her long brown hair and green eyes made him forget the past. He worked at the time with his abandoned wife's uncle and brother, both of whom had big-time crime connections in Puerto Rico with a car-parts and dope-smuggling ring. One day, so the story goes from Titi, turning the corner, coming back from lunch hour, he saw the two men talking to his manager. He did an about face and was never seen again. Titi and Marcos eventually got thrown out of the apartment, unable to pay the rent, and ended up in Family Court, with Marcos placed on a PINS petition, "person in need of supervision." I always thought the name of this legal document symbolized the pains and pricks of life the children inherited, people in need of supplication. Often, it was the parents in need of supervision. In the "screening" interview, Marcos spoke the way his mother did, long pauses between words, forgetting what he was saying, repeating himself, but when prodded, speaking rapidly and then losing steam and focus. It was as if a haze invaded his attempts at concentration. Like his speech patterns, he was bursting with energy that came out all at once and then lost purpose. Compounding this boy's attempts at self-description was that these initial interviews almost always occurred with my complete ignorance of the child's background, the papers accompanying him mercilessly bureaucratic, names, dates, reason for placement, little more. Usually a case-record would show up days or weeks later, but sometimes they never would or were so sketchy that one had to conjecture and fill in the dots.

"So tell me about your family a little."

"You mean well, oh alright, well, my dad, you know, my dad, you know, I don't think I can remember, I don't ... think....My mom tells me he loved, ugh, loved, ugh....things."

"What things? What do you mean?"

"I mean... I don't know. He liked good stuff and left out to... to...get away."

"I know your mom is very concerned about your behavior at school. You've been cutting a lot these papers say. Here you have to go to school every day, no mess ups. You want to get ahead and help your mom and yourself, right? You want your mom proud of you right?"

"Yeah but she don't know and I, I think... she isn't feeling good....but... I don't know."

"What do you mean not feeling well? Come on, Marcos, speak to me. You're going to live here with us and we want to help you and your mom."

"I can get, I can get new clothes? Juan said so."

"Sure you will. But your mom, why isn't she feeling good?"

"Errr, my mom Titi, yeah ...." He laughed at my puzzled expression. "Yeah, I call her Titi, Momma Tee-tee.... she likes that. It's what my Pappy called her."

"What's she not feeling good about? Tell me. Maybe we can help her."

"Oh right, right. She's just not happy, you know, just not anymore because of, well, because..."

"Because?"

"Well because, because of me. I don't know... she says she doesn't want me to turn out like my dad or her dad."

"Why is that?"

"Ugh, you know, ugh, I guess, wild like him, you know. Just runoff. And...and... I want to be good for my mom. She needs me to be good."

Marcos's face went from smile to grimace to smile as he spoke. He snapped out of where he drifted, smiled, spoke, then sputtered into some dark place in his mind and had to be prodded out of it again. After three months in the home, everyone liked Marcos who was seen as something of a sap, harmless and starving for acceptance, willing to do just about anything to make contact with someone. He would cut school just to tag along with anyone doing something exciting. School sent him into the dark cloud inside, confronting him with tasks he couldn't figure out. He was impatient with his own confusion and wanted out. He'd do anything to avoid facing what the grimace reflected, misery and more misery, especially endless worrying about not pleasing his Momma T. who was sick about him. I sensed the panic of hopelessness inside him and requested a full battery of psychological tests for him. Piling him into the agency's van, I drove to the Manhattan headquarters where the agency psychiatrist Doctor Bironi interviewed him. The doctor was a heavy set man of about sixty, nearly bald but for the white and gray tufts of hair that stuck out over and from his ears. He would look from above his long pointy nose past tiny reading glasses always poised below his eyes. He was the unending butt of jokes from the boys.

"Takin Marcos to Dr. Exploding Head, Mr. D?" José asked. "Maybe Marky will make his glasses fall off."

I told the doctor I felt something was about to go off in Marcos, that something was making him feel panic deep inside although his mother lived only a mile away and saw him just about every week. He was attending the same high school before placement and so there was no big upheaval in his life except for much better food and clothes. Spend two minutes talking to him and you can hear a bomb ticking louder and louder inside, to the boy's utter distraction. Dr. Bironi dryly reported to me the results of his interview as he scribbled his notes into some form.

"No bomb here, Tony. No bomb. Just a confused kid feeling like he has hurt his mom and she's getting ready to abandon him in your house."

"Maybe his fear is..."

"Yes, yes, of course, he's scared," he interrupted. "Wouldn't you be with his future? Just some separation anxiety. He's fourteen years old and has got some growing up to do. He says he doesn't know his father and he calls his mother Titi, 'momma Titi.' OK, so her name is, let's see here, yes, Tatiana, but what's this first name stuff with his mother? Get a case-worker over to her house. BCW's got to do better than these scanty notes I received. But no bomb, Tony. Just that the boy's scared. He'll calm down. Just reassure him he'll be alright. He needs some hand-holding. Heh, don't we all sometimes?"

He patted me on the shoulder.

Then, one autumn Wednesday night a week later, Fernando knocked at my door.

"Mr. D., Mr. D. wake up, wake up, come quick."

I scrambled to my feet.

"Fernando, it's 2 in the morning. What's the matter?"

"Sorry, Mr. D. but Marcos is freaking out. He's outside yelling."

Grabbing my robe, I tumbled out of sleep down the stairs and opened the front door. To my utter astonishment there was Marcos at the corner of the street up a stop sign, hanging onto the top, yelling for all he was worth something like, "the Nixon got my Titi. He got her locked." He was rocking back and forth up there, crying wildly, yelping like a puppy stepped on.

"Marcos, what are you doing? Come down. Come on, come down, you're waking up the whole neighborhood."

Lights were indeed being turned on. Across the street, beneath a high gable, Mrs. Haberstrom was glaring down at us out of an open window, shaking her head. Marcos suddenly jumped down from his outpost of misery and crumpled on the curve of the street, between sobs trying to speak. Then he stopped crying suddenly and looked up at me with utter hatred in his eyes. Calmly, without a hitch in his speech, he made his accusation.

"I know you got her upstairs there with you, Mr. D. Get her out of that closet you locked her in. The Nixon put her there. The Nixon stole her. He took her. Gave her to you. And if you don't let her out, I'm going go right up there and get her out. You got no right."

Fernando had by this time joined us, heard the story, and, laughing wildly to the other boys now all looking out from windows, shared the revelation. The boys from the group home next to us had also awakened by this time to glare at the spectacle, their counselor nowhere in sight, probably sound asleep in the basement of that home.

"Yo, yo, Marcos says his mom's upstairs in Mr. D's closet and..."

Here he paused to get control of his hilarity.

"The Nixon kidnapped her."

The boys broke into wild glee, with John standing in the front doorway rocking back and forth like a buoy during a storm. My wife called down from our upstairs window.

"Are you alright? Anthony, are you OK?"

I left Marcos to whisper up to her.

"Call the police. The kid's freaking out. He must be high on something."

I turned to the guys.

"Close the windows and get inside. Everyone go to bed."

Marcos suddenly bolted at me as I stood in the walkway to the front entrance.

"I'm getting her out of there, I'm getting her now."

I couldn't let him in the house in his state, thinking of the open door to my apartment, my wife there. I tackled the boy, grappling with him on the lawn for a while, by this time my wife screaming down, "Help him, John. Fernando, help."

As the two boys heeded her call and ran towards the two of us wrestling there, Marcos broke free, flying directly at the house across the street where Mrs. Haberstrom's sickly husband now stood in the doorway with her watching aghast as the boy charged towards them. I ran after Marcos, throwing myself in my best football fashion at his fleeing knees. We both fell heavily onto the street curb, his knee crashing my hand into the steel edge of the curb. I applied a full nelson to the boy as he lurched in every direction. Fearing he would break his neck struggling to free my hold, I let go and he attacked me viciously, flinging arms and legs at me. I fended him off, blocking blows with my arms.

"Do him, Mr. D. Do him," José called out. "Drop him, drop him," he yelled, assuming a boxer's stance, delivering roundhouses into the air.

I could hear my wife yelling down, "Let him go, let him go." I didn't know whether to run in the house or somehow restrain the boy again. He just kept coming at me, crying now as if he had become the helpless puppet of some force inside him. Mercifully, the police car came flying down the street. The neighborhood was in for an all-out, eye-popping scene. Two young officers flew out of the car. Both knew me from my many previous calls, usually to report AWOL boys, and immediately grabbed Marcos. One pinned Marcos to the street face down, with his billy club horizontally held across his back. The slender framed boy somehow was still able to lift himself up with his arms pushing against the pavement. The other officer joined in, adding his weight to the pile but still Marcos was able to almost lift himself free, this slight boy of 100 pounds playing David to Goliath, some divine-like strength welling out of the boy. They held him down with all the force they could summon, one officer pressing his hand flat against Marcos's face with his whole weight behind it to pin him there while the other officer had his knee and full weight pressed on the small of the boy's back.

"Stop struggling, stop." The boy wouldn't, scrapping his face on the street wildly in utter convulsion. "Stop, damn it, stop," the officer yelled again, this time delivering two blows with his billy club to Marcos's legs. Again he drove his knee for all he was worth into the boy's back.

"Now stop, relax, relax, we don't want to hurt you. Calm down, calm down."

Finally, the boy or whatever was gripping him inside gave out, and he dropped into jelly-like calm flat on the street, sobbing, "ohhh, ohhhh." The boy was handcuffed, put into the car, and I was told they were bringing him to the emergency room. "This kid's on something." The police drove off with Marcos.

"Oh thank God," Lisa yelled down, "Are you alright?"

"I think so."

I glanced at the boys who now were completely silent, having witnessed probably the most baffling scene of their lives although they had already seen so much chaos. I felt a sharp pain and looked at my left hand. The thumb looked distorted.

"I've got to bring the kid's medical release papers to the hospital, Lisa, and then I'll be right back."

"Why? They'll treat him anyway. It's an emergency. Just please come to bed."

"No, no, I've got to go but I'll be right back. Guys, the party's over. Get to bed."

I didn't want to tell my wife about my throbbing thumb. Apart from her, there was no mercy about.

"We're going to close you down," a neighbor yelled. "Close you down for good this time."

The scene at the hospital continued the bad news. In the emergency room, I was amazed to see Marcos burst a strap of the straight jacket he was in while on a stretcher. He had the strength of a demon still inside him. Whatever it was, it was now also occupying my thumb, a bluing mass of pain. An injection knocked

Marcos out. As for my thumb, it was put in a cast but luckily, no pins had to be inserted. Adventures with it would continue, however, as events proved the cast on my hand to be nearly fatal in its impact on my life. One doesn't know the value of the body until parts begin disassembling, leaving one astonished at the degree one can suffer a sudden erasure.

The inevitable report the next day told us Marcos was on angel-dust, as it was called, technically elephant tranquilizer which he had inhaled with a dash of mescaline. No wonder Nixon had appeared, become fused with me, his supervisor, his Russian mother in my closet. But why had he kept crying "the" Nixon? It made me think he had abbreviated the phrase "the one and only" as if he were introducing him or something. And now, for your ultimate amused horror, the one and only Nixon will kidnap your Titi. I tried to wrestle some humor out of the whole thing, wanting it to mean something beyond the insanity of it all: the stop sign, the Nixon, the mother in the closet, her child the would-be savior. Marcos merited further consideration. He was an allegorical poet in our midst, at least to my mythical inquiries of him which saw him as a kind of sleeping giant Willie had roused through the open market of drugs now being funneled into the house. Willie had been supplying Marcos freely for his surveillance work on my bedroom and other pranks and mischiefs. Perhaps Marcos's closet dream came from his recollection of his mother's groans now projected on his eavesdropping of another chamber. The image of Marcos atop the stop sign yelling Nixon and Titi in my closet haunted me into near delusion. I wrote this poem to exorcise the memory to no avail -

At the Orphanage of Dreams

In a struggle with a mad child
I broke my finger, the proud one,
which in pain steals away my mind
until I am a child of his darkness.

The boy had seen faces in the rooms
while other children slept.
He had heard his mother's cry
beneath my door in a wilderness.

All by the windows, aghast we stood,
watching the boy transformed as if
a giant had stepped out of his head
to set up home atop a traffic pole.

Fool that I am, I played hero to the loon,
asked him to come down as he wailed
back and forth astraddle the steel edge -
if only sanity had a rim of metal

to hold us in, immune
to the acid of dreams! I pulled him
down. A typhoon was in his eyes
lifting me with the strength of bulls.

I was aloft in a whirlwind
swelling out of a puny boy.
Now the child rests, his fit gone under,
but the pain summoned up

over an abandoning mother
lives in my hand, and I reel in wonder.

The poem leaves out Momma Titi and Tricky Dick. Who would believe any such poem? The poem's title implies dreams abandon us – or do we them?

The home, however, grew wilder than any dream with the arrival the very next Monday of Adam, a new placement sporting a broken leg. He had fallen out of an apartment window in the Bronx. He claimed he had no home. The Family Court decided a maternal aunt in Staten Island might be a resource, and so into the home he came. His leg and my thumb in a cast immediately linked us in ways I could not imagine.

The new counselor I had hired arrived the same Monday for his first tour and must have thought the place a battle zone. John's rocking appeared like shellshock, and José now decided it was time to train for the Golden Gloves. Fernando lifted Willie's deadweight to impress him that there was a price for disturbing Fernando's peace. Fernando was a linebacker for the local high school. Willie begged Fernando to put him down as the house trembled with the boy like a torpedo hoisted into the air. Tony, always on the prowl for an opportunity, began to smoke his joints in the house by carefully making a hole in the half bathroom's window, placing the lit end outside the window and closing it so that all the smoke went either into his lungs or into the alleyway, none in the house.

"Mr. D. sure to be laid up a while," Tony said, "and my curfew's looking good."

He laughed, "tee hee, tee hee."

This boy-adult always had the most money in the house, the local banker in fact, as he worked hard and stole well, having made friends with neighborhood kids who were the sons of a contractor. He had connections.

The new counselor Al I would soon be calling Albie as we hit it off immediately, telling him he had to wear a helmet on duty to make sure he'd make it through his shift intact. The look on his face told me he didn't know whether it was polite to laugh.

"Stop worrying to death. You can always sue us if you get broken bones or go on compensation. Easy money, Al."

This cheered him up as did our trip to the pantry where Al sized up all those ivory soap bars, cans of chili and tuna, towels, soap-pads, and the ample meat stored in the freezer.

"We eat well here, Al. Help yourself to anything as long as you use it and leave it here."

Al took this very literally, inviting some of his friends to eat with the homies. I remember the day I came down to see this one very large bald man eating the sausage and meatballs. I didn't see him at first because as I came into the dining room, I watched in horror as Willie dumped ketchup on the spaghetti along with American cheese slices.

"Willie, there's a sauce Mr. Al put on the table. Mrs. D. sent it down specially and you're using ketchup?"

"Mr. D., Willie's got rocks in his head," Fernando declared.

"Yeah, Willie thinks he's Mr. Sloppy Stupids," Tony tee-heed.

Then I saw the large guy in the corner of the room, eating away.

"Yeah, Mr. D., that's Mr. Green, the new boy," José laughed.

I welcomed Al's friend to our table as the oldest home boy I had ever seen.

"Hi, I'm Richie," he told me.

"What's with Mr. Green?" I asked José.

I heard Al laughing in the kitchen. "Because he's extremely tight with his green backs."

"Oh, I see...well, tell him the massive plate of food he has in his hands is not free. He's got to help bring the kids to the movies now."

A special kind of humor came into the loony bin at this time, fortunately for all of us. We would really need it.

Chapter 3

Terrorism

Sleeping in my bedroom the following Saturday afternoon, finally off duty, the fiery pain in my thumb slackening, I awoke to a figure fiddling about in my wife's drawers, his head and shoulders working through her jewelry boxes like a little squirrel digging for acorns. The kid had the audacity to raid my own apartment in the very room I was asleep in and scurry about while he had a broken leg.

"Adam, what the hell are you doing?"

"Oh, oh, Mr. D, Mr. Kevin told me to take some money and go to the store."

"Well, this isn't the office, bud." I grabbed the kid by the arm and scooted him down the hallway and out the door of my apartment. "Never come in here again unless you have my permission."

I escorted him to the stairs, encouraging him to go down, and when I let his arm go, he turned and stumbled down a couple of steps, held his balance and ran quite well out the door, cast and all flying in the air. He was nimbler than Tinkerbell but the next day told the social worker that I had hurled him down the stairs, reinjuring his leg which now hurt badly again.

"I have to report this to the agency and fill out a report to the Bureau of Child Welfare too," she told me.

"You must be joking, yes? OK, ok. I can understand you're required to do that, Ms. Dana. Please mention this kid broke into my home and was rifling through my wife's personal effects in our personal apartment. How do you think he broke his leg in the Bronx? Cat-burglar, the case notes say."

"What caused the broken leg is not relevant, Mr. Danilo. What did or did not happen at the head of the stairs is the issue, and I've got to report the boy's claim. There's a lot of controversy right now, you know, with the dead foster child last month in the city and all the problems at Dawson Street. My responsibility is pretty clear cut in this case. I'm just reporting it, not accusing anyone."

Dawson Street was another agency group home where the supervisor was under investigation. Her reporting me now was really alarming as I had already bruised my reputation at the downtown headquarters. During a large meeting I had lost my temper and made a grandstand, throwing a chair, raving for more help on the front and complaining about all the cars the administration had assigned to them as personal vehicles when two group homes had to share one vehicle. Administration would be all too glad to fire and evict me.

Meanwhile, despite the intense monitoring he was receiving, Willie held to his guns. Items of my wife's laundry began disappearing, panties and bras mostly, one by one. I searched the house one day while all the boys were at school and found nothing. I didn't want to question the boys because I didn't want to draw attention to the thefts. Whoever was doing them - and I had no doubts who was behind the pilfering if not directly the bra-burglar himself - would take wicked glee in my embarrassment. Then, Ms. Sheila told me she came upon a pile of burned undergarments in the back staircase. I was too outraged to speak. After a long walk in the park, I resolved of course to get more support in helping Willie and not tell my wife how we found her clothing but still warn her about the dangers of being alone downstairs in the home when outside our locked apartment. This decision not to tell her, in line with other concealments, did not sit well in my conscience. The practical course said why worry her about a vicious detail when the big picture was known to her and already enough to worry about? On the other hand, I was speaking for and not to her (I was reading Levinas at the time) when the burning question directly concerned her intimate belongings. My not telling her felt like a dirty secret that soiled me. But that was my decision, my burden, heavy on my tongue and hard to hide in my eyes when I next spoke to her face to face. I would bring Willie downtown to the agency for a session with the social worker, psychiatrist and my immediate supervisor. Somehow we were going to impress upon this man-sized child that his war was hurting himself, that he was on the brink of being relocated although in truth, this was not a strong option since Willie was free for adoption, making the agency his legal guardian. We were family.

Lisa told me she felt very uneasy about her disappearing garments, and I emphasized that she needed to be aware of who was in the house anytime she left our apartment, which we had to make sure we kept locked in view of what Adam had done. She shook her head at the adolescent frustration involved when I told her Ms. Melissa, a part-time counselor who would do night shifts occasionally, also had had dirty clothes taken out of her laundry bag. We wondered if perhaps Juan was wearing the stuff. Meanwhile, most of the boys were very polite to her, she told me, and she felt while the thieving and snooping was prankish, it was also a warning that we had to be more careful. We considered, again, the limited job opportunities I had while I was also attending grad school full time and teaching part time as I was. The work I was doing in the home had never been so hard until the last few months at that time. Maybe things would lighten up. In truth, most of the days in the home went smoothly, with lots of structure, humor and sports activity. I made sure to play ball with the guys a few times a month. On the field or court, I was just another dude, not the boss man. That felt good to me and the boys who enjoyed tackling me or planting a hard pick as I showed them to do to my chagrin. Overall, Lisa and I both enjoyed living with most of the kids, some of whom would have been devastated if we left. So we decided we would be patient. Leaving the home was not necessary and not at all convenient for either of us. Lisa was attending graduate school, a masters program, and hoping for the director's job at her library once she obtained her qualifying degree. I was in the middle of writing a dissertation. Plus, by not paying rent for what was a nice apartment, we were saving enough one day for a down payment on our own condo or whatever, and at the time were planning a trip to Spain.

We were living under very unusual circumstances that needed careful planning and adjusting to and if we did, our work would bear fruit. Yes, in fact, most of the days were, I guess, pretty normal given that we were a house full of teenaged boys, a kind of happy chaos. Full moons did let loose weird behavior from the boys, I kid you not, as did some new placements, but six of the boys were very stable or I should say typical adolescents. So on we went.

Then the noises at night started again and I lost it. I charged down the stairs at three in the morning, grabbed Willie by his pajamas and gave him a bath with toilet bowl water, putting a sponge in it to wash his face. This time I had crossed a line even if for a long while after that, Willie was on his best behavior. The next day we had another long talk, and we both apologized to each other.

"What I did was out and out wrong, Willie. I lost my temper. I wanted to shame you the way what you made my wife feel fear and embarrassment the last few weeks."

"No hard feelings, Mr. D. I deserved it. Just don't tell anyone about it."

"I won't but you can tell, Willie. You can call the social worker and make a complaint about what I did to you, washing your face with toilet water. Her number is on the refrigerator where it's always been. No one deserves what I did to you, Willie. Just as what you've been doing to my wife and me, we don't deserve that either. Agree?"

"Yeah, yeah, I understand. Just don't tell anyone, not even the counselors. I ain't gonna say anything. I'm sorry. I'll tell Mrs. D. too."

"That's good. She needs to hear that. Maybe we can figure out a way to be kinder to each other. We do live here together so it's best we treat each other with respect for everyone concerned. What do you think? Shake my hand?"

Willie smiled in the way that would light up his face and eyes, one of his impressive powers, and taught me the current cool way of shaking hands, fingers interlocked and then putting our fists together. I knew what Willie thought of as normal was exactly what had been happening probably all his prior life, harassment, cruel pranks and much worse. I had to somehow break this cycle, not succumb to it.

I continued to bring him grocery shopping with me one on one, an activity that caused some jealousy with the other boys. He enjoyed pushing around the massive carts of food in the market, helping get stuff from the shelves. We would make jokes about what and how people ate or how they acted in the house. He told me his love of ketchup came from times when that would be his whole meal. I told him we would teach him to eat balanced meals that would help him control his appetite. He did want to become a guard on the football team next year he told me. Three boys from the group home were already on teams. So things could fall in place. I apologized a few times for the bathroom incident, and each time Willie swore he would fit in more and listen. It was much later when a more complete case record turned up that I learned of the attempt on the boy's life by a john who tried to drown him in the tub at his aunt's house. What does one do with such pain he had to have inside? The shame I felt over what I did to him was linked to all that he had experienced elsewhere and that had been carried right into our lives together. A chain reaction of violence and pain. A vortex. I felt ashamed and ashamed that I felt ashamed. I still do.

The social worker filed her report regarding the alleged incident of my abuse of Adam. It struck me as ironic that Adam, whom I had not abused, phoned in a complaint while Wille didn't. I was summoned to a meeting downtown, the result of which was that a follow-up report would be made to the Bureau of Child Welfare which in the meantime had cleared my continuing work with the children. They probably would interview me soon. I begged administration again for more staff and more staff hours and was told that more counseling hours would be assigned to the house, some double coverage provided, two counselors during the hot hours of 3 to 11 during the week. Also, for some weekday nights, I could hire a sleep-over worker. So far, only on weekends was such help available. But I had heard such promises before made during meetings with all the group home supervisors.

Christmas was looming on the horizon, shopping for ten boys, arranging home visits if possible, helping them to deal with their pain of separation and loneliness from families during holidays even though many of their families were places of battering and addiction.

Adding to the stress, Ms. Dana, the agency social worker assigned to my home, now saw me in a different light and began suspecting a pattern of abuse in the way I worked with the kids. She interviewed all the boys. She told me all the boys seemed to like the home, and they said for the most part got along with me and the staff. Some did say it was a fun house, but others seemed reluctant to say anything bad as if they had been coached. I told her they hadn't been and that I was glad to hear some of the boys thought living there was fun. We played regularly at the school playground up the block, with Juan cheering us on. Fernando was on the high school football team along with two boys in the group home next door so that there were lots of sports talk and exercising going on. José was now training for the Golden Gloves at least in his own mind and was practicing at school. Juan was always practicing dancing and was thinking of taking lessons with my encouragement. Adding to the positive mix of things, a new boy Kevin from Bedford-Stuyvesant arrived in the house, tall, athletic and something of a gentle giant. He was a sweet kid everybody liked. He also loved to play and talk basketball. The counselors and I always kept the silly jokes flowing as did John, Fernando and Tony among the boys. Quiet days were that way because they were often merry ones, and we had lots of these. Some of the older boys and I would often end up in the kitchen sometimes past their school bedtimes just trading funny stories.

"You should have seen Juan looking for that meatball that fell off his fork. It got stuck in his pants and when he stood up it was just hanging there."

"Guess he's got a third one now he doesn't know what to do with."

"Got stuck cause Mr. Al be cookin with glue or something on his fingers."

"No, that be Mr. Kevin with the Vaseline."

I would just shake my head, suppressing laughter. "OK, guys, enough. Just remember to clean your hands before and *after* you eat."

Then we'd all laugh.

Marcos returned to the home and we all made a special effort to talk to the kid. Everyone including Marcos laughed at the crazy thing he had done. I brought him to a local drug rehab and got some counseling for him. But he didn't have a drug problem really. Just lots of confusion, understandably, and the angel dusting was an isolated incident.

Ms. Dana told me she was pressing the Bureau for them to interview me because she felt she was learning more and more about how things were in the home and wasn't convinced yet that all was well. She was fresh from grad school and had lived all her life in a big house in Scarsdale. She was in a bit of culture shock although I knew I had indeed crossed the line with Willie who never let out a word about what I did because he'd have to say what he did.

"This stress you feel, Dana, in the house comes from my need for more staff. We're always harried here, troughs and peeks, two weeks of calm though busy routine providing for ten boys followed by a day or two of mayhem that causes problems for a week. I need help, workers, not investigation, and I need your understanding too. No one can live here and work as many hours as I do with these kids and not get upended by it all sometimes. As long as the kids are happy - and I know they are telling you nice things about the staff and my supervision here - why prolong this investigation? Adam is OK, isn't he? He told me he loves this place."

"Yes, he claims but yet he also told me you did throw him down the stairs. No, luckily, his leg wasn't reinjured but still I have to see some kind of resolution here. I am only doing my job."

I thought of the agency psychiatrist who had not foreseen Marcos's crisis, and now this social worker overlooking that we were making the best of a difficult situation. The lack of support, of more workers in the field, had led to a burn-out syndrome increasingly evident in my actions. This incited poor decisions though it did not excuse me from them. Adding to my despair and anger was the rumor that the agency headquarters had received lots of valuable Christmas donations, expensive stereo systems, electronic game boards, leather coats, expensive cologne, etc., and had it all locked in a large room for a while. What was being given out were only blow-up footballs, blankets and card games coming the group homes' way. Another supervisor had seen an administrator hauling the stuff away in hand trucks into his agency-assigned car, with all the other administrators suddenly showing up in blue jeans that day. When the group home supervisors asked about this one angry meeting, we were told by the director that foster homes were targeted first and then group homes for distribution, but I again raised the issue of why administrators had personal cars and why there were new hires for administration but not child-care staff.

"We need cars to get around in the field, the Bronx and Manhattan, not just the Island, Tony. But since when are you the chief officer here assigning resources or personnel?"

What set me off more than anything was the way the official talk about the mission our agency performed was couched by administrators in all this religious good-will stuff when in fact the per diem rate we received for the boys was uppermost in a "bottom-line" mentality.

"If we fold, then all the good we are trying to accomplish is over with, and then where do these children go? We've got to maintain a high occupancy rate. The figures don't lie."

This is the speech we'd get from the director while the chief officer would make references to the work of God we were doing. True, to my mind, the agency's mission was the loftiest one any organization could have – to help needy kids. There were far from enough agencies out there doing this kind of residential work. In New York City alone there's tens of thousands of kids in some kind of placement, and many more tens of thousands who need help. Still, it was easy to speak such things from the arm-chair distance of an office in Manhattan and the paid transport of a free car back and forth to work. But try to live in a group home for a while, we would tell downtown, see the day to day reality of the limits of what we can do. The chief exec would say he was praying our work would succeed. "Send the children to me, Jesus said. We're here to welcome them in."

At the end of another bombastic meeting, the director announced another high-end administrator had been hired, no doubt paid six times or more than what we were. Rumor also had it the Cardinal had just installed a new carpet on the top floor of the building, the regal domain of his Eminence. I decided to take some action beyond speaking out. Right after 5pm, with almost all of the office personnel gone, I went to work with my protest. I gathered a few crucifixes from the offices, packed them all into the elevator and sent them up with a strong note to the top floor to the head man, the Cardinal of the Archdiocese of New York. "The group homes need help now, your Eminence," I wrote. As my crowning touch sure to get attention, I put a little lighter fluid on a cross, set it on fire and then put it out, pushing the button for the top floor. I wanted to leave a strong smoky impression. I was out of my mind with despair and frustration. This was clear to me but did not stop me. As a fire alarm went off, I flew down the stairs.

I also decided to take out my frustrations by doing mischief to the social worker. I followed her car to another home of the Island. Thumb in a cast and all, I decided to pour a little sugar into the tank of the agency car she drove. It was very difficult with one good hand getting the sugar bag to pour correctly into the funnel I placed in her gas tank. A little old lady walking down the street stared at me in disbelief. I just looked at her, smiled and said, "Hi, it's a beautiful day, isn't it?" The sugar did the trick. Her car broke down the next day, she suddenly quit the job, and the heat was off me as far as her investigation went. I met with a Bureau worker downtown and with no social worker from my own agency stirring the pot, the interview went well. I also knew this Bureau worker who really understood the severe constraints that live-in supervisors experienced daily. She sympathized.

"Sometimes these kids need some really clear lines drawn. Just don't cross the line yourself, Tony," she told me. "I know from my visit last year how much the kids like you and the home there. I think you're doing a good job. I hear Judge Gedy does too. Just take some time off. I will also recommend more staff assigned to your home."

And so that was her recommendation. For a time, things did indeed calm down. Of course, even when we were calm, the other homes on the Island sent us a constant stream of disturbing news. Three girls had run away from one home and were living in an abandoned building. One of these girls, Gena, was the sixteen-year old sister of the boys Jimmy and Sammie in my home, their father the Chevrolet cowboy of "ten g's in the Tunnel" fame. Upon being brought back to her group home, she claimed she was desperate to return to her mother's home, and by running away, she had hoped to show her mother how miserable she was. Truth is she and the other girls had had a grand old time for a few days. But her cover story worked. She was returned to the mother's house. The mother to her credit had long since managed somehow to get the wayward father out of her life, but her own penchant for self-destruction brought an even more violent man into her home. We all knew from the case notes that this boyfriend known as Rocky was dangerous, with prior convictions for assault and battery. For several years now, however, he appeared reformed, working full time and supporting a growing family. Gena went home to join him, her mother and a newly born half-sister. A few months later, I made a home visit to see if the home was safe enough for the boys to make some weekend visits. When I arrived at the two-bedroom tenement apartment, Gena, the mother, the baby and eventually Rocky were there. Their unease was evident. I asked about living arrangements. Rocky was proud to say he slept wherever he wanted. To my horror, the mother told him, "Yeah, you bastard, you got my daughter pregnant." So there it was, the mother with her new born, the daughter pregnant with her mother's lover's child. If Gena's father heard about this, he was sure to shoot the mother and Rocky. Her brother Jimmy, when he eventually heard about the pregnancy from Gena, indeed wanted to kill Rocky and had to be warned against it everyday. During my interview at the home, Rocky glared at me the whole time. I kept my best poker face on as my heart raced and stomach turned. I too wanted to throttle the guy. I asked how many weeks was Gena pregnant and whether she wanted the baby. "Two months or so pregnant," the mom said. "She's not sure what she wants to do." Gena just nodded, letting her mother do the talking. I told them I would file my report with BCW and have our social worker make a visit to help Gena out. When I left the apartment, I puked outside and then wept a while in my car. I called all the social workers, court workers, administrators, everyone. The girl had to be removed from the home even against her wishes. The safety of her coming child if that's the route she took also was at stake.

The misery her child would likely endure born into such a family made me wonder about how no child asks to be born or picks its family, name, nation, place or date of birth. I thought of baby Oedipus with the nail in his feet placed in the wilderness to die at the order of his father the King, a play I was teaching in a nearby prison at the time as an adjunct professor. The secrecy of the murder in the ancient myth was much like the secrecy of children's misery in their own families. It was hushed up or ignored by society. The city newspapers, to my mind, should run a column every day near the front page on a child who ends up in placement, why she was there, what the future holds, above all, how we could help out. Of course, pseudonyms would protect the identity of the children involved but attention, urgent attention, had to be focused however painful. The hopelessness and despair inherited by innocent children cannot be tolerated in a society that would remain sane. Such misery expands exponentially in the course of a battered life, hurting everyone in its wake. The whole system of childcare to me feels like a band aid given to someone with cancer. And yet sadly, in so many cases, the child is better off in placement than in their natural home just as some people in mental asylums need protection from supposedly sane people outside the institution. I also found that the inmates I taught in a medium security prison were among the best students I had ever experienced in a classroom. Top down inversions, the least among us, first.

For the time being, my wife and I made an escape, taking our Spanish vacation, enjoying the beaches at Malaga, the wizardry of the Alhambra, the splendors of Madrid, sangria and paella.

My daughter Ariana went to live with my mother only too glad to help us out. The home had round the clock coverage, arrangements I had to rethink desperately at the last minute when one staff member quit just before we were to leave. I vowed to forget where we lived for a while but I couldn't help perceiving things differently because of it.

When we visited El Escorial, Philip II's austere palace outside Madrid, I thought of all the Hispanic kids I lived with, and how the big frame of history really does account for what children get born where and to whom, for the conditions of life into which we're all born. The haves and have-nots divide up the world not according to some mysterious plan set in stone by nature or God but from the brutal relations that underpin political sovereignty gained at the point of a sword or gun held in some warrior's hand while the other hand waves a flag with a cross on it. King Phillip II's obsessive control over his global empire, perhaps the largest history has ever seen, made me think of some vast Bureau of Human Welfare, sending out inquisitorial caretakers all over the world, to the Netherlands, Mexico, Peru, Chile, the Caribbean, Florida, the Middle East. The Spanish crown created the *encomienda* contract with Columbus that entitled Spanish nobility, mostly second-born sons investing in global conquest, to many thousands of hectares of land in the New World - including the native peoples on it. The black legend of history, with capitalism a form of legal theft for the most part, is certainly not peculiar to a Spanish quest for empire, as the histories of Portugal, England, France, Italy, Belgium Germany, Japan, Russia and America show. Strolling through the halls of his granite castle, I thought of how Philip II, *imperator mundi totius*, would hear mass every day in a little chapel near his royal chambers and then off to a towering pile of memoranda sent by hand from and to nearly every quarter of the known world. In my head, I heard the bass baritone of the king singing in Verdi's *Don Carlo, "Col sangue sol potei la pace aver del mondo"* – "With so much blood, I have paid for the peace of the world." In the throne room, I imagined the king, who oversaw every little detail in his vast empire, sign his imprimatur to a commission sending 200 mules to Mexico to help plow, drain and haul, taming the wilderness, bringing Christ to the barbarian, a-mass-ing the wealth that would be used to conquer the Moor, secure Jerusalem and defeat the detested Protestant Cause of the Dutch and the English. Perhaps in the afternoon, the somber king would visit his Titian paintings just outside the royal chapel. He'd ponder the figure of a heavenly Venus, her shining flesh only a dim emblem of the divine light too bright to be seen directly by mortal eyes, the reason why the goddess as often depicted by Titian looks at a light from beyond the space of the canvas that a lute or virginal player cannot see, their backs turned to it but towards her. The king no doubt would struggle to look past her voluptuous form, his hand over his furrowed brow, half-looking, the way empire-builders have to see past the human misery that their ambitions cause, past what the poet Virgil calls "a dire lust for domination," *dira cupido*, a stern flying little god of lust, a longing to look out beyond and down upon the human world, as it were, a lust for other worlds implicitly said by Virgil to belong to the emperor Augustus, declared a god by the Roman Senate in his own lifetime. The emperors and pharaohs of history think they belong over and beyond us, we the little people, according to their own self-serving vision of grandeur and an impossible future reaching beyond death. But the gaze of the eternal, Titian, crafty philosopher of a painter, awarded to Venus with a wink of approval from her son Cupid. This is the light of love in the world from a source beyond it. I thought too of Bartolomé de Las Casas, whose mission had influenced my own life. How he fought against legalizing slavery in Venezuela and against slaughter in Hispaniola and Cuba! The legacy of this distant past, the black legends of empire, if one could trace its effects upon generations of a family line in the "New World," might well end in the streets of New York City, to a Family Court, a PINS petition.

These things are interconnected in ways we can spell out and fathom. Chance and destiny may be locked in a love-hate embrace but human acts too, the signing of memo's, the digging of mines, the wiping of blood from the flanks of caparisoned horses, add up a toll of mighty accountability.

The anxieties of the group home Lisa and I tried to erase from our minds for a little while cast strange shadows everywhere, even upon our arrival to and from our place of escape. The airport in Madrid was patrolled by uzi-bearing soldiers watching the flow of people from ramparts above. What were they expecting?

"Never know about those new placements coming in," I told Lisa who advised me wisely to let it go.

"Please no more job creep. We're on vacation."

Outside the door to the airport, a poster for a Bruce Willis flick in Spanish set me astride my mental hobbyhorse again. Today's man of the gun, yesterday's man of the sword. A good gun pointed against a bad gun, terror against terror creating terror by attempting to execute it once and for all. In this effort, killing someone else is not called murder but war or justice. And yet for peace to occur, a gun has to be turned on itself somehow, turned against the need for a gunman and what brings him into being, a so-called hero free in a time of martial-law exception to use violence. No flag or cross burned or raised would stop the terror but only furthers it or falls victim to it. This is why God asked his son Jesus to commit suicide for the sake of mankind, to stop the cycle of violence. I had this last dizzying thought as we left the chapel of the emperor.

"You love brooding," Lisa told me. "This cynicism of yours has a really wacky, funny side, no? You forget to laugh at it."

"OK, so let's laugh to forget and get drunk too and quickly. Sangria, please, or Lacrima Christi."

Chapter 4

Party Time

To be a group home supervisor meant you joined a tight clique and became certifiable, like a rower in the bilboes on a sinking ship, and we live-ins knew it. We'd get together at some bar on a Wednesday night or have one opened on a Monday morning after the kids left for school, to drink, smoke, joke, rib, complain and brag about how we few, the chosen ones, withstood the suffering and the lunacy. Our collective social life really took off or plummeted, depending on how you look at it, when one Ronnie Byars arrived on the scene to take over the group home next to mine. My wife and I had grown to be close friends with the previous supervisor and his wife, playing cards together, watching films and stealing drinks off upstairs terrace we shared as well as helping each other. Seeing them leave made us sad and jealous. Walter would still work for the agency, though, as my boss, Borough Administrator of all 8 group homes. The new supervisor next door and his wife for some reason received a red-carpet treatment from Manhattan. A whole new apartment was to be built for them, and to my astonishment, it was to be built in my house. My wife and I and all the boys in my home would switch houses with the group home next door. We'd move into a smaller apartment upstairs while the basement in my current home would be converted into an apartment for Byars, his wife and two children. This would also free two full bathrooms for the boys, one in each home. That was the only really positive outcome. The disruption this top-down decision made on our lives was considerable, with twenty boys bringing their stuff from house to house and all kinds of furniture and supplies transported in every which direction. Some of it disappeared apparently to add to someone's slush fund.

Ronnie Byars was a big time charmer. He had gone around the same block many times, in and out of drug rehab, but not recently, and he vowed he was standing on his own feet, "with God and my wife's help," he said, putting a Baptist preacher's tone in his voice for a moment and laughing. We hit it off right away despite the enforced move which he apologized for. The director of the agency was a long-time friend of his, and so he had received another chance to get his act together and raise his family. His vows marital and otherwise did not last long. Ronnie quickly became the largest liver among us, a powder keg inserted into our parties for live-ins only.

First of all, we now went into Manhattan to escape. Ronnie and Mr. Will, who by this time had his own home to supervise, a girls' home, knew of a place called "the Mud Hole" somewhere in the West Village. Off we went, tumbling into a van at 10 PM one Friday night, Ronnie bringing his own car in case he met up with someone, I guess. Mr. Will was a New-Orleans born giant of a dude who loved to eat, talk and laugh. I was the constant target of his gentle prodding. "O boy Tony, you gonna fly tonight, you gonna break out," he said as I piled into his emerald-green Cadillac along with another supervisor Ted, our boss man Walter, and my counselor Al who had long since become a friend. Inside the very crowded Mud Bath or whatever the place was called, Will managed to find a stool to place his massive body next to the bar. The other four of us stayed in a dark corner near the entrance. The place was deafening and jumping with people in all kinds of outfits as if ready for cameos on *Star Wars*. We watched Will jabber along with some lady friend he apparently knew before. Then I saw his bear-like head jerk back and forth in riotous laughter. He immediately called for me.

"Tony, heh Tony, my man, come over here, someone wants to meet you."

I worked my way through the crowd and asked Will what was up.

"Lawdie, Tony, see this lady here? This is Missie Lorna and she wants to dance. She seen you bopping your head and knows you want to dance too. I told her you are a right proper man, a scholar and a gentleman, and will protect her out there. Yes, siree. Go on. Take her out on the floor. Give her a spin."

"Hello, how are you? Nice to meet you."

"Good God, Tony D., loosen up, she ain't gonna bite you, are you, you sweet thing? Say something nice to the lady. This ain't no downtown meeting."

I looked into her sad eyes in the dark bar, the constant noise, laughter, the loud music swilling everywhere. It felt like carnival time with Will the parade mascot. She was tall and lanky and smiled knowingly at the male ego I was trying to summon up, mostly not to disappoint Will.

"Go head, go head, T. Have some fun. Ask the lady to dance."

"Do you like to dance?"

"You don't even ask a lady her name," she whispered so I had to lean in. "Well, it's Dora, and yes, I like to dance. But this song's too fast. Something slower would be nice. I'm feeling a little drunk, you know."

I guessed Will didn't get her name right? Maybe I didn't hear her or him right? Anyway, Will was now a bundle of merriment writhing in spasms of glee.

"Good golly, Tony, take her by the hand. She really wants to dance now but she's shy. Go head, step up to the plate."

We moved a few feet to the side of the dance floor, making our way slowly through the guzzling crowd. A band I couldn't see was playing Boogie Nights. In the strobe light, her pink boots kicked to the beat. She saw me notice them and raised her leg up and shook it in the air. "Go girl," I shouted. We laughed.

Someone suddenly tapped me on the shoulder. It was Ronnie. "Let's go. It's way too hot and I can't even move. I know a better place. I told Al how to get there. I'll meet you guys." And he was out the door. I waved good-bye to Dora and went back to tell Will at the bar it was time to split, Ronnie's turn to pick a place.

"OK, let's go, but you go back and invite her to come. At least step in there and get a kiss."

I turned around and there she was. She had followed me back to the bar. Dora looked at me dreamily and bent her face towards me.

"Go head, in there, give her a kiss, T-man."

And so I kissed her on the cheek lightly and told her to have a nice night. Will nearly fell off the stool he was laughing so hard. "What kind of a kiss is that? Give her the real thing, T." Outside in the cool night air, he said to me, "Here, Tony, take the keys. I'll let you drive my baby. I'm too happy." We tumbled into the big green Cadu and I took off for the next place, taking Fifth Avenue.

"What's so funny?" Ted asked Will.

"Ho, ho, let me catch my breath, good God, this is too good, lawdie, have mercy, mercy, um, um. Well, my man T here kissed that missy, but you know what, I was checking her out before you got there, Mr. T. And I just got to talking a little and she was real friendly like so I just slipped my hand down there and guess what, good God, guess? Dog gone. She had a joint bigger than mine."

I instantly grew red and the guys were all over me, yelling and pushing me as I tried to keep my eyes on the road.

"T., lawdie no, you going up Fifth, turn my baby around."

And so I did instantly, now doubly red in the face, with Will acting out a scene for us.

"But Officer, I was only going one way anyway on this one-way street here and plus I just smooched a queen and my head's reelin."

The next stop was even more strange, even to Will who had no doubt bent a few bar stools in his day. We followed Al's directions given to him by Ronnie. It looked like a regular bar from the outside. The five of us walked in as an old woman opened the door for us, telling us to be respectful. "This is a quiet place, just relax and behave," she said, winking at Will. It was indeed quiet, dark and very dank. Admission included a drink at the bar so we walked right up there, no crowd, no noise, complete contrast to the Mud Place. Then as we were ordering, we heard a kind of slapping sound coming from the right in a room beyond. I could see just a few people seated at small tables and watching the entertainment. I looked round the wall. In the corner on a slightly raised platform, a man was locked in a pillory and was getting his behind whipped by a dominatrix who was taking deep pleasure from each stroke she delivered. As if this wasn't strange enough, a man and a woman, I think, greeted each other at that moment by slapping each other firmly in the face, saying "hi there, you naughty one," and "yeah, long time no slap, baby."

We were too stunned to laugh, and all I said was, "well alrighty then, let's finish our drinks and leave." We turned around to scan the rest of the place and now we saw down a hallway behind the other room people were walking in and out of doors, some wearing little towels, some in bizarre gear. "O my God, did you see what Mr. Loony Tunes had on back there? What is he, Napolean or something?" Al asked. "Yo, Captain Marvel, you fall off a spaceship or what?" Ted yelled. We laughed too loudly and the dominatrix shouted something at us. "This isn't a ballgame," I think she said, as if I was about to mistake her for a goalie. Then Ted saw a billiard table in a different room, and we went there to recover our shaken sense of things.

"Where's Ronnie?" Al asked.

"I thought I saw him when we first walked in," Walter observed.

"Well, let's get out of here, go back to the Island, and hit McGuire's before it closes for a last round. This place is a bit too out there in tootie-fruitie ville," Al said.

"You might enjoy getting your butt slapped," I said. "I hear you and Mr. Greenbeans bump heads a lot."

"O really? I know you and Juan exchange teddy bears."

"Someone tell Ronnie we're outta here," Walter said.

Walter and I went separate ways to scour for Ronnie, looking into dark humid rooms that at least to my surprise had saunas. Into and out of locker rooms I walked, eyes all over me. "Heh, where's your towel, sweetie?" some guy asked me and I just shook my head in disbelief, trying to suppress my laughter. We couldn't find Ronnie. Finally, Al grabbed my arm and bringing me before a door, told me to look in the back of the sauna. Through bubbles and haze, I peered, making out Ronnie's little goatee. He saw me through the window, raised a glass of champagne and called out, "Join us, her name's Brenda and her friend's Annie. Don't worry. They got the right plumbing, Tony."

"Errrr, don't think so there, Ronnie," I told him, opening the door. "We're back to the Island, McGuire's, if you want to join up."

So we took off, amazed at Ronnie's plunge in the tub.

"Man, I guess he likes dark stuff with little thinny legs," Will said.

Forty minutes later we pulled into McGuire's to have a beer or two before heading back to our respective prison homes. Suddenly we heard a voice from the other side of the bar call out, "My boys are here, they're here, drinks on me, everybody."

It was Ronnie. Somehow he had managed to haul himself out of the sauna, dress, jump in his car and beat us to the Island.

"Yo, Ronnie, you got a helicopter or something?" Will asked.

"No, Brenda put a prop on his head," I said. "Or something else he'll be itching tomorrow."

It dawned on us all that Ronnie was in a league of his own. He was further out than we'd go, and I'd soon find out how distant his orbit was and how far I had to keep it away from my sphere of things. This is not to say I didn't have issues of my own. I had been drifting away from who I thought I was, feelings twisting out of control, anger and grief carrying me along, developing from some melancholic tendencies. Lisa and I had had long talks about some of my concerns, and I had written her disturbing letters before we had gotten married. Maybe I had overdosed on Kafka or Hamlet. "I'm a loner, free-spirit type, subject to tantrums and ranting," I wrote her one cold night I spent in the group home before she moved in, a bride entering a male bedlam of dysfunctional families, ten boys trying to escape the desperation of the adults who dominated over their lives. "My love for you is so real and yet marriage has always seemed to me about obligations, not freedom but duties, not pleasure but security. I fear the contract side of marriage will curdle my soul over time, damaging our love and my ability to love. I would never want to hurt you." These feelings expressed in a letter to her two months before our marriage were more than a bachelor's cold feet. Lisa knew it and she worried about the risk of marriage to me. I was an idealist leftover from the sixties, a peacenik without a war to protest. I courted loneliness all my life, a "monk" as my engineering father called me. I was most impractical in his eyes, loving literature so much that I was dedicating my life to its teaching and writing. From counseling in a home during college to moving into one as supervisor, I was pursuing some crazy mission to do human work which more and more felt like holding a bucket under a bleeding wound so that the "red carpet" of society, the glittering fabric of American life, would not get too obviously sullied. The boys in my agency's care were mostly sorry victims of history and circumstance, their numbers legion, their lives not regarded. What could one do? Yet there I was.

Now Lisa had married a hippy-monk running his orphanage, to use my father's description of me and my work. Her own Roman Catholic background had been strict. Her childhood home was ruled by a Sicilian-American matriarch, her mother's mother or *Nonna*, who lived in the upstairs apartment of the two-family home that she and her husband owned. The men in her immediate family were mostly silent and gentle, especially her dad who always did what he had to do to provide for the family, rarely complaining, only saying positive things about and to people, often in a good mood. Lisa wanted to rebel against the part of her culture that in her own experience retarded the independence of women. *Nonna*, for one small but telling example, had forbidden the closing of Lisa's or her sisters' bedroom doors for fear they might spend too much time combing their hair. This was never an issue with how her brother had been raised. I commiserated with her and asked if a fear of something bigger than vanity was at stake? Lisa laughed and said, "You mean afraid we might touch ourselves? O no doubt." The Church too, in her eyes and mine, forbade women's independence by denying them sexual rights equal to a man's. In my mind, I told her, even the whole way one must speak today of "rights" for the sake of maintaining one's political freedom, already indicates a diminishment of a person's humanity. The glorious potential in a woman's nature is always there. I encouraged her with such talk even as I privately savored but also feared the circumstance that I was the man who had "taken" or been gifted with her virginity. It's a beautiful myth but no more than a myth. Still, I felt its hold on me. My own sisters had been made to live it by our heavy-handed father. Lisa and I talked for hours once whether or not Mary, the mother of Jesus, had the choice to say no to her impregnation by the holy spirit. If she had no choice, then the Annunciation scene I so loved in Medieval and Renaissance paintings was a rape scene. "That goes too far," Lisa told me.

She wanted a career for herself, a desire that baffled her parents who, in terms of their Sicilian Old-World culture, largely saw husband and children as the true destiny for a woman. Like me, she was in conflict, sixties values crashing into Old-World conservative ones. But her religious faith as a means of self-discipline or self-constraint, having been indoctrinated for over twenty years into her by the two looming matriarchs she had lived with, sat far easier in her soul than in mine. I was in steady clash. The group home was my unplanned-on version of making a living within a commune or monastery, a strange way of connecting warring values, my way of dropping out and remaining committed, libertine and martyr, I thought to myself. As with Lisa's troubled connections to her own upbringing, one's ability to analyze one's lot in life does not evacuate the emotions, the deep-seated feelings, one has about it. One cannot stand outside one's fishbowl though trying to see it for what it is, is both necessary and difficult.

Where Lisa and I faced moral and philosophical dilemmas, the boys in the home were caught up in a life dilemma, the lot handed them much less privileged than ours. It was far more handed down to them than chosen by them, the heavy, even tragic circumstances of their lives having closed down on them usually right from the start like an inscrutable decree of fate. Unlucky in the parents as most of them were, they were more puppet than ventriloquist, as it were, made to live the consequences of a life not their own. This is not to say they were completely without choice when it came either to better their lives or wreak havoc. I had to help them locate and foster that choice, help them understand and acknowledge that they had to create a choice as well as take advantage of opportunities that came their way. Above all, I had to help them see they were not doomed to repeat their parents' life. The fate-like forces of social rank, race and class were also admittedly in the mix. Mostly from poor families, the kids had much fewer options than Lisa or I had growing up, coming from middle-class families as we did. Fortune's wheel appears arbitrary in terms of who gets what at the start of the race. The long lens of history proves it's not so random. Though we're all subject to forces beyond our control, some are less so than others for reasons that can be dug up and revealed.

Unfortunately for us, a spell of lunacy waxed again in the group home with the arrival of a boy named Ray placed voluntarily by his irate military father who lived in a small house near a beach on the Island.

"He's a wild kid, Mr. D., but he's mine. You feel free to keep him in line," the father told me. "Keep me posted, and if you need back-up with the discipline, I'll be here front and center, you know, the enforcer. Spare the rod, spoil the child."

"Well, we're here to help him discipline himself, Mr. Rowson," I said.

"And if he doesn't, he's not coming home. I'll just leave him be so he can fetch for himself like an animal if he wants, live here with the other messed-up kids. I don't want to see him until he gets his act together."

Rowson was an ex-Marine, or so he claimed, crew cut, hardened jaw, black polished shoes, jeans and a denim jacket with a US flag stitched on one sleeve and an eagle on the other. He thought the group home was like a boot camp or at least that's what he told his son.

The image of this boy now living among us animals fused in my mind with that of another boy, one Thomas Savage, like some inescapable allegory. I had just read a brief note about Savage in the account of the sixteenth-century planting of Virginia by Captain John Smith of Pocahantas fame. Little Thomas was traded to Chief Pohatan as part of a deal that the Captain made for some native corn. He was thrown into the bargain as a keepsake and pledge of trust that the Chief probably had taken a shine to and that the captain had grown tired of maintaining on sparse meal. The name Savage was an ironic reminder to me of how barbarity exists even in the naming of it, in the accusing of others of it. Mr. Rowson was trying to tame the wild by using his own form of savagery on it. 14-year-old Ray had gotten the real message. He was upfront about it.

"I'm here because my dad hates me for being like him."

"What do you mean?" I asked.

"I mean he does his things, drinking and stuff, and when I hang out to get away from him, I do my things. Then he hits me for it, hits me for being like him."

"Cutting school is not your thing, Ray, and you can't hang out here. You've got to go in the best direction for your own sake, and we'll help you find that but you've got to follow the simple rules."

"It looks cool here, Mr. D. The guys say you're cool and I love sports. I'll do my best."

"And we don't use physical punishments here so you don't have to worry about that. We use incentives."

Ray's depression and candor, the sad knowledge he had about his father and his relationship with him, was disturbing to witness. It was too much for any 14-year-old to know much less describe it so precisely, "he hates me for being like him." This boy struck me as very intelligent and I wondered how he put his natural wit to use while cutting school. I was soon to discover how. I got word from the weekend counselor that Elvie, the woman Willie had been pimping, had again been found in the house downstairs this time with a shame-faced Ray. He told the counselor, "Just meetin the neighbors, Miss Melissa. She's Tony's friend." I suspected more black marketing by Willie, the king of the underworld in the house, but what was Ray going to do for Willie? Why was Tony mentioned again?

Tony flustered. "Mr. D., I don't know, this new kid thinks he's in with me. I've got nothing to do with Elvie anymore. I told you that, Mr. D."

"You better not be sleeping out at her house anymore either," I told him.

"Mr. D., ask Ms. M. and Mr. Al, ask all the counselors. And you see me all the time. I'm sleeping here and I'm not into Elvie no more. She's just gross. Ray knows her from Jimmy. I only slept at her house when I got real tired from all the hours I was working at the bakery next door to her, that's all. And you know I quit that job."

"And what's going on with your construction friends, Joey and Frankie, why are they coming here looking for handouts?"

"Te-heh, te-heh, they were just fooling around with Mr. Al, you know, wanting to get the same treatment his friend Mr. Green gets, the freeness, Mr. D. But they don't steal."

The guys had a real party brewing, however. Returning from a weekend long trip when I refused to call, I walked into a quiet house 7AM Monday morning. I found Fernando in his room alone.

"Where is everybody?"

"Mr. D., I don't know what the hell's going on. It's getting crazy again, I think, Mr. D. I saw Anthony, Juan, and John leave this morning for school. The rest of the guys took off late last night, I think, I don't know where. I don't think they came back."

"What do you mean, took off? Where's your brother?"

"Don't know. He wasn't here for dinner last night. I don't know what's with him. You better ask the counselor about the other guys but he doesn't know much, I bet."

I awoke the counselor Lou who had worked alternate half-weekends for us for about two months now. He was a laid-back older family man with two grown children. He loved the idea that he could get paid while sleeping.

"Where's the guys?" I asked him.

"What do you mean? I wasn't feeling good yesterday so when I got here on time at 3, I made a big pot of chili for the guys who ate. Then some left to play some ball. I just fell out down here at about 10 or so. Sorry but I still have some fever, I think, but you know, I came in anyway. I know how you needed coverage because you were away."

"Fernando tells me most of the guys snuck out last night and never came back."

It dawned on me then how José had said to Willie that the agency van was a party car for Mr. D. and his friends. Just a joke I overheard, but it was actually something of a warning from José to me. He knew I was within earshot.

"Where's the van?"

"Outside, down the street a little. I saw it when I got here."

"Where's the keys?"

As the counselor checked the set, he discovered the inevitable. "The van key's not here."

Shooting up the stairs and down the block, I confirmed my suspicion. Missing van, seven missing kids, party time, their style. I think also what set them off was the rumor everyone was hearing now about Mr. Byars, that he was a "party head," with all kinds of people visiting his basement apartment late at night over the last two weeks since his wife and children had gone to visit family in Puerto Rico. Any hole in our authority over these kids led instantly to massive revolt because beyond our rapport with them, we really had no other means of working with them. If we seemed as "wild" as they did, well, no boundary to cross over to and find quiet a harbor was left.

I called the police, gave them the story and the license plate, filed missing persons report, called the Bureau and changed the population count for the day with my agency. It was no fun contacting the parents. Only José's unofficial stepmother was sympathetic, sorry for her son's trouble. "Why he can't be more like Fernando, I never know," she said. Of course, I did not want to remind her that José had a different mother with her philandering husband who always denied the child was his. José's mother was a single parent, hairdresser who suffered from bouts of mania and depression. She had once in a while brought to the home roasted pork or pernil cooked in the Puerto Rican way with platanos, rice and beans. She was so proud to see us savor every bite. We all appreciated her tasty generosity. Then she went off the grid somewhere about a year or so ago, possibly back to Puerto Rico.

The police the next day located the van outside Clove Lake Park. Apart from some burn marks in the backseat, beer cans and junk food strewn about, the van was fine. The boys involved drifted in separately during the course of the day, Jimmy, José, Ray, Willie, Marcos, Stephen and Robby (we had 11 boys in the house at the time). They had gone on a joyride, Mr. and Mrs. D. away and the counselor ill.

"José, why you?" I asked him alone as I spoke to each boy separately as they came in.

"Mr. D., Willie paid me to drive. I'm the only one who knows how. I figured we'd just cruise around a bit. Then Ray had some guy buy beer and Stevie had some joints. I just said 'I'm outta here,' and left the van right there at the park. I walked back, slept at Frankie's house and went to school."

Ray and Willie were like nitroglycerin together. Jimmy was just a tag-along and Stephen and Robby were prone to thievery and violence. The last two, Judge Gedy's favorites, felt above the law. Robby was the one I really had a hard time working with. He had been living with his maternal grandmother, a sweet old woman named Lilian Daniels. He was allowed to visit her on alternate weekends, too much for her to watch him every weekend because he was a wild kid. His father had been arrested repeatedly for fraud, larceny and assault, while his mother dropped in and out of the picture, committing to his care and then disappearing, running off with some new boyfriend. Her mother really raised the boy but her illness and age made it harder and harder.

One Monday I had called her to see how the home visit went. In her brogue accent, she told me,

"O not as I hoped, Mr. D., not as I hoped. I don't know when I can have him visit again."

She was reluctant to say why but I was able to get the truth out of her. She told me between sobs.

"Because he's not just a wild one now, he's mean, Mr. D. I don't know how he could but he hit me last night when I caught him in me purse again. That boy's got a cruel streak. I think he wants to lash out at the world and he took it out on me."

She said he bloodied her nose and blackened her eye.

This attack gnawed at my stomach. Robby appeared like the apple-pie kid, very blonde-hair, very blue eyes, and a chipper attitude. He was into karate and was taking lessons his grandmother was paying for. I confronted him over the assault of his grandmother, arranged for social worker meetings with him in the office, and grounded him to the house on weekends until further notice mostly to prevent him from visiting his grandmother. He barged out of the office when I told him of his grounding, knocking me out of the way and then turning on me in a karate stance.

"You must be joking, Robert. Don't throw a punch or you'll be taking a big risk."

He flashed a drop kick in my direction, I lurched out of the way, grabbed him by the back of the neck and instantly pinned him against the wall. He broke free and ran into the front yard. "C'mon, motherfucker, I'm waiting for you," he said. "You'll wait a long time," I told him, yawning at the door. And I closed the front door, so as not to give him an audience. The karate show was over for a while. He would do chores for attacking me. He might burn in hell for attacking his grandmother, I felt like telling him when he came back inside for dinner. "How can you hurt such a woman who has helped you so long?" I was very conflicted working with this boy after the harm he did to his grandmother. His presence in the joy-ride group that included two of the kids who had been with me for years was very disturbing, showing how quickly even the best kids in the home could change allegiance. Even Fernando, José told me, knew about the joy-ride and was paid to shut up. Juan too was involved because he owed Willie money and had paid him, thus providing party money. It was an open revolt, a mutiny. I grounded the whole house for two weeks with a routine of extra chores. I was hoping to break the bonds forming around Willie and Ray whose idea it was to steal the van. The older boys who had a job were excluded from the grounding only so they could work.

I made a group announcement. "No girlfriends. No phone calls except to family members. The only time you go out is to school or out with a counselor or me, always under supervision."

There was really not much I could do beyond daily rapport and as a last resort, the reward and punishment system. And I was way too angry and disappointed to dovetail the consequences to each child depending on the degree of his involvement. By not doing so, I realized I fed into a feeling of us against them, something I had not felt so sharply before, with even Fernando now glowering around the house. I kept talking to each boy privately, reminding him to think of his path to the future and not get trapped in a fun house that turns dead end. It was time to grow up a little.

Party time then grew violent, however. One fine Saturday morning later, I walked outside to find my private car's rear window smashed, a weight lifting bar through it. Livid, I got all the boys out of bed, smiling at them, talking nicely, saying I had good news. I lined them all up in the living room, with Fernando, the tallest kid standing at the head of the line.

"OK, guys, it's football time," I winked at Fernando, and I pushed him as hard as I could so that he fell back and nearly the whole line of kids fell like dominoes, flattening the new cocktail table that sounded like a gun going off. My pent-up rage had fired its load, half wounded beast, half caravel discharging cannon shot. The guise of sports helped diffuse things, preventing a brawl I would have lost in handcuffs. I hadn't planned out what I would do when I had called them all out of their sleeping beds that Saturday morning. Turning it into something of a game was a gut reaction that proved a wise move, taking me by surprise and saving us from a riot.

"Any questions here? You guys want boot camp, here it is. Anybody want to say something to me? Go ahead, now's your chance. You know what happened, you know what you did or who did it. It's my play time now, my time to ruin your day like you did my car."

The boys at first were stunned, Willie most so, shortest of boys at the end of the line who had totaled the cocktail table. I had just carried it home from a thrift store the day before, hurting my back. José and Fernando shook their heads at me and smiled sarcastically as if they knew I couldn't be serious, pretending it was some kind of contact sport. Stephen, Robby and Ray just smirked, unafraid. Only John had missed out on the lineup. When he walked into the room, the boys were sprawled out or just picking themselves up. I turned ready to deal with someone coming from behind me but then saw John's big eyes rocking back and forth towards the ceiling. All he could think of was Doctor Guerino. "Want me to call Doctor Guerino, Mr. D? Anybody hurt?" His recent visit to her popped in my mind.

"No, John, unless you're full of constipation again."

Fernando was the first to laugh, followed by a chorus of howls. A little comedy put rage to bed for the moment, from near riot to belly laugh in the time it took for John to shuffle his feet. I laughed the least this time. And the weight-lifting bar, as I'd find out, would come back to haunt us all like a lead cloud that wouldn't go away. On the other hand, I can't say I wasn't relieved when soon after this incident, Judge Gedy arranged with the downtown office and BCW a new placement with a different agency at Stephen and Robby's request. I was glad to see them go frankly. They needed more help than my home could give and, with Robby's abuse of his grandmother, more help than I was willing to give him.

Chapter 5

Cauldron

Many a night the older guys and I would hang out in the kitchen talking. John was both stimulus and jovial butt of talk. Fernando had a lot of common sense, was gentle and fun to be with until his friendship to Mr. Byars began to worry me. Ronnie Byars was a charmer. He would rub his nose quickly with the pointer finger of his left hand, with the pinky extended, to accent one of his clever remarks followed by a bubbly laugh. The guy got to you, ready for whatever was going down, and when Ronnie first arrived, he had a good effect on everyone. We lived on humor, and Ronnie had lots of it, a fresh infusion. Then he went off, back to his old ways whenever he got a chance which usually meant when his wife wouldn't find out. Fernando had taken to the guy, kind of like the father who hardly had anything to do with him, rumored to be a rogue. Ronnie began to guide the young man regarding colleges, and I felt shunned. Mr. Will also felt uneasy about the magical influence of Byars.

"He's got lots in his bag, and why your director boy Leo in the office is so chummy with Byars, well, tells me something funny, you know, Tony."

"Ron may have some sordid connection with Leo. I mean c'mon, they build an apartment for this guy, make twenty boys exchange places, move me and my family for him and his family."

"They trying to drive you out maybe."

"Well, getting fired might be the best thing for me and for Lisa."

"You know, Lisa's a good woman. I mean how many women would move into a group home? She must love you, Tony. So maybe she'd trust you enough for you and me to go to N'Awlins," Will laughed. "Just tell Lisa, you're going for a haircut."

I imagined Will and I busting down to New Orleans in his huge Cadu by way of Brooklyn to pick up Will's Brighton Beach girlfriend. Will knew the city well, from Harlem to Houston Street, he'd say, from Katz Deli to some downhome cooking on 123rd. Despite his living large pleasures, he tried to be a loving if not very good father to his daughters and loved his Caribbean wife Hermione or Mimi, as she was called, who was a great woman. She either loved people right off or didn't want to come near you at all, but she was always sweet and polite and would cook for anybody who came into her house. I passed on the trip to the deep south but told Will just the idea of it was vicarious pleasure enough to keep me out of bars, living the cruising life in my mind, group home gypsies. Lawdie, have some mercy. Will went anyway, much to his family's worry but returned, happy and larger than ever. The girls' group home he was in charge of was really run by his wife so Will's absence from it was not much of a problem there. The girls did have a big problem with running away. They would just decide not to return home for a couple of days, living with their boyfriends or out finding one. Will would blow the whistle and come down hard on them, and they'd behave for a while, then do it again. There were three girls involved in this. One of them decided to cover her tracks by claiming that she felt forced to run away because Mr. Will was peeping on her. She described how he would sit in the closet, his three-hundred-pound bulk jammed into a dark corner behind a slightly ajar door, or he would flit by in the hallway like a giant Peter Pan turned voyeur. I thought of Will trying to duck detection tiptoeing about in the dark, a pyramid of a man acting like a gazelle. So her story was a bit suspect but it launched a BCW investigation anyway. Poor Mimi.

I did know Will's effect on my own boys when he was my counselor was very positive. His worldly wisdom kept them out of lots of mistakes even though he himself could not avoid some of them. Fernando was one of his favorite kids as he was mine so we consulted each other about how to raise the boy. This reality of raising other people's children created a tremendous pressure on everyone involved. What parent does not feel sometimes as if he or she were groping in the dark when a child is troubled or difficult? Even more so when you're a surrogate parent. Plus most of these boys had been betrayed, abandoned or abused by adults in their life and so had learned to trust nearly no one. The stress from these various conditions of neglect and poverty radiated into all our lives. Lisa felt I was spending way too much time with the boys while the boys, at least the ones who were long-term residents, felt they could not get enough of our talks and jokes. I existed in this divide, feeling great about being so needed and on the other hand feeling the stress of trying to work an impossible job that drained me emotionally while at the same time attempting a "normal" life as a husband and father of my own child. Lisa and I felt we lived in something like a boys' scout camp for the wayward and rejected.

As for my own parents, my peacenik ways had also been a source of conflict in my own family. My father wanted me to be an engineer or architect, the same line of work he worked and had married into to boot. My love of poetry and something I vaguely called "world peace" was without any traditional career paths. So we banged heads a lot, snarling arguments over the supper table. I was the monk reading Engels and Marx at sixteen. This did not endear me to my very Catholic mother either who saw me as a free spirit, but she respected my freedom-loving ways and was worried that I was tying myself down to responsibilities I would come to resent by marrying and moving into a group home. My father, however, just saw me as weird. I was not the son he had hoped for, and I knew that and felt his wrath so often I had simply internalized it as a kind of self-hatred. This led to my over-identifying with the home boys. Lisa sensed all this conflict inside me. On her side, her desire for a career, to do something with her college education, seemed a bit perverse to her very Catholic parents. To them, college education for a woman was really to make her attractive to a husband, a means of landing a prize supporter, preferably a doctor or at least a lawyer, and of course Italian and Catholic, all the better. Lisa became my liberation project, and she told me I was like her knight in shining armor. Moving into the group home, however, was more like living in the dragon's cave for us so the knighthood and freedom project were in serious doubt.

The long-term home boys, some of whom would live with me for five or more years, walked something of an emotional tightrope in their own lives. I was their father and not their father, I was their friend and their supervisor. As their supervisor, I reminded them of their feeling of living in exile from their family as well as their need for support of their future. I learned the hard way any pretense at being a surrogate father led to heavy resentment of intrusion into their private life. On the other hand, if they sensed a counselor or I was just punching a timecard without any real involvement in their lives, they would create upheavals to get the attention, even negative attention, that they so craved. Fernando told me and the older boys one night during our carefree talks, "Mr. D., it's a little hard to see myself in college or anything past this."

"Things will shake together for you, Fernando, you've got determination and intelligence," I told him.

"Yeah, shake, rattle and rollin like Dr. John here," our new homie, a second boy named Anthony, Anthony F., said, an 18-year-old who had transferred into my house, after his long-term placement in the home next door and a brief unsuccessful stint in the real world following high school graduation.

"I see you're not talkin, José, no more Dr. Drop, no more rockin anyone?" John asked.

"You still rockin John," José said.

José's Golden Glove dream had come to a crashing halt. For the very first bout he was scheduled for, both homes had piled into two vans and went to the large gym in Brooklyn where a ring had been set up. José's opponent was a muscle-bound tough looking Italian kid. José never came out of the boxers' area where we had left him, shouting some final encouragement to him. His name was called over the P. A. and when one of the boys yelled out, "Dr. Drop Dropped Out," all the guys had to laugh. I knew the boy's spirit would be broken for a while, but the dose of reality was inevitable and welcome. We would be spared his practice jabs for good. José would grow even sheepishly self-humorous about the whole thing.

"No, no, I ain't fightin no Bronx mob dude. You'd been scared too, John, gettin in the ring against that guido. O sorry, Mr. D."

"No offense, José, but don't talk that way in school."

"Yeah but John knows how to bob back and forth pretty good. What Mr. Al say? John's gonna get a job as a buoy."

John laughed at this prod from Fernando, who felt sorry for his brother's boxing disaster and was trying to divert attention from it.

"But Fernando," I said, trying to return to the shred of self-revelation Fernando had let out, "why did you say that you can't see yourself past this place?"

"Because it's so crazy, it's like getting cooked or something. It changes you. Kind of brands you."

"What do you mean, cooked?" I asked.

"You know, your goose is cooked when you wind up in a place like this with all these crazies in here."

"Well, a cooked goose isn't the worse thing in the world especially if you're hungry. Heh, come on, you going to get into college, and there's more good things ahead for you to do your own cooking with."

"Yeah, he'll eat himself up," Anthony said.

"OK, OK, but let's not get all worried about the future all at once. It's a day-by-day thing. Just do each day what you have to and don't get lost. Time on task. Eyes on the prize. Life's not a smooth thing. If it were, we wouldn't have to pave roads."

"Mr. D., I so want to get my permit," José said.

"Yeah, so you can jack up the van again," Anthony teased.

This kind of late-night banter had some real value in connecting us together. Serious feelings were let out in playful ways, creating camaraderie among us as they perceived any future adulthood from a common ground that in their own eyes set them apart from "normal" families. This bond of shared estrangement and survival humor, however, was always put to the test by the uncertainty that would often enter the home with the arrival of a new placement. A whole fresh load of troubles could turn up, and Fernando's cooked-goose idea no doubt came from this feeling of being trapped in a simmering pressure cooker of woe and misery.

Ricardo was one such boy who made us look directly into the fire. His seemed a typical new placement situation at first, no father in the current picture, child living with his mother in the South Bronx and getting into trouble on the streets. The mother had taken out a PINS petition. Ricardo's placement in Staten Island was the Court's attempt to distance the boy from the gangs he was getting involved with. He was Hispanic, sixteen years old, quiet, polite, good-looking, and athletic, and so he fit in right away with the population of the two homes. Because he was a streetwise kid from the South Bronx, some of the boys listened to him with some respect. This kid knew what he was talking about. Only Fernando and Anthony disregarded his stories at the dinner table.

"And yeah, the South Bronx is a really cool place to hang out if you want to go nowhere," Anthony told the guys at supper one night. "Willie, it'd be perfect for you."

"Me too," Marcos said, not getting the point.

"You wouldn't be so tough in my neighborhood, Willie," Ricardo said.

"Yessum and no way in mine too," said Kevin, whose Bedford-Stuyvesant neighborhood also left him indifferent to much of what passes for suffering and hardness in the world. But pretending to have no boundaries is of course what being macho is all about. Willie's life in Georgia, as difficult as it was, really was no ticket to the top of the pecking order in the house. Since the van incident and the smashing of my car window, he had lost credit with most of the older boys. Although they liked to laugh at his bravura, they above all hated getting into trouble at home with me. It was biting the hand that fed you. Now Ricardo instantly seemed high in the order just from his good build and from where he was coming. He underlined his claim to power one night at supper, having little respect for any support system because of his tough-guy image.

"Everything's cool here, but no one better mess with my stuff and I'll be cool with everybody else. Anybody touches my gold chain, well, they die."

"That's right, Willie. So stay out of people's rooms. I don't want anything in my room from you that's somebody else's," Fernando told Willie, who remained Fernando's roommate.

Marcos, however, failed to hear the seriousness in Ricardo's voice. Ms. Sheila told me about the gold-chain comment. I spoke to Ricardo who told me the chain had been given him by his father the week before the father left for good. The plate on the chain said, "Be strong," and for Ricardo, the chain was the last link he had with his father. I told him we usually don't let expensive jewelry just sit around in a drawer and it was better to let me hold it. But he insisted that he keep it.

"Mr. D., this is me, this chain, it's my father and me. I've got to hold it on me because that's all he left me. So please be chill with it. I can't let you have it."

So I acquiesced but told him threatening others was never acceptable. All the boys had similar items, keepsakes from missing parents that they held onto for dear life. Usually it was a letter, postcard, photograph or watch, and it was sad to see such attachment to souvenirs of what might have been. The objects had a talisman-like quality for the boys like a piece of their identity and so represented something beyond sadness. It was a tie to the past that they carried into the future. I saw Ricardo's link to the chain in this harmless, pathetic light. He wore it all the time, dangling it above his bathrobe in the morning and carefully removing it at night, placing it at the foot of a bookmark showing the crucifixion. It was the center piece of an altar as well as his claim to standout.

Two days later one Wednesday evening, as I sat in my apartment reading one of Petrarch's sonnets, the speaker pondering in a forest the image of his absent beloved, I rose to answer a faint knock on the door.

It was Ricardo.

"Sorry to bother you, Mr. D., but there's no counselor on duty. You better call an ambulance. Marcos got hurt. Maybe dead or something."

"What do you mean? Where is he?"

"He's laid out in the street, bleeding a lot. He took my chain from my room, and I caught him down the street. I hit him over the head with this, just like I said I would," he said calmly, handing me a weightlifting bar. Ricardo turned around, walked into his room, flipped on the television, and laid on his bed.

I tore down the stairs and out into the street. There was Marcos, face down in the middle of the street in a pool of blood. He was motionless but still breathing. I called out for help, Jimmy stuck his head out the window, and I told him to get Fernando. Fernando came running out of the house, and I told him to stand over Marcos and not move him, just prevent him from getting runover, and I tore back into the house to call an ambulance. My heart was beating a million miles an hour as I thought of poor Marcos and the cruelty of Ricardo, a sixteen-year-old calmly watching tv in the room upstairs next to my apartment, straight from an attempted murder. The ambulance came and I jumped in, getting the counselor next door to watch my house too. At the hospital, I called Marcos's mother, telling her that her son had been hurt, leaving out the details until she arrived later. Marcos received twenty stitches in his head and had a severe concussion. Thank goodness his skull wasn't fractured.

"My boy, he, he might have been killed. What's up with that house of yours? My boy ain't safe there? I better take him, oh, oh, oh."

She wept uncontrollably.

"This is really me, my fault, my fault...."

Her bottomless misery was too much for anyone to bear. I put a hand on her shoulder and wept with her. Things fairly under control at the hospital, the boy out of danger, I flew back home where my wife would be returning very soon. I kept thinking of Ricardo, what he was capable of doing. Getting back, I walked past the closed door of Ricardo's room where I could hear the tv and went nervously into my apartment, not knowing what to say. What do I do, dock his allowance for attempting to kill someone?

"Hi, honey, how's everything?"

I looked at Lisa and began to mumble, fighting back tears. How could I tell her whom we were living next to in the room right outside our door? I explained there had been an attempted murder, and she looked at me with horror. I called the police, something I should have done before I left for the hospital, but my mind at the time was focused on getting Marcos medical treatment, and I had overlooked the danger of Ricardo. Most of the boys were also stunned into inaction, mulling about like zombies in the living room.

"What's up with Ricardo? That kid is sick," Fernando told me.

"How can anyone be so cruel?" Juan asked me.

"Just goes to show he likes that chain of his more than anything," Willie chimed in, happy not to be involved for once. "And Marcos, he's just stupid. He must have known Ricky would do him up, Mr. D."

When the police came, they interviewed Ricardo, and I filed a report. There was nowhere to bring the kid for the time being so he had to stay put overnight. The police and I together told him to stay in his room. Ricardo remained matter of fact.

"OK, no problem with that. Like I said, he crossed a line. He paid the price."

The next day I called Family Court to obtain a hearing as soon as possible. I wanted this boy out of my house. A Court session was scheduled for two days later. The agency social worker came the next day and stayed with Ricardo an hour or so in the house, talking to him. She also called his mother who could not see how we could be right in accusing her son. "He's just messed up a little but my boy's not like that," Marlena told me bitterly over the phone. The Court session was also a striking example of denial. The social worker told Judge Gedy that the whole incident was just a misunderstanding as Ricardo had explained to her and to his mother. She told the Judge a curtain rod was the instrument of attack.

"I know the report says attempted murder but would a curtain rod really kill anyone?"

"Your honor," I called out, "that's not what he hit Marcos with. It was a weightlifting bar."

"You're out of order, Mr. Danilo," the Judge told me. "You'll have a chance to tell your story."

And I did, looking at the social worker in utter disbelief. Ricardo kept his head down the entire time of the hearing. The Judge ordered the boy to be taken to Spofford Detention Center for Juvenile Delinquents, a lock-up that would secure his person overnight and keep him under strict supervision all day. From what I learned later, Ricardo spent two weeks there under observation, receiving psychological testing. He was then released into the custody of his mother, back to Simpson Street in the Bronx. Just another kid on the streets, just another fire lit in our home, leaving behind scars and absolute astonishment at the violence even young souls are capable of. The sadness of it all.

Chapter 6

Upstairs, Downstairs

About this time, Ronnie Byars was in full swing. He had hired one Ms. Charlene, a lean, tall green-eyed black woman striking in her gaze and demeanor. She was very good with all the kids who looked up at her as a hep older sister. She had great rapport with nearly everyone except Ronnie's wife Harriet. I sensed some jealousy there as Harriet would often not get involved in conversations whenever we sat around some evenings swapping stories. She was usually high strung, and Charlene's easy ways and connections with the boys made her seem even more nervous and stiff by contrast. There was constant tension in the house next door.

My house settled down for a while with the usual antics of teenagers slightly upending things once in a while. There was the incident of "Victoria's secrets" as these were called, referring to a beautiful twenty-year old neighbor Vicky who insisted on getting undressed down the block with the window of her attic bedroom open. I learned of this one night as I passed Anthony's upstairs room next to my apartment. Looking in, I saw him standing on the windowsill, leaning out as far as he could.

"What in the world are you doing? You can't fly. Get down before you give the neighbors a heart attack."

"Mr. D., Mr. D., check this out. This neighbor's giving me more than a heart attack."

Mounting the windowsill, I leaned out and almost fell out. Vicky was in full swing, dancing in her room about two hundred feet away stark naked, her body appearing every ten seconds in front of the window as she swayed back and forth.

"Whoa there, Anthony. Get down anyway. It's not right."

"C'mon, Mr. D., you're looking too."

"Well, yes, but only to see what you're doing."

I made Anthony get down and closed his venetian blinds. The next night I heard a commotion in his room and left my apartment to see. There were six kids standing in line with two on the sill, all hoping to get a glance of Vicky's open secrets. I yelled at them to get down immediately, but I knew this was going to be a recurring battle with the word out. Next thing I knew even the guys next door began hanging out windows at all hours of the night as Vicky liked to rouse herself for nocturnal dances whenever the mood struck. And it struck often, gathering audiences. One boy next door decided to climb a telephone pole and almost got killed falling ten feet down on top of a pickup truck. Vicky heard the ruckus and closed the curtains, only to open them the next night. Mr. Al came on duty and found out what was going on. He knocked on my apartment, and Lisa opened the door. She was having a faberware party with five other women, including the cook who occasionally worked for me as well as other staff wives and friends. Lisa directed him to my den where I was sitting reading, and he asked me what all this peeping was about. Closing the den door, I decided to show him. The next thing I knew the door flew open, the light flicked on, and my wife and some of her friends were crammed in the door watching Al and I fight over the binoculars. Al and I almost fell out the window as the women began to taunt us, Lisa and my cook Susie leading the way. Al and I claimed we were looking at a strange bird in a tree, and Hilary, a supervisor's wife, said, "Sure, a bird with just about two of everything." So we were part of the show now, and I felt like writing an anonymous letter to Vicky, informing her of the depravity she was inspiring down the street. But I didn't have to.

Two days later, after our continued patrols of the windows failed to keep the guys hanging out the windows, Vicky's very large and very angry brother Harry, a policeman in training, knocked on our door and called out all the guys on the front lawn for a beating.

"You guys in there are a bunch of perverted niggers and spics and you Mr. D. man, are just a fucking idiot leading the tribe."

We all crouched down in the house, hoping Harry would just scream himself tired. But he didn't. Lights across the street were going on as neighbors heard his yells. I finally answered the door and talked to Harry in as low a tone as I could muster.

"What's the problem, Harry? How can I help?"

"You can get these guys from being such demented perverts. They're snoopin on my sister, I understand from your boy Jimmy. I caught his stupid ass trying to climb up a ladder in my backyard. He thought he could get on the terrace. I almost killed his ass. He tells me he wasn't breaking in but was hoping to get a look at my sister. He says all you guys do it. What the fuck is going on here?"

The thought of how desperate little Jimmy was struck me as somewhat humorous and I fought back a smile.

"Just teenage boys acting stupid, Harry. I think your sister Vicky should know about her window there. It's pretty visible and with twenty boys in these houses, well, word gets out."

"You telling me my sister's asking for it, huh?"

"No, just that she's innocently getting undressed in front of windows and dancing about and these guys are teens, that's all."

"I hear from Jimmy here even you're peeping with the counselors."

"Jimmy is covering himself. I certainly have punished these guys for doing it, and I respect people's privacy way too much for such things."

"Any more of this bullshit and next time I'm in the house and your spics are going to pay big time."

For the next few days, mercifully, Vicky closed the curtains. Then, riling the boys to Dionysian frenzy, the curtain was lifted. This time, Vicky's sister joined in, as I understand from Anthony, with both women trying on gowns. Vicky's sister was getting married.

"We all kissed the bride over the weekend, Mr. D.," Anthony told me.

"Yeah and these jerks were hanging out all the windows, Mr. D., after hours with the counselor asleep," Fernando told me. "I can't stand this stupid stuff. I just went to bed. It's embarrassing to live with these guys. And no way you want that Harry dude going off."

But the show went on. The counselors and I really put the clamps down on the window peeping, docking allowances, grounding kids. One weekend we had a house load of frustrated peepers sitting around the living room, doing extra chores, the steam of deterred voyeurism cooking their brains. Then James, a boy next door, just went crazy for a while for reasons undetermined. It was getting close to July 4th, and one morning my whole house awoke to the sounds of a loud explosion and then a rigorous chase going on around our house. The counselor Mark and Ronnie were pursuing James who had a "cherry bomb" in his hand. Looking down from my window, I could see they had cornered the boy against garbage pails, and he stood there, lit lighter in one hand, cherry bomb in the other.

"C'mon, c'mon, mess with me, c'mon, and I'll fuckin blow yous up, blow yous up."

"James, relax, relax, no one's going to hurt you. You're only going to hurt yourself. Give us the bomb," Ronnie coaxed.

It was a strange scene to see the three of them in sleeping attire, Byars in expensive slippers and velour robe, the counselor in tattered army shorts and t-shirt, James in underwear festooned with a Michael Jackson portrait, white gloves on either side of the crotch. After a minute of tense silence, Ronnie pretended to give up.

"OK, James, OK, go ahead, do it, do it, I haven't had my coffee yet. Get the damn thing over with so all we can get our breakfast."

Obligingly, James Bluefield made his break, lighting the bomb, hurling it at the two men and dashing down the alleyway. He went AWOL in his underwear, surprisingly not coming back for three days. He must have fallen in with Michael Jackson groupies. Bluefield, needless to say, was a very disturbed young man from Jamaica, Queens. His last name stuck in my head as an emblem of his reality. He seemed always brooding about something. Tall, good-looking, and very dark, he sulked in corners, often mumbling pop tunes to himself like a blues performer on the road gone crazy with loneliness. No wonder. He had never known his father, and his mother had inevitably failed miserably to take care of her eight children. Her oldest, James lived to see all the shambles of the life around him, his mother's boyfriends coming and going, the street violence, the occasional evictions. Six of the eight children had different fathers, apparently, a figure only topped by Juan in my house, whose mother had sixteen children, perhaps ten different fathers, as far as we were able to tell. James had gone inside, into a blue space of melancholy to protect himself somehow from all the turmoil of poverty and pain in his life. Whenever someone spoke to him, he would snap out of his funk long enough to smile, welcoming the attention, then begin to drift before one's eyes back into his inner space, unable to concentrate. There would be occasional outbursts of violence, such as the time he held the whole home at bay with a wooden chair over his head at the supper table, eventually slamming it right into the platter of fried chicken. He had been thoroughly thrashed by the boys for ruining the supper before the counselor had disentangled everyone. Now the cherry bomb incident. Vicky's open secrets for a time had drawn James out of brooding. At least, when looking through her windows, he did not have to peer into his own deep, painful spaces, I guess. James was eventually located in Queens when his mother called us to say she had gotten word he was living with one of his paternal aunts. The thought of James' getting all the way to Queens from Staten Island with only his Jackson briefs on boggled the mind. Some sleepy eyes must have been raised on the Ferry that morning, no doubt. I imagined the Ferry crossing in front of the Statue of Liberty bearing on its famous decks a pure product of America, a home boy running from a home he never felt home, free, crazy, and nearly without clothes. In every direction James went, fields of blue. He stayed on in Queens, and Byars dropped off the rest of his wardrobe, including some new clothes he bought for the boy. "We couldn't help him but at least he'll think well of his time with us. Don't want anyone to think we walk around half naked in the group home."

I found out two weeks later that despite our successful attempts to patrol the windows, some of the boys had set up surveillance down the street in a vacant lot from where they watched Ms. Vicky dance. They had binoculars from Willie who had another boy steal them from some neighborhood friend. By this time, Willie, realizing there was no way to get to the top of the power structure with all those older boys from tough neighborhoods in his way, had decided to go underground as his main amusement. He was fully operative in a black market, dealing in goods stolen from local break-ins, the vacant lot a warehouse. He had gotten another boy from next door to take advantage of any open windows in the neighborhood. Again, the lag time between this new wrinkle in Willie's operations and my finding out was something Willie could count on with all the craziness going on all the time.

Another version of upstairs and down was occurring next door. One afternoon I had to find Ronnie so he could give me the ledger and receipts for the revolving fund he wanted me to drop off in Manhattan the next day. I found him upstairs, kneeling at a door. He put his fingers to his lips to silence me and brought me away into the hall. "I'm fixing the door," he said and winked. Then the bathroom door opened, and Ms. Allison walked out, a public school teacher who worked as a tutor with some of the boys.

"More ice tea, Allison?"

"No thanks. I've had quite enough."

After she walked downstairs, Ronnie whispered in my ear, "I sure like making her pee." My eyes opened like an alarm had gone off. I felt like I should tell our boss, but I knew this would put us all in a very tense situation. I'd be seen as a betrayer of male trust and our clique, but what about Allison? My head was spinning as he handed me the envelope bulging with receipts that were to be refunded by the agency. How many of these receipts were taken off a store floor? Another day early one morning, I went to pick up Ronnie for a trip to the downtown office. Knocking on his basement apartment's door, Harriet answered sourly.

"Yes?"

"Good morning, Harriet. I'm looking for Ron."

"So am I."

"You mean he's not here? We have meetings downtown all day and I'm driving in with him."

"Oh, check upstairs in the, uh, what's he calling it now? The counselor's room. Yeah, the counselor should know," she said in exasperation, closing the door in my face.

Walking up the two flights, I wasn't sure what the story was but it revealed itself quickly. Knocking on the counselor's door, I heard some scrambling about, low voices, and then Charlene cracked the door a bit.

"You know where Ron is?"

"Who's that? Tony?" I heard Ron say from within. "OK, T., be there in a sec."

I waited a few minutes down the hall, the door opened, and a beaming Ron came out.

"Little private session there," he told me, rubbing his nose with his pointer finger.

"Ron, you're not... well, you know I knocked on your door downstairs, and Harriet, well, she, she..."

"Come on, she what? Knew where I was and had an attitude again? She always does. Come on. I'll fill you in on the way downtown."

He told me half the story. He and Charlene were friends before he hired her. She had run into a little trouble in Newark where she was living with her brother and needed some help right away. They were more than long-time friends, he said with another wink. He figured he owed her some support so he hired her, and she'd live in the home in the counselor's quarters until she found a local place to live. In the meantime, they were enjoying each other's company.

"Ron, what about your wife? I mean, come on, she's there with you, two flights down, and you and Charlene are upstairs having, well, your thing, and that doesn't bother you? What about your two kids and all? And the boys must know or will find out soon too, no?"

"Tony, sometimes you just gotta do what you gotta do."

"Ron, if downtown finds out..."

"Leo knows Charlene and her family too. He knows the arrangement and just told me to keep a low profile."

"I can't believe that. He knows she's your live-in lover?"

"Live-in friend."

"Come on, Ron. You can't be serious. Your wife knows, guy. How long until things get crazy, violent? You can't do this."

"Tony, please understand here. You're not going to go around telling people, are you? Make your judgments if you want but come on, I'm confiding in you. Harriet and I have been having a lot of problems. She's going to take the kids back to Puerto Rico where her family's from. In the meantime, well, Charlene really needed help. I can't tell you all the details right now but they're coming down the pike. When it's time, I'll let you in on things."

"Ron, I really can't go along with this. If your boys find out, my boys find out, and you know how crazy they'll get knowing you're upstairs banging the counselor with your wife downstairs. Ron, you must be joking here, no?"

"Tony, when the wife moves out, we're getting separated legally. In the meantime, I just had to help out Charlene. I mean she was about to get arrested for being involved with some things her brother was into. I really can't say anything more."

After the morning meeting, four of us live-ins went out to lunch at a small bar and grill on the East side of Manhattan. We sat at a booth, ordered lunch and were waiting when Ron broke out an envelope, dumped a little powder on the table, cut it into a line and was about to snort when Mr. Will, the first to realize fully what Ron was doing nearly jumped out of his seat.

"Good God almighty, Ronnie, what the hell you doing? Trying to get us all arrested? Put that shit away, man. Go in the bathroom for God's sake if you gonna be tootin."

"I know the owner here. He likes it too, and who's going to see us back here? Help yourself to some if you'd like."

I sat there in astonishment for a few seconds as Ron did a line and then another right off the table in a busy restaurant. I was about to leave when Ron put everything away and told me to relax. Ted who was also there just shook his head and said, "Just don't know why anyone would want to do that crap." Meanwhile, Ted, married with kids, was dating a policeman's wife. Talk about courting danger. We ate in silence, and when Will and I were alone for a while heading to the office, we shared our utter disbelief at the incredible brawn of the guy, doing lines off a table in the middle of the day with all kinds of people around.

"That dude's a wild man, and he's got something going down with Leo, I be tellin you, Tony, something going down, something, a ha, a ha, something no good. He's a wild dude."

I choked on my words, almost telling Will about Charlene but then again, if people knew I knew and something blew up, I'd be seen as Ron's associate in debauchery and now drugs. Then again, Will was Will, and if I couldn't trust him, I might as well not trust anyone in the whole agency. Will had become a good friend. Bouncing it back and forth a while, I decided to tell him.

"Lawdie, Tony, I knew it, that guy's way out of control there, T, and you better duck low too because when word gets out, you two will be seen in bed with her together or in a sauna at the Mud Club," he laughed, a big hand-slapping laugh, head twisting side to side. He looked like a frenzied tuna caught in a net when he laughed this way.

It relieved me to tell Will and hear his jolliness and concern for me. It made it feel as if living now next to bedlam, let alone living in one myself, was just a crazy story one heard about, a story about the unbelievable things people do, hellbent to destroy themselves for what? What? I thought about the broken families of the boys. How often was it just gross irresponsibility that led to parental neglect or abuse or outright abandonment of children? How much genuine insanity was in the mix?

But the behavior was just the surface of it. I thought of Juan's mother and her sixteen kids, the barely known fathers, one of them in the prison where I was teaching. My experience teaching college literature in a medium-security prison is a whole other story I have to tell. I also thought of Kevin's mother whom I had visited in Bed-Stuy in Brooklyn as part of a routine home visit to see if the boy could safely go home on weekends. I went to Bedford Avenue to section 8 apartments, walked through the graffiti-splattered hallways, over some broken glass, into the elevator that had experienced a fire. Down the hall on the eighth floor, I knocked on the door. A husky voice asked who I was and then opened the door. Standing before me was a large, round woman with huge soft eyes wearing a long checkered nightgown and sneakers.

"Y'all come right in, Mr. D., yes sir, Kevin's told me about how nice you are to him and what a nice home you running. Sit yourself right down there on the couch."

"Thank you, Mrs. Morton, glad to meet you. Kevin is a really sweet kid, and thankfully too because he's a big guy. You know he just made the high school basketball team."

"He been tellin me, yes sir, Mr. D., and I want to go out there and visit him but I'm diabetic and with my weight and all, have a hard time movin around. Oh no, I see you looking at that little baby there sleepin away. Not mine, oh no, not at my age," she chuckled, "no thank you there, please. I take care of lots of babies here in the building, gettin some extra money like I need."

"How many babies do you care for?"

"Oh bout three or four, different times of the days, you know, with the mothers workin part-time and what not. Yes, sir, that's what the good Lord would have me do, take care of the babies. I also get some sistance, some food stamps. You know I got another son bigger than Kevie and older too. He be sleepin in the bedroom. He sure wants to meet you. I'll wake him up."

"No, no, that's OK" but she had already disappeared into the room.

Then a giant of a man emerged, walking towards me with hand extended.

"Oh yessum, yessum, my name is Jonah, Jonathan, what's your name?"

"Already told you, Jonathan, and watch out, you almost steppin on Mr. D.'s feet. Step back a little."

Jonathan proceeded to give me a big hug, and I disappeared into his huge arms and chest for a second. He was drooling heavily too, and as he rocked me back and forth, I could smell his foul breath and body odor.

"OK, Jonathan, OK, Mr. D. knows you like him and preciate his caring for Kevie. Now go back to sleep. You know how drowsy you get this time of day."

"Yes, Jonathan, thanks for the welcome, and I will take good care of your brother."

He disappeared back into the bedroom, and I relaxed quite a bit, wondering for a moment there if I was going to get crushed.

"Don't you mind him too much there, Mr. D. He's harmless. Retarded all his life and I been taking care of him for thirty years now. Yes, not easy, not easy, but he's my son."

We spoke for a half-hour or so. She had no qualms about Kevin coming back to visit now that she had a court order of protection from his alcoholic father.

"And where does he live?"

"I don't think he's in that apartment of his no more. Shoot, you probably better off askin round the park if anybody seen O. T. lately. He's probably drunk under some bench. This ain't been easy, no way, no how, but I gots to care for Jonathan. Kevie, well, he deserve better than what I can give him, with his brother here and the babies I got to care for and that no good father of his botherin us. Kevie wanted to break his jaw last time he was here because he showed up drunk as usual and was tryin to take my money. Kevin ran him off down the hall. I don't want to see Kevie in trouble for that no good father. And the neighborhood here, well, you can see for yourself. Kevie deserve better. He's a good boy. And God know that too, yes indeed."

"He is a good young man, Mrs. Morton, and he's doing well. You should be proud of him. Now I see where he gets his niceness and manners from. I can tell he's your son."

I left her home wondering how this woman managed things for herself with all her health problems let alone her son's. She sustained a good feeling about her life that persisted among open misery and past failure. It showed in the pressed curtains, the carefully organized living room, the clean counters, her invitation to me to sit and relax in her home. And where did she have this courage that she would not see as courage, just an acceptance of her lot in life? It had to be her humility. She was far more than holding on or getting through life. She was inspiring at the most basic level of life, a blessing to her in any form it comes. Where did she get this kind of strength I could only wonder at? Things at the human level are a lot more complicated than any explanation because they stretch backward into time, hiding under fact sheets, birth certificates, death notices, far beyond bank accounts and the material qualities of one's life, the physical attributes of one's body or health. Mrs. Morton had held to her faith and her sanity somehow against incredible odds. I thought of all those infants she was taking care of probably for years now. I imagined the apartment when three or four were wailing, diapers being changed, milk being warmed, cradles being rocked. In such work, faith and care, human lives are sustained. Mrs. Morton's life was a testament to this reality as was the kindness of her son Kevin.

Will and I entered the office that afternoon to attend a drug prevention seminar. Twenty live ins sat there round a table, nervously drinking coffee, exchanging tales of the mild to extreme chaos we experienced day to day. The Bronx supervisors always had more mind-blowing tales than we had on the island. One home had decided to give all new placements an initiation. The boys would stone a kid out on whatever drugs were floating in the area and leave him in the middle of the night miles away from the home in nothing but his underwear. Word got out as to what they were doing when a boy turned up on the side of the Cross-Bronx Expressway wandering about in a mescaline-induced delirium. It reminded of training to qualify as a shaman among Southwestern native Americans. If you survived a solitary a one-hundred-mile trip on foot in the desert with little water and no clothing while high on peyote, you qualified as a high priest or warrior. For these boys, the end result of initiation was the right to sleep in a bed, refuge from the desert of New York City streets often less merciful than vultures. So what could we be told this afternoon about drug abuse that we didn't know already?

Leo, the director, droned out his welcome and introduced the "expert" speaker who had worked in rehabs and residential treatment centers for many years, having survived his own difficult teenage years and learning from his experiences and training in counseling to give others insight into the dynamics of drug abuse. Slumped in my chair, I looked around the room for an unfamiliar face to rise when I heard Leo say,

"So without more ado, here's our agency's new expert in these difficult issues, Mr. Ronald Byars, one of our own."

Will choked on his coffee. My jaw dropped. Byars, sliding a finger under his nose quickly back and forth while looking at me in the eyes, rose and began his lecture about his life experiences. He stood there stoned himself, expert in addiction, indeed. No one besides the three of us who had witnessed his tooting at the cafe table knew he was high. We three had an interesting silent commentary to make through hand and eye gestures. We had to suppress our laughter, always the funniest laughter when forbidden by ceremonies of law and order that might be seen through by barbs of hilarity directed at them.

"And you never know when one of these kids is high unless you know exactly what you're looking for," he said. "They have ways of hiding symptoms, coming home smelling of beer to mask telltale signs, pretending they're excited about something you like, acting very concerned about their chores, whatever it takes to make you think their behavior is coming from elsewhere than their drug of choice, speed, dope, coke, crack, pot, whatever."

In a few weeks I discovered how even more open Ronnie was with his own symptoms, not caring to hide. By this time, his wife Harriet had left with the children, and Charlene had moved into the basement apartment, with lots of late-night guests coming and going. As it was our bi-weekly routine, I picked him up one morning for a trip downtown to the office. I knocked on the door, and Ronnie yelled out, "Come on in. I'm in the shower."

I walked to the kitchen table, and Ronnie came out wearing a towel, telling me to help myself to some coffee and whatever else I wanted.

"Even this," he said, going to the freezer where he removed a quart-size freezer bag and tossed it on the table. "Help yourself. Do some up. It's Rosie's bag but she won't mind you tasting it."

He went back to the bathroom with a wink. I sat there in the early morning light streaming in through the basement window, staring at all that cocaine powder and then at the strange zigzag pattern in the dark orange carpeting, at a loss to see where Lisa and I fit in in all of this. Had we become part of a system that was corrupting kids by the very assumption it could provide a surrogate family let alone the often sorry people who had come forward to play the role? So much was left to chance as in many job situations. A worker or a boss could be good, bad or indifferent, but when children's lives were at stake, far more than corporate loss or efficiency was involved. And yet, the daily rate per child per night was what kept us afloat. Money per child, how vile the equation, yet we were all involved in this way of thinking that seemed to me, staring at the inescapable pattern scattered in the glow of a strengthening sun, the solution and the problem, the cure and the disease. A price on everything. The bottom line was the burden and the motivation, the foundation and the crack. The noose around all our necks. I was dizzy from these feelings. All I could do was keep in the right direction. Avoid despair, do what I could to help people in my care, and move on when I obtained my doctoral degree, hopefully obtaining a professorship although the odds of that were growing increasingly slim in a diminishing job market. The study of literature was increasingly being phased out, not providing technical skills directly pluggable into the marketplace. But what of the leadership abilities the study of literature had once upon a time helped foster? Was not Ulysses a model of how to survive by wiliness and his poet of how to do justice to the world? The gods had given Ulysses moly to avoid a foul transformation at the hands of Circe. What could prevent it from happening to me? Drifting back from such thoughts, I saw the bag of coke on the table. Here was the modern lotus plant of America, toot and forget. Ronnie came back fully dressed.

"Come on, T. Help yourself."

"No thanks, Ron. Coffee is about as far as I'll go this morning. It'll have to be lotus enough."

"Lotus? You mean your man Will, the Otis man?" Ronnie chuckled.

"No, no. Heh, what do you mean this is Rosie's? Who's that?"

"Rosie from the hill."

"Oh, our Rosie."

"Yeah, no wonder her house budget is a bit steep. She loves that nose candy far more than me."

Rosie was another live-in, a single woman running a girls' home that was known as the most chaotic in the agency. I was surprised to hear she was so heavily into drugs because she was always so chipper and direct. Now I knew why she was so up all the time. At thirty years old, she had gone through a difficult divorce from an abusive guy rumored to be heavily connected with the mob on Staten Island. He worked as a guard in a huge home on Todt Hill that supposedly had three subterranean floors. The guy began to bring the violence of his daily life into his own home, hating Rosie for putting on weight, not appearing like the "doll" I guess mobsters require in their line of work. But to her credit, she managed to leave the guy and ended up moving into a group home to support herself and do, as she told me one time, "some real good work with kids who grew up like I did, all busted up with no place to go but down." So I respected her for these reasons, her hard-won independence from a brutal marriage, her commitment to helping kids, but now obviously, things had unraveled. She knocked on the door just before Ronnie and I were about to leave for the office. Her eyes were hollow, her body appeared weighed down, and she spoke in quick phrases. Ronnie told her he had scored for her, and she jumped up into the air, suddenly becoming for a moment the person I remembered her as. Out of her purse, she took a roll of cash and gave it to Ronnie.

"Heh, Rosie," Ronnie said. "Hope you got enough receipts for that. If you want, I got some extra ones on the counter there. Love that carbon copy, sweetie."

Ronnie was referring to the way we did our budgets, documenting with receipts how we spent the funds which would be replenished according to the amount we had spent. Just about every two weeks we would need another infusion of funds. I was proud that I was dead center among the sixteen homes the agency ran, neither too high or too low, "the standard," Leo told me, for how much should be spent. My kids and I ate well and wore nice clothes. Needless to say, Ronnie and of late Rosie's homes were way up there at the top, big spenders for now obvious reasons.

"I'll wait for you upstairs," I told Ronnie, feeling nauseous at the drug transaction, feeling more and more implicated. Upstairs, some boys in Byars's house were scurrying to get out to school on time.

"Yo, Mr. D., wha's happenin?" Jesus shouted out to me. "Play some ball this weekend?"

"Sounds good, Jesus. How's the varsity going?"

"It's going good, good. Scored a touchdown last week gainst Monsignor High. And my mom was there."

"I hear she cooked up a storm, rice and beans, platanos, roasted pork, the whole deal."

"Yeah and we're still eatin it up. Just had some for breakfast. You want some?"

Gathered around the dining room table were four guys devouring omelettes stuffed with roasted pork.

"How's crazy Wille boy, Mr. D.? Still drivin you nuts?" Miguel asked me. "He better not move here or we'll all starve."

"Got that right," Carlos yelled.

"And how's your man Freddy?" I asked Miguel.

Freddy was a neighborhood man who lived alone. Eighty or so, he had lived in the same house for about forty years and watched the area go from nearly all green with mostly farmland to nearly all concrete walks and semi-attached homes. Miguel had taken a shine to the old man with his talk of things past and his constant barrage of laments regarding the current state of Staten Island and American politics.

"Built that damn ginny gangplank, Miguel, that stupid bridge, and all the riff raff from Brooklyn spilled over here. Used to be a getaway out here, a forest place with streams and all kinds of deer and wildlife. Used to have eagles flying through. Now just got the stupid traffic and the biggest landfill on earth. I read it can be seen from outer space for God's sake like the freaking wall of China."

This was Freddy's constant lament, and Miguel would just listen to the crabbed talk and laugh. The way Freddy spoke of the past and the forests reminded Miguel of his memories of Puerto Rico.

"Mr. D., Freddy's not been feeling too well," Miguel told me.

"You mean he's moaning against reality again? What else is new?"

"No, I mean, he's...what did you say the other day about that counselor who quit? His hands went straight up in the air and he said, 'I'm gone.' Well, I told Freddy that one and Freddy said it's like that for him only serious. 'I'm gone too,' he told me, 'out of here. My time's up. Only I'm not out the door. I'm headin for green fields in the sky. Bad heart problems."

"Oh no. I noticed he hasn't been standing on his corner spot."

"Yeah, he can't tell you what's everyone doing in the hood no more. He's not Mr. Eyeballs anymore as you call him."

"Miguel, seriously though, you must be worried about him."

"Yeah, kind of like the guy, I guess."

"He's been like a grandpa to you. He always waved to us too. Whenever I spoke to him, he always had a piece of news, what storm was coming, who was moving out, fighting or coming home late. Well, I hope he's OK."

"I don't think so, Mr. D. This time he says it's real serious. Heh, got to go sometime, I guess."

"Well, he's a tough old codger. He'll probably hang in there. And you know what? You've given him a lot too. He loves talking to you. You're like a grandson to him. Maybe tell him that. He'd love to know you felt that way if you do."

"Yeah, I know, I know. I'm going to visit him again after school today. See if he needs anything from the store. He's losing his breath a lot. Can't even get to his old corner. So his hands are going up, Mr. D, maybe. Out of here myself. Got to get to class."

Miguel spoke in flickering tones of sadness and humor. He was fighting off the despair he clearly felt inside for the possible loss of Freddy. His going over there to help him was just part of the way Miguel was. He might not tell someone he loved them but he'd do just about anything for them if considered a friend. He had a kind heart though an exterior toughness had to be kept up to fit in with the other boys. It was something of a male code of honor. Often their childhood experiences had taught them they would be hurt if they had strong feelings for someone in the home or neighborhood. Fear of love stemmed from their heavy sense of how fragile life is, with home thought of as a place of exile rather than a root. Children, counselors, social workers and supervisors came in and out of their lives just as their own parents and siblings had done or were doing. Any deep allegiance was a danger. You just had to protect yourself. Unfortunately, the exterior shell too frequently took over the person, with emptiness and cynicism becoming the main feelings of the day. Even Miguel, so capable of kindness and thoughtfulness, had come to see a bitter, violent side of himself once.

Boys from both homes and I had been playing softball up the street in a large schoolyard, one home against the other. We had good athletes in the homes, Miguel one of the best. This one game was hotly contested. Jimmy was not anywhere as gifted as some of the other boys but during this game he rocked a hit over Jesus's head deep into centerfield and ran the bases for dear life as if a lifelong fame were at stake. Miguel, playing third base, ran home to catch the ball because the catcher had fallen down. Jimmy and Miguel collided fiercely at home plate just as the ball arrived into Miguel's mitt, Jesus having made a dead-on, one-bounce throw to the plate. Jimmy threw out a leg as he slid, kicking Miguel in the face and dislodging the ball. It was a walk-off inside-the-parker.

"Are you fuckin crazy!" Miguel screamed. "You fucking kicked me in the face."

"Heh, that's the breaks. You dropped the ball. We win, we win."

"I should fuck you up."

"Tough shit, spic boy. You dropped it, dropped it."

The racial slur was the last straw. Miguel grabbed a baseball bat and was about to beat Jimmy with it when I jumped in between the two.

"Put it down, Miguel, calm down, calm down."

"Get out of my way, out of my way. No one's callin me that, not this little shit, no way."

"Miguel, come on, calm down, don't do something crazy. Drop the bat."

By this time, all the boys had taken a few steps back, staring in astonishment at the usually placid and very well-liked Miguel.

"Get the fuck out of my way, D man. You want some too, huh, huh?"

As he said this, he lurched towards me with the bat and took a swing, barely missing my chest because I had leaped away. I fell backwards into Jimmy, knocking him down and falling over him. Miguel just stood there over us, bursting with silent rage, looking like a caveman with a club raised up, his whole body shaking. Jimmy and I scrambled to our feet. Everyone backed away from Miguel who stood there at home plate. All went silent. He just let the bat drop and stood there with a blank look on his face, his head cocked.

"OK, guys, game's over, game's over. Let's go home." I yelled and clapped my hands, thinking if we all just walked away, there'd be no big drama over male honor or whatever was on the line.

Everyone still stood there frozen, contemplating the suddenly murderous Miguel.

"Come on, guys, you heard Mr. D. Let's go home. Game's over, over," bellowed Fernando.

When we had walked well out of the park, I turned to see Miguel. He had dropped to his knees. I told Ronnie, his supervisor, who promised to have a long talk with Miguel. Ronnie put his hands on my shoulders and looked me in the eyes. "Are you ok, T.?" I was shaking with outrage and despair. I lied to him, saying, "I'm fine," but not in a dismissive way. "Wow, he almost knocked you out of the park." Ron's touch of concern and humor helped me regain some balance. He advised that the three of us should talk and then the three of us with Jimmy after he cooled down too. Ronnie, despite all his problems, was very good at intervening, knowing what to say, using his training and personal experiences to find the right tone and gesture, a mix of insight and humor. I was impressed with Ronnie's skills especially the first few months of his employ. This is why his turnaround felt so tragic later on and why I was so conflicted about reporting his drug-dealing and sleeping around to anyone. I still can recall Miguel's tears and how dumbfounded he seemed when I finally talked to him about the whole incident. Ronnie had already gotten to him in a good way.

"Don't know, Mr. D., what got me that way. But the spic talk, the spic talk. Still, shouldn't have let it get to me, not against you anyway."

"And you have something else to say to Mr. D. too, no, Miguel?"

"Well, yes, yes, Mr. D., I just know how to... well, I can't say I was sorry to have gone after Jimmy. I shouldn't waste my time with him. You, though, well, when you got between us, I just felt you were taking his side and that's where I went off. Off."

"Come on, Miguel, something else too to him, yes?"

"Yeah I want to apologize to you. Mr. D. I just went off, I guess."

He sobbed a little when he said this and then turned his head away with some anger, a strange sight, tears shed in anger.

"You guess, Miguel?" Ronnie asked.

"Ok, ok. You're right. I was totally wrong," he said, still looking away.

"Miguel, you can do better. Look at Mr. D, please."

It was hard for Miguel to say he was sorry to me though we had become close. His manhood was at stake. In his eyes, I had sided with someone who attacked his identity. This connected with some bad experiences he and some of the other group home kids had in the high school they all attended. Slurs were made such as "that's a homie boy" or "welfare boy" or out and out racism, "spic head from the deadbeat home." These insults often cast before a crowd cut to the bone. The boys were easy to single out as a target of bullying and scapegoating. They were simply different, living in a home, refugee and exile from their own family, sometimes cool in their peers' eyes though weird, sometimes treated as just weird, outsider, loser or butt of racism. They felt how they stood out all the time. When I stood across from Miguel that day in the schoolyard, I think all of these feelings exploded from him, the hands gripped on the bat frozen with hatred, driven by his bitterness at his plight. That's more or less how I put it in the house log for the day and in the official report I had to write. Miguel's attempted assault on me was much different from Ricardo's actual assault on Marcos. One was unplanned, done in a fit of passion grossly out of character. The other one wasn't. It was icy and brushed off like a deed mandated out of honor to a lost father. Still, who would have thought Miguel had such deep rage inside him? Both attempts filled me with a nauseating mix of horror and wonder.

Finally, Miguel came round after the three of us stood there in an edgy silence for a minute - and how long time feels in such moments, ten seconds concentrating sometimes years of feelings in them. Then Miguel said weakly, looking at the floor, "Sorry, Mr. D." At last, he raised his eyes, looked into mine and said, "Sorry, Mr. D. Don't take offense, please." He blushed and looked down again.

I hugged him. We both cried a little. I was more surprised by my tears than by his.

"OK, Miguel. Got ya. Got ya. I accept your apology. Just learn a lesson here, OK? No rage is worth hurting anyone over, much less swinging a lethal weapon at someone who wants only the best for you."

Hard to tell what a person hides inside, hidden even from one's self sometimes. Probably the worst case of an exterior behavior masking deep feelings of hurt was a fourteen year-old I had worked with in the Bronx when I was a counselor during my college days. The teen named Chris was the house clown, a raucous, clever fast talker who was always cracking up everyone or trying to. He was compulsively silly. Silliness at the right time is a great gift but it's a curse if done all the time.

"Oh boy, oh boy, that was a good one, a good one," he'd say, surprised sometimes by the quickness of his own wit. He would often fall afoul of his uncontrollable tongue, getting into trouble and then sulking for hours. He would try to explain himself after the long brooding and cook up trouble again instantly.

"That's right, let's eat like pigs. We fatty hatties who shit in the potty and smell like sneakers," he'd say at supper, amusing some but making others snap back, "All the dumbass things you say."

"Can't help myself, I just shoot it off like a gunslinger. ZBang, Zbang. You know, Mr. Tony, you know. You got your own little bullets. You mumble machine. You trouble bubble. Just sayin what you're supposed to say. Eat, sweep, study, go to bed. Robot Tony. Robot man."

"Chris, we all know you're clever. But you don't need to make jokes all the time. It must be so stressful for you to keep it up, no? And I'm not one of the boys here. Drown your tongue in your head before fishing for trouble because you're doing it right now."

"Oh boy, oh boy, good one there, good one. I'm swimming upstream. Catch me. Mr. T, if you can but you gonna need a bigger hookey."

He had one giddy comrade among the boys, Gerry, his roommate who acted as if he and Chris were two of the three stooges. We put them together on purpose. Another less risible roommate may have tried adhesive tape or at the least ear plugs. His banter often provoked an inopportune laughter in the staff, turning us into sidemen even when we were telling him to do his chore or something. He'd make it sound like we said something funny – "Chris, clean your room or else" – "Tony, clean my room for elks?" - breaking the moment to his favor although the live-in supervisor, my boss, Bob O'Brian, having lived with the boy for two years, had had more than enough and refused to get taken in anymore. Chris would sing a crazy song - "Mr. O. He mad. He make Chris sad. Mr O. O No. Ya know? Ya know?" Bob would just wisely dead-pan or frown, letting Chris get the last word or singsong but not a retort. His incorrigible wit could get one's dander up if you let it, always clowning at the wrong time. He also had sulks that were impenetrable, showing a black mood of silence out of nowhere that could last a day or two followed by more torrents of comments, silly and abrasive at the same time but advanced for his age, maybe for any age, in his verbal agility. "Notice that sweet smell coming from afar, from distant fields of flowers blowing in the wind," he'd say and then lay a fart in a crowded silent van. "Last night's chicken, today's spirit." Amusing insults were his specialty. "That kid's got more problems than a dog with two legs, four feet and an owl for an ass with fleas on it." Or, "nice supper there, Mrs. L., did you discover it in the oven or mail-order it from Jack in the Crack down the block a ways?" Or, "Gee, this is a great place to live if you're a horney toad in a pond full of idiots." Or, "OK, so you don't have a brain, we can see that, but what's looking out of your eyes there? Is it a squirrel gathering nuts? A jellyfish? Plus I have a big pecker. Deal with it." Anything was liable to come out of Chris's mouth. He'd bark or fart on command usually when a staff member was making a point or enforcing a rule. Each witticism would push the envelope until he'd wear down his opponent, usually leading to an attack on him by one of the boys. He was satyr-like, a compulsive jester, a combination of Don Rickles and Diogenes at fourteen, committed to walking backwards for the contrarian hell of it. His mouth was an adventure, dragging him along towards what he thought was a truth or funny flash of the moment. The sulks, however, as I learned later, were hooked up with some big engines of despair inside. His parents, the father an addict, the mother simply AWOL, had left him to his devices at seven years old with an old maternal aunt who was nearly deaf, very wealthy, and eventually too sick to care for Chris. He was deeply bitter about this abandonment, understandably, and could never address this profound sense of betrayal in any serious way. How hard to bring words to it at any age much less at fourteen. The endless drollery was his attempt to prevent looking inside, an avoidance of the harrowing introspection his wit indicated he was capable of. One sensed lots of self-hatred inside, the compulsive humor distancing himself from others and himself, often earning the negative attention he felt he deserved.

I hadn't seen or heard about Chris in three years, with my having left the position as his counselor in the Bronx to assume the live-in position on Staten Island. I ran into my old boss Bob one day in the office. He had left the agency a year or so ago but had returned to the office to lunch with a friend. When I asked about the boys we used to work with, he told me about Chris.

"You know, Tony, horrible news a few months ago. I ran into a friend of mine who worked with Chris after he left our house. After you left, we had transferred him to a foster home, but he messed up there and then wound up upstate in a reformatory. One day, he was found dead in a barn nearby. He hung himself. Seventeen years old."

This was grief beyond words. I was at a total loss. Had we all been complicit in his self-destruction, trying to ignore or laughing with or at his compulsive humor? We should have realized it was a plea for help. We all knew how nearly unreachable Chris had been, the joking his way of putting up a wall between himself and everyone, between himself and himself perhaps, his occasional sulks a reaction to the impossibility of the task. I've fumbled for words for years thinking about how Chris acted and what he did, trying to make sense of it. I have read in the philosopher Maurice Blanchot words to the effect that the hand that delivers the suicidal deathblow belongs to another self, hoping for relief from the broken self it would destroy. It is the killing hand that rejects despair and pain but cannot free itself from them except through death. The act of suicide is thus a twisted one of hope, a step towards a better life as if death were a state of being one could enter. Such a step never lands. Poor Chris had this split in his life. How sad he fell into it. Why hadn't we reached out in a more compassionate way to the Chris beyond or hiding beneath the court jester? He used words as a way of staying afloat but they were like the flailing arms of a drowning child. These strings of thoughts and feelings have carried on for many years in my mind. I cannot accept that the laughing dimpled face framed by the round curly hair was somehow gone from the world forever. Chris perhaps had run out of words and fell into blankness, the self-hanging a way to hold himself up, to gain a final reaction from others that he would never see. Somehow I had to shake free from the gloom before it ate me up.

Chapter 7

Ghosts

Shortly after news of the suicide, we celebrated Halloween, an event we had been planning for several weeks. At the time Helen and Walter were still the live-in couple next door, very nice, respectable people, with Walter going on to become the borough administrator and Ronnie Byars replacing him in the home. Helen and Lisa had decided to take charge of Halloween with a costume party, inviting counselors and supervisors from other homes as well as family members. The boys were all given a chance to come up with a costume. Willie predictably chose a devil's outfit. He told me, "I know I'm the devil here, Mr. D. Admit it. You think about me this way," laughing his infectious series of short chuckles. In fact, his costume broke some of the tension as we all came to realize that we had demonized Willie. He was on a path of self-destruction, so it appeared, and he relished the attention he received from raising hell. Though more bite than bark, when silent, most plotting. The other boys fell in line with this self-stereotyping in costume. José was a boxer, Fernando an angel, Jimmy a cowboy, Juan a danseur, Tony a "Brooklyn guido," that is, hair slicked back, gold chain, t-shirt and tight sleeves with a cigarette pack tucked in, and pointy black shoes. Marcos dressed in sheets, saying he was a ghost but really looking more like a patient in an asylum. Fernando tried to get John to dress like a buoy since that was going to be his job. "A human buoy paid by the rock, or maybe a park bench," Fernando told him. John deferred and dressed, well, like himself, hard black shoes, white socks, baggy pants twisted strangely high around his waist, white shirt sticking out, his hair in a state of havoc, with his eyeglasses forever slightly crooked or dirty. I dressed as Robin Hood, borrowing green leotards from Juan who for some reason had a pair in his closet way too big for him. I had to have the story from him. "Thrift store, Mr. D. I was going to turn them into leggings." Juan clapped his hands in glee when he saw my daughter Ariana dressed as a ballerina, which is what she said she wanted to be in life. But the real winners were Helen and Lisa. They carefully made these two giants' heads that they lifted over their heads, dropping the huge masks to their waists. So they were walking heads, their faces painted with lantern-like grins and wide-eyed stares with long lashes.

During the early evening, we closed all the lights, and each one of us had to recite a story in the dark. Everyone had been told a week beforehand they'd have to tell a story. Out of a bowl, we drew lots to see who'd be first. Willie was number 1. To my surprise, "demon" Willie was reluctant to say anything at first. He always wanted the spotlight but not this kind. This one was officially approved and given to him, without his having to merit it either way, and of course, it was a negative focus Willie thought he craved, working hard to earn it. We all urged him on, and after some silence sitting there with all of us in the dark, in a low voice, he began his tale.

"So I work in a dark cave for these dudes whose faces I hardly ever see, and they work everybody hard and everybody hates them but there ain't no use. They just have you. The whole world is this way, everybody working for these guys who wear nothing at all but little shorts. They got some whips and stuff to keep people in line. The work I gotta do is pretty gross. I gotta gather up all these worms in the cave and feed them to people, no, not just to anyone, sorry, don't mean to ruin the story, but I give the worms to the boss men who feed them to girls, yeah, especially the pretty girls," Willie laughs.

"Figures," Tony yells out. "Tee hee, tee heh. That's as close as you'll come to pretty girls."

"So this goes on all the time. I get the worms in buckets from the stone floor. They just keep oozin' out all over the place so it's not really hard to find them at all."

Willie went silent for a while. The whole house was silent too, some twenty people spellbound by this odd tale coming out of this man-child seated on a stool in a dark corner, wrestling inside with whatever was driving him. With his past, even the little we were able to piece together from what Willie was willing to remember, there was a host of nightmares leaping at him from all sides. Out of his silence, a strange laughter rose.

"When it's feeding time, the dudes start chanting, everyone starts chanting to the girls, 'Eat the blood, eat the blood, the blood, eat the blood.' And then the babes do, they do, they eat because there ain't nothing else. They get blood all over their skirts..."

"OK, Willie, I think you better end the story," Walter said, seeing his five-year old daughter beginning to cringe, gripping his arm in terror.

"OK, OK, Mr. W. Well, OK. Yeah. Well, after this stuff goes on for a long time and I'm gettin' old, real old and tired of everything, too old to bend down much and pick up the worms, I decide to just go to sleep, just fall out on the stone benches they got carved out of the walls. And so I do, and as I fall asleep, I remember I can fly.....yeah, that's it, that sounds right, I can fly, and I notice up above me all of a sudden, there's a hole in the ceiling, and it's just big enough to get out all the way and I see a blue sky there up above the round hole. So I start flapping around a bit but I really don't know how to fly yet and I'm banging into the walls and the dudes are after me, trying to pin me down and I'm laughing now because they can't really get their hands on me. I'm too fast even though I'm banging around, hurting myself to get away but I'm still having a good time. It's like the first time I've had a good time the whole time I've been in the cave, the only time it feels that way anyway.... That's the whole story."

"Willie, there's no ending, do you get out or what?" John asked, rocking furiously.

"Yeah, Willie, like you're just flying around, drop someone, drop one of those dudes with a leg kick, like this," José yelled out, kicking towards a candle we had lit on the table, making it flicker.

"Take a chill with that," I tell José.

Juan also told a story that rolled around in my brain for quite a while, connecting, as I felt, with Willie's bloodworms. Juan loved to perform and rose to tell his story. He bent slightly to one side and then another, giggling off and on, rolling his eyes, flapping his hands in the air like he was a bird trying to take off, letting us know he was making the whole thing up right there unlike Willie's strangely half-memorized tale. Yet the point of his was just about the same.

"OK, OK, so a group of kids crash on a desert island, no adults, the pilot dead in the crash, and they're all afraid. They didn't really know each other because it was the first day they had met, taking a plane ride to a camp in, um, in, um, Europe somewhere, no Africa, yes, the Gold Coast somewhere, I think. The Gold Coast's in Africa, right, Mr. D.? OK, OK. Anyway, they're on this island, and it's really beautiful with all kinds of stuff to eat, falling right from the trees, pineapples and coconuts and there's plenty of water to drink from these incredible fountains. Anyway, they just keep wandering around. They're eating and drinking all they want and they don't have to worry about anything, about sleeping out or anything because the weather is perfect, perfect," Juan emphasizes spreading his arms out over his head, "Just perfect. And so everything's really cool until, well, until something weird starts happening. One by one the kids start disappearing, just like, well, not being there anymore. Everyone would wake up in the morning and someone would be missing. Finally, I decide, yes, of course, I'm there, I mean it's my story so I might as well be in it, I decide to stay up all night and see what the hell is up with this. So everyone is sleeping packed tight together and I go off all alone under some palm trees behind some bushes so I can't be seen. Although everyone is scared, they all fall asleep in the middle of this night, a really thick night, I think, yes, so black I can't even see my own hand in front of me. But I'm awake just like I promised everyone. I'm on guard and I'm going to find out what's going on. Then all of a sudden, what happens is this strange cloud moves across the sky. First I see a little light way out to sea faraway, a little blink on the horizon, and it gets closer and brighter little by little until it is right over our island. I can now see it right over ahead. It's all dark all around the outside of the cloud but inside there's this weird light all twisted up in darkness rolling around. Then I see something coming out of the cloud, it looks like a giant hand, yes, a giant hand except it's got like teeth between the fingers, kind of like a shark's row of teeth but between these glowing long fingers, and it's reaching down towards everyone and I start yelling out to everyone and then instead of going at the kids sleeping, the hand that is really a jaw comes right at me, right into the bushes like it's got eyes, not just teeth. Everything it has can eat things, eyes, hands, mouths, it's all one thing all twisted up together coming out of the cloud, and it grabs me, it starts lifting me up, up, and as I'm going up, well, it, yes, it starts eating me, I'm disappearing into it, and it watches and holds and chews me all at the same time and, and, and well, I'm dead now. Thank you." Juan bows to us, and after recovering from a stunned silence, we applaud.

"Yeah, Juan, wouldn't you like to be eaten up," Tony taunted Juan who sticks his tongue out.

"You're just jealous because you can't make up any story worthwhile."

"Yeah right, I'm going out with my friends later. Like I'm really into this Halloween in the group home routine."

"OK, Ant-knee, you're just too cool for all of us. Enjoy your night out. Of course, your egg-throwing will be much more sophisticated than what we're doing here."

"Yeah, eggs with joints sticking out of `em," yells Jimmy.

"Yeah, like Juan's hand with the teeth, eggs with joints eating your brains," Fernando calls out.

"Guys, cool your engines. We have little kids here," Walter reminded.

"Yo, Mr. D, tell us one of your corn-ball stories, all that old stuff you read, pick something corn-bally out of it," Reuben, a boy from next door, calls out.

"Yeah, c'mon Mr. D., chuck one out," Tony said. "Give us a horny one."

"Tony, take it easy, it's a mixed crowd, OK?"

"Well, I've got ten minutes before I split and I want to hear one from you."

"Oh, ohh, Maria's waiting for you, right, Ant-knee? Huh, huh, ohhh," Miguel teased.

"Least I've got a girl, not like you guys with your magazines stashed away, going nowhere fast because you just came back from nowhere. Ain't that right, Mr. Al, isn't that what you say?"

"Alright, alright, calm down, calm down," Al called out from the kitchen.

"OK, OK. A quick story then."

"Right on, Mr. D., you're dying to tell one, we know, we know. Even Mrs. D. knows how really good your stories are, right Mrs. D.?" Jesus said, laughing and rolling his eyes.

"Of course, yes, Jesus, Mr. D. has practice, lots of practice teaching his classes that always pay so much attention to him. They love just his stories – at least he thinks so," Lisa said, prodding me with a private allusion. I had accepted phone calls from an older students, a thirty-five-year-old woman in the middle of a difficult divorce - and which one isn't? - and was reaching out to me for advice and solace, to use an old word for friendship. I was getting involved with her, no doubt, and not just out of compassion as I had told my wife who didn't need to hear me tell her this to understand. But more of this latter.

"OK, so here's my story. Imagine a time when there were no cars or supermarkets or phones or anything we would call modern, everyone living on farms in small villages with really no way to get in touch with the world outside. You live in your little village amidst fields and endless forests, and this little village probably would be the place where you would die too. Everyone knows all about everyone else, and everyone practices the same religion and customs and believe in the same things. Well, Halloween is a really big holiday for these people, especially in ancient Scotland. It is the time of year that the flocks of sheep and herds of cattle are brought to their winter pens at the end of the fall. And the people feel there were spirits who live in the forests and fields where their animals graze, spirits of the wilderness and spirits of the dead. These powers of the wild and the past have to be given offerings to show that the people appreciate all they have been given by them. At Halloween, they leave baskets of things harvested out in the fields, putting them as gifts at crossroads in the woods. The spirits would be called to come and feast on these treats so that the spirits would not play any tricks on them during the winter. This is why we still say trick or treat. Another custom on Halloween night is to light a huge bonfire on a hill. People dance around this fire and sing songs and even prayers to the queen of the witches, queen of the spirit-world. One of her more famous names in the ancient world is Hecate, a name given her because of the many offerings made to her or the hundreds of millions of ghosts she rules over in the world below. The tradition is not only to dance around the bonfire but to leave behind in the fire little stones or pebbles, and the heat from the fire warming the stone would give the person who left the stone heat and warmth throughout the winter."

"Yo, Mr. D., John would have to leave his head with the rocks in it that he has," Willie said.

"Ha, ha, Willie, and you'd be out there eating all the baskets like a pig, oink, oinker, oinkiest," John jived back.

"Ok, Ok. Now here's the story part."

"C'mon, Mr. D., get to the good part if there is one." Tony said.

"Yeah, it's like we're in school or something," Jimmy complained.

"Well, there was one girl nine years old who had taken a nasty fall from a horse and walked with a limp that looked like it was going to be permanent. She cried and cried over this damaged leg of hers because she loved to run in the fields and climb rocks and trees and skip through streams but now all that was over. She knew how powerful the witch goddess was and her tribe of spirit people so she thought and thought and decided that maybe if she left some part of her life in the fire, the spirits would take her with them and maybe heal her since her mom was always telling her how they have the power of life and death over things that grow or fade away. Had not her leg faded away? Couldn't the spirit people make it come back whole again? So that night after the wild dancing with her family and fellow village people around the fire..."

"Yeah, tee hee, the village people, those dudes from Greenwich Village that Juan baby would love to meet," Tony called out.

"OK, OK, story's almost finished. Hold your horses. And stop taunting Juan, Tony, or you won't go out tonight. Anyway, this little girl named Lena decided to put her tooth in the fire that night after all the dancing. Leaving a personal possession, she had been told, was always forbidden unless one wanted to be taken away into the spirit world. But a tooth, to her mind, paid tribute to their world beyond, one that was always on the other edge of the forest, just beyond the light through the trees. What could be the harm? The tooth would carry part of her there and show her trust in their powers. It was a pledge of her faith in them to heal her."

"Excuse me, Professor D.," José said raising his hand. "Can I go to the bathroom?"

"Yeah, he's got to leave a tooth. Dr. Drop's got loose teeth," Tony said. "What the mirror punch you back?" The boys exploded in laughter.

"Sara likes the story, Tony, this is good," Helen added, referring to her five-year old.

"Me too, Dad," Ariana said, holding up her arms, trying a pirouette.

"Well, thank you, Ariana, Sara and Helen. I appreciate the support. So Lena left her tooth in the bonfire and returned home and then snuck out during the night to see what would happen.

She crept out of the window while everyone was asleep and slowly made her way across the field to the top of the hill where she laid down behind a rock, watching the embers still flickering about a hundred paces away. She waited and waited and then she heard the wind stirring up beneath the full moon, bringing with it strange feelings. She saw on all sides of her people staggering about. From their clothes, she thought them exceedingly poor, people without homes, people with open sores and broken limbs, and they were everywhere. A cry went up into the air from hundreds of mouths calling out: 'Great Mother of the night, keeper of the animals and forests, guardian of the moon and the flow of the waves and grasses, heal us, lift us into your care and carry away our pain, o great one of the world below the moon.' Lena had never seen so many people with problems similar to hers. She raised herself atop the rock and saw people in every direction looking up to the sky and crying out. There had yet been no greater feeling in her young life than this, a sudden sense of strong kinship, a friendship with all these strangers, all hoping to be saved or helped, for some great power to come down out of the stars, healing everyone in one great sweep. She felt great warmth flooding into her. She felt she was letting go of pain deep inside, breathing in a spirit of togetherness, knowing others felt such pain and suffering too. And she thought it's not skies that heal, no, no strange force out of forests need come to make everyone whole, but only people already together now feeling together and sharing their search for healing as the best way of healing. This is the way to go forward and grow tall. She went down from the rock and walked her way home, the hills empty but for the glow of the moon, the guttering fire, the horizon distant on all sides without relief, a dark border beneath the stars. She felt how hard her life would be but how harder it would be to look to some force to heal other than the people she knew and loved and lived with day after day. She was on the path to being her own brave self, her own powers that she would carry every day within, and for the first time in a long time she felt the presence of hope in her own strength."

"OK, Mr. D., that's really nice, I can feel that, very nice," Juan extolled, taking Ariana's hand and twirling her around slowly.

"Yeah but she still lost her tooth and her leg ain't fixed, and she must feel like a fool out there now too," Willie mocked.

"Sara wants to know where the witches went," Helen asked.

"They went into the fire they left behind," I said.

"Ha, ha, good one, Tony, sell that one to Disney," Walter chuckled. "We can cast some administrators as warlocks too, to cut down the cost of the production."

"Yes," I said. "Give all the proceeds to Catholic Charities unless Disney is going to gobble them up like a hungry pumpkin."

"But don't let Leo get his hands in the till."

"OK, guys, it's a nice moment. Don't mess it up," said Helen.

"That's Tony's forte," Lisa added.

At this time, despite my fable, I could not be further from feeling that, outside my small circle of family and friends, camaraderie with others could help alleviate human suffering or lay ghosts to rest instead of being haunted by the misery that had reigned over the past. Working with so many kids suffering some form of trauma was taking its toll on my faith in mankind. I was also teaching two classes for the local city college, both off-campus, one at a medium-security prison, the other at a grammar school where twenty-five women, mostly in their thirties, were taking my literature course. In the prison, I taught some forty-five inmates World Literature, beginning with Oedipus Rex or as one of my captivated students called, "Eatie Pussy." In all justice to them, however, they proved one of the best classes of students I ever had, thinking hard about fate and destiny and the illusion, to their minds, of free choice. Every Tuesday for a semester, I went from the group home in the morning and afternoon to the prison at night where I'd be frisked before being allowed to enter. One of the inmates was probably Juan's father, fortunately not in my class. I thought of the revolving door syndrome, how many of the kids whose lives ended up under the jurisdiction of Family Court went on to having their futures decided for them by Criminal Court, a chain of grief and fate-like failing that began with shattered families pulling people apart. The family itself in so many of the people I worked with had been a place of exile rather than support and love. My student-inmates identified with Oedipus.

"I'm like Oedipus," one inmate told me. "It felt like that all during my childhood, just one thing coming down on me after another."

Another student wrote an essay about how he too preferred being blind like Oedipus at play's end rather than have to face what he did to his family, the shame of his own knowledge both the result of self-reflection and an obstacle to it. He could not undo what he had done. And the issue of justice was powerfully noticed, how Oedipus "killed his pop and slept with his mom and belongs in here with us," I was told in class one night. "If he's an unacknowledged hero of justice, like you just said, professor – yeah, I got it here in my notes - where's the justice when the hero is in exile? Seems mighty hypocritical to me." "Right on, right on," a few guys said.

This point was made by a fifty-year old man named Freddy who knew a lot about how tables could be turned suddenly and what one thought one knew about justice and love could be turned upside down very easily. Freddy wrote in his essays about how his father was ground down by a string of part-time jobs in the city, how his mother was chronically ill with mental problems, and how he hung out in the streets to learn how to survive the hard way. "Raising four kids on minimum wages is like being employed by the sphinx. Someone else's riddle is always coming at you, new one every day to devour you if you don't get through it. That was my father's life."

I learned a lot in that course about how one's place in the social scale of things almost determined how one lived and thought. I shared a passage from Freud about how if people don't solve their Oedipal problems, they become like Oedipus, an exile from their own happiness, which should not be expected to be more than an ordinary kind and not unachievable. "Can one be happy with what Freud calls ordinary unhappiness?" I asked. "Easy for you to say, teach. Try ours on for size," someone chimed in. My inmates were like Oedipus, in exile from their former lives but endlessly reflecting upon them. From the perspective of social dilemmas they had inherited, not merited, the way Oedipus was assaulted at birth by his own father the King, they were more victims of fate than shapers of their own destiny. This was not to absolve them of responsibility for their crimes, which were mostly related to drug-use, but to see their responsibility as a ripple in a pool that spread outward throughout society and backwards into times long distant from their own life. I mean what chance did most of the home kids have compared to other kids? They were innocent kids born into conditions of horror and squalor sometimes passed down for generations in a seemingly unbreakable link. In truth, often conditions of conquest from centuries or decades ago were at the root of the dysfunction and the poverty, not DNA. It was no mystery or scourge from nature or beyond. It was a matter of the brutal facts of world history.

I'll never forget the first day I met with my inmates slash college students, a captive audience twice-over. No other teacher at the college apparently wanted to teach in the prison, so the class was given to me as a graduate student, getting his feet wet as an adjunct. But it was a literature course, and I was excited to teach it. I would have taught it to a school of bluefish or to Willie's bloodworms if they had asked me. But to inmates? I thought of the writers Boethius, Sir Walter Raleigh, and Wole Soyinka. Imprisoned, they relied on philosophy and poetry to get them through. One can imprison a body but not a mind. The assistant warden first prepared me by reading a bit of a riot act. Without looking up from his pile of papers, he rattled off a list of do's and do not's to me. "Don't turn your back on the class for a long period of time like a minute or so; don't bring expensive things to class such as a gold watch or fancy pen; don't walk between the aisles; have your five-minute break at the same time all the time; don't let students gather to discuss in class things that have nothing to do with the class; don't let them gather around your desk; don't tell them personal things about yourself or life like where you live; avoid talking about provocative things like sex or violence or drugs; consider wearing a jacket and tie to send a message about professionalism and the formality you want to maintain; above all, any sign of violence like someone talking way too loudly or out of turn or getting agitated, notify the guard. That's why there's one outside the glass wall. He's there to help you and to keep an eye on things. That's his job. Any change at all in your routine for the class, tell the guard well in advance." Needless to say, I was terrified by the whole prospect but still intrigued by the experience.

Entering the classroom in a closed-off section of the building, I introduced myself to the guard seated at her desk outside the glass wall of my classroom. She was the only woman I saw in the whole complex during my semester there, and one of the few women at all my students saw. "Sure, Professor," one witty student, a former English major in college, would tell me. "All these stories about men and women, but that guard there is one of the very few females we can check out. You get out of touch in here with what it feels like to even see a woman much less be with one. So maybe the guard there ain't bad but heh, she's like Medusa. If she's checking you out, it means you're on her report. She's stoning you."

The first class was unbearable to me. I never felt so different, so uneasy in my life. I stood out there at the front of the class, stiff as a board, trying to remember to breathe correctly and project. A lot of guys were wearing doo-rags, a strange sight to see as if they were all imams and wise beyond my years. I was the youngest person in the class and one of five whites in the class that was about eighty percent black. I would hear speech-patterns and accents from all over the world, from Brooklyn to Jamaica. But this first class began in eerie, tense silence as the guys, arms folded, legs crossed, watched me closely. I handed out a brief syllabus and started reading it in a nervous voice. After about fifteen anxious minutes and lots of eyes rolling and throats clearing and blank looks coming my way, I received my first question. "Yes," I said to the hand raised, "can I help you?" "Yes, sir, you can," the student said, rising to his feet. I saw the guard from the corner of my eye look up from her endless paperwork.

"My name is Lee, Lee Farley. Now I don't know what you was told `bout us but let me tell you. We ain't bout to steal your pen or poke fun at you or kill you or each other. You look like a cool dude. Relax, relax, it's cool. Literature's cool too, man. We respect you for that."

Lee broke the ice. I broke into a smile and laughed. "How did you know about the pen advice?"

"They always be puttin' teachers on alert. We're used to really stiff, scared old teachers here, but you're young, probably from the

Bronx from how you talkin, and the stuff you been saying about dreams and stories, yeah, that's cool, cool, we got dreams too, long ones that go on all night and get us by in the day. Uh-huh, the day, yes-sum, the long days."

"That's right, Professor," said Larry, who told me his name when I asked him. "We know a few things about, what you call it here on the paper, the power of dreams and stories to change people's worlds? That's what you wrote. They help forget the world too. That's why I read novels and stories and stuff. Take me elsewhere, please. Anyplace, just not here, not here. I read to forget where I'm at."

That became a major idea in the class that we wrestled with, the function of story. A lot of the guys were writing poetry, mostly rap as it would come to be called, this being in the early eighties, and the poetry was almost always about unbearable pain, about what to do with it, about how to live with it. Many poems - and I was given some of them to check out - were about the families they left behind for the last few years. Wives that were waiting for them or claimed to be; wives that had divorced them; children that had grown into adults in the ten to fifteen years they had last seen their father out of a cell or "cube" as they called it. Several inmates were in prison for over fifteen years, sent down from a maximum-security prison to this medium one for good behavior. Taking a course merited additional good behavior points as I was reminded at semester's end when the assistant warden asked me to fill out a profile of each student. I refused because I felt it was unethical to weigh that way what and how something was said, a clear violation of free speech which to my mind had to be protected especially on the so-called margins of society and in a college classroom. This inside-out view of things influenced my thinking about the metaphor of a "mainstream" society. We're all in a fishbowl, able to see out of it, but not able to see it or the world outside of it without it. How fragile our lives, how imaginary our view; how hidden the wandering flows that make up the mainstream; how different we all are at the intimate levels of our lives where we actually live and dream; how we all use stories to cover up and escape as well as open up perspectives outside the workaday world of daily routines. Through my students' lives, I pondered the difficult unhappiness of even ordinary life, of loved ones left behind sooner or later, the lived misery and painful recollections even in the most blessed of lives much less the lives of inmates and those they had victimized. I thought of how Plotinus at the end of his great philosophical treatise describes the truly wise person as living a life that turns away from the pleasures of earthly things, "a flight of one alone with one alone." And yet these pleasures are mostly what one lives for to relieve the daily grind.

The other class I taught also involved ghosts of the past who would not die away but like Willie's bloodworms kept coming out of the very walls. The woman who had begun calling me was going through a horror of a situation. She had been sexually assaulted two years ago, and her husband had told her not to draw any attention to it but to forget the whole shame of it. That was just one source of suffocation of her life in her fishbowl of a marriage. He had also been dead set against her education, and, working a full- and part-time jobs to pay the bills, he was not there to help her with the three children, one of whom was severely handicapped. The list of her frustrating obstacles to developing her impressive talents in art and music went on and on. She had sought me out because I had brought a message of hope to her, reading Alice Munro, Sappho, D. H. Lawrence and Kate Chopin in my class, a near revelation to her. I guess I was something like a guru in her eyes, and I soaked in the adulation because it fed my craven male ego. She was also beautiful and extremely intelligent along with all the talent. I was giving her my heart along with my sympathy and advice. I began to see her after class, one thing led to another, and soon enough Lisa found out because when she asked me point blank if I had feelings for this woman whom I kept talking about, I said yes. We can't seal ourselves off from others, I rationalized to her. Interconnected lives are all over the place. Each connection involves many pathways of lives converging, some leading away from the past, others leading back to it. But she knew I was just trying to cover my tracks.

"This is not some project here, Anthony, with this woman," Lisa told me. "It's your choice based on your wants, these wants you feel for some reason. If you want to save the world, join a soup kitchen. I'm not buying that this is some kind of experiment in social progress. You're having an affair or about to have an affair. Period."

"I don't know what I'm doing, Lisa. But I have feelings I don't know what to do with. I've been pretty upfront about them. I'm confused. I'm sorry."

I was overcommitted, to say the least, and about to run into walls partly of my own making. I had a penchant for melancholy, and with the world the way it is and the work I was doing in it, I had plenty of suffering to find, plenty to brood about. Karrin, the woman in my class, was a prime example of yet another person living with fire under a bucket. I felt myself loving how she saw me as the one person who could ease her pain by listening, not judging and intuitively understanding, as she termed it. I warned her not to think I was advocating free love such as the kind we read in class by Shelley in his three sermons on free love. I was a messenger, someone who spoke the message but did not live it. I was an agent of ideas I did not necessarily practice or believe in, just an aspiring open-minded dispenser of them, professing nothing but the need for an open mind. But even I did not heed my own warning. She found the message powerful and liberating, helping her get some perspective on her life and her husband's resistance to her education. As we drifted further into each other's life, I realized to my dismay I was bringing her more suffering, not less, that I was losing my own fragile hold on my dull happiness, most of all that I was being divided from Lisa. A poem by Elizabeth Bishop began haunting my mind, expressing my own feelings in an honest and therefore terrifying way:

> The weed stood in the severed heart.
> "What are you doing there?" I asked.
> It lifted its head all dripping wet
> (with my own thoughts?)
> And answered then: "I grow," it said,
> "but to divide your heart again."

How deep the root was the question that worried me as Karrin and I grew closer. Even the brooding on such a question watered the divide. I thought of my child and her three children constantly, one of whom was severely malformed, and how what we were feeling often led to broken families, sometimes to the displacement of children. Was I recruiting a future population for my group home? I was quickly travelling down a path of no return to the shock of Lisa and my own bewilderment.

The class of mostly housewives, almost all of them older than I, loved our discussions. We would argue all class about the difference between married love and romantic love and between men and women. Women's magazines were brought in by some of the women, with articles such as "How to make love like a single person" or "A hundred ways to make your husband beg for sex again," providing evidence that marriage harnessed desire and that men once married were insensitive to the needs of their wives. They had to fantasize about women they could not obtain to stay married, but the fantasies often prevented them from complete love of their wives. My counterargument, more in the spirit of devil's advocate than conviction of my own, was about the institution of marriage itself, a prime example of deferred gratification, the main strategy of civilization, to delay pleasure and make you pay, in the capitalist mode of things, for material things to compensate for the lost pleasure postponed until when? Retirement in Florida? Heaven? Do people kiss in the afterlife? I recited some lines from Marvell's "To His Coy Mistress": "The grave's a fine and private place, but none, I think, do there embrace." Marriage like any institution had its plusses and minuses. The terms we use for it are telling: the bride "bridled" sexual desire, and the husband "plowed" the field otherwise considered wasteland. Bridling meant attracting desire and holding it in place, channeling it without quenching it to keep it going, hence the acquired need to use cosmetics, women being taught to think of their body as an image factory to hold the male gaze. Men were taught to think of plowing the field of wifedom, commitment and responsibility the cost of satisfying desire which in fact does not respect boundaries of "thou shalt not" or "mine not thine" but has an unruly rhythm of its own. The god of desire Cupid is a bastard with wings and arrows for a reason. This is why Lady Chatterley falls in love with a game keeper outside her marriage, a symbol of desire's transgressiveness into fields not one's own. We all keep an animal inside us. To Lawrence and many other modern philosophers, writers and artists, the natural conditions of desire were not necessarily compatible with marriage vows. Far from a natural behavior, it's more like training a caged monkey to behave than allowing it to follow its own inclinations. Most of the women in our class, however, had an ideal view of marriage even if theirs was not particularly satisfying. When you find the right person, there's no reason the love can't last a lifetime. There will always be problems and conflicts but if you are happy deep down, then it makes everything worthwhile. The class wanted me to give my deepest thoughts on the subject, the only male in the class and nearly the youngest. But I felt I was drowning.

I wanted to play out a scenario for them, asking them what would happen if they met with my other class of students, the inmates. Where would their sense of things fall then when they encountered very different views of American society? When they had a chance to speak with people who felt left out, even exiled, partly by their own actions but partly by the odds set against them right from the start? Would the status quo and all its conventions seem so justifiable then, on the chance or speculation that some people out there are happy deep down? I was also realizing that I styled myself a disaffected intellectual who had something of a savior mentality and a libertinism in constant jar. Neither class would let me off the hook, always wanting to pin me down though I had been trained in reading the ambiguity of things, with the assumption that the better the poem or story, the wider its range of implications. One woman, Sylvia, told me in class I lived a monkish life and dreamed of free love. I told her love that is not free is not love but enchained friendship, thinking of Milton, Shelley and Lawrence. Without vulnerability, love dies between people. The freedom to say good-bye is what keeps love strong – such could be the pop lyric of the day. Once the sense of debt and owing sets in, it's duty and payment. Passion and longing drop out of the picture to go underground. Hence, the constant fantasizing in America about sex, especially about young people's passion, that dominates movies and television and magazines, with the image of the beautifully trim body always in uppermost view, with women especially trained to think of themselves as an image for men to consume. But they wanted to know, where are you committed emotionally, professor? Where are you in this analysis? I told them I was unimportant, a drop in Aphrodite's ocean, as Sappho knew herself to be, and the views that were available, not holding to any one of them, were what we wanted to consider as critical thinkers. Nature is always larger than any human convention, and certainly love is the most dynamic, elusive and strongest of emotions, the hardest to define or control. We do not choose whom to love. They appear in our horizon of things, a strong chemistry, an infatuation, so-called "puppy love" a phrasing belittling the experience that liberates certain persistent and deeper aspects of the personality or soul, call it what you will.

Two women in the class were most vocal in telling us they too felt the split in American society. They were housewives with two children each and working-class husbands who usually ignored them, wanting to be with their beer-drinking, sports-loving buddies. But these two women worked together as belly-dancers and did quite well on weekends. I told them they were not being truthful, that I could not imagine them belly-dancing. They said I was seeing only the student-side of their lives. They knew the desire-side very well. Even women would envy, perhaps desire them when they danced, and the men were just head over heels entranced when their dance wound them round. At semester's end, they showed up in full belly-dancing gear beneath their coats. With a tape-cassette blasting out the swaying rhythms, they danced for the class that applauded and laughed with vindictive glee. Their astonished, wide-eyed professor turned red. Then, about ten of the women took me out for lunch at a local diner and awarded me a new book bag. They thanked me for a controversial, stimulating course and would miss my cranky idealism.

Karrin and I refused to miss each other, however. We could not separate. So entwined had we become, absence from each other proved painful. Before we had met, she told me, she and her husband had agreed to divorce. She planned to still live with but not sleep with him until she graduated from college and was able to pay her own way in life. Now here was an unconventional arrangement, or so it seemed to me. Her husband had agreed to this apparently from purely financial reasoning. Her getting a job would greatly improve things for the children, and if they divorced, she would have to drop out of school and get a poor paying job, hence the arrangement. Where was I now? To my horror and pain, I felt the weed growing stronger and stronger inside of me, still loving Lisa but giving my heart to Karrin. Could one love two? Painfully, yes. I was hardwired to be monogamous, but my empathy for Karrin turned to something much more quickly. She had told me she had been forced last year to give up rights to her severely handicapped daughter, and how the care of her for so many years had hurt her, her marriage and her other children. She admired how I was a group home supervisor. Her feelings renewed my idealism. Our first kiss was a seal of our fate. But the situation, both of us married with young children, was intolerable for everyone involved, but there we were, hooked into each other. There were also professional implications for me, a professor dating a student, unequal positions that did not foster true love, it would seem. It was a hopeless, dangerous, exhilarating romance. I was astonished to find myself in the middle of two contradictory sets of emotions, one drawing me towards Lisa to protect her from the harm I was doing to our marriage, the other towards Karrin. Love conquers all indeed. I felt vanquished by the conflict of a guilty misery and a reawakened freedom. I was just burning up. At the same time, all the emotions in the spectrum of things one can feel were pulsing through me in such an intense way, I felt immersed in a sea as vast as the universe, cut free of a destination, giving me the illusion of not seeing where I was and putting a luminous edge on everything, a glow. It was a strange feeling, to feel so alive in some ways and to watch oneself get taken over by emotions. Where were the resources to gain control? Karrin loved me deeply, and she was incredibly wise and beautiful inside and out, as I would tell her. We were connected. Even our hands were of the same shape and size. Were we related somehow? My mom had been adopted, never knowing a thing about her biological parents beyond their nationality. She must have felt their ghostly presence throughout her life. Now so did I, with Karrin's mom looking suspiciously like mine. I shared with Karrin a poem I had written about first hearing my mom had been adopted:

Citizens of the Universe

When I found out at seventeen
my mother was adopted, the purity
of my blood proved so much snow
in July. Thought old enough
to know the truth, I looked at her
with new eyes. She too was told
at seventeen by her mother.
My own shock gave way to hers,
how she must have suffered,
how she must have wondered.
Half-Irish, half-German, was she
the abandoned product of the great war?
I embraced her the way children do,
not needing to know each other's names.

Chapter 8

Rising

I had to struggle to hide the cleft inside me. Increased responsibilities were coming my way. To my surprise, Walter would leave the job as administrator of the borough and Ronnie Byars was promoted. He was now my supervisor. He lasted a few months. With his wife and children gone back to Puerto Rico, he was living wild. One time he and his girlfriend-counselor asked to borrow my personal car for a couple of hours, and like a fool I gave it to them. They came back two days later. I found a note under my door: "Thanks for the car, Tony. Sorry for the inconvenience. Have to get away. Best - Ronnie." And then he and Charlene disappeared for good. I began to wonder if my car was being sought by the police as a getaway car or smuggling vehicle. Eventually I heard the story. The girlfriend's brother was a big coke and gun runner in Newark. In fact, her whole family was being sought by the police, and Ronnie was involved up to his ears or I should say his nose. So he was gone. The group home he had abandoned had been run by the older boys for a while. I soon discovered this and reported the lack of staff. This led to the realization that Ronnie had simply erased himself from the scene, his apartment nearly empty, the budget money gone too. Into the fray, I was pressed by headquarters, given the promotion I had been mysteriously passed over for when it had been awarded to Ronnie. I wanted the promotion and didn't want it. It was too stressful and little by way of financial reward. But I took it like a good soldier for the cause, also hoping to lose myself in work.

Now responsible for seven other homes, I quickly learned how badly things can and do fall apart. I received a report that one of our girls' homes was running riot, with no one answering phone calls from downtown. The daily headcount was not being called in, prompting the concern. Off I went to the other side of the Island where the group home was in a large former convent of several stories in gray cobblestone. I entered the home from the backdoor, the front door locked, and found an eerie silence. The girls, all twelve of them, were nowhere in sight on a Monday morning, not necessarily strange given it was a school day, but a tour of the bedrooms revealed problems. The rooms were in shambles, food and liquor all over the place. I couldn't find a counselor and the live-in supervisor's apartment was open but empty. I knew his wife was away on a visit to California for a month but where was Terry or a staff member? I continued to search through the large house, going down to the basement. I heard a weak banging sound coming out of the laundry room. From behind a locked closet door, I could hear someone whimpering. Not finding a key, I located a screwdriver and forced the lock. There was Terry, the supervisor, tied up and taped over, with dried blood on his forehead. He was so gagged and wrapped round with rope and tape that he looked like a half-undone mummy, the look of dreary terror on his face making him seem a man buried alive. And he had been closeted for a day or so. I unfurled him and called an ambulance. Suffering from a severe concussion, he eventually came round to hear the bizarre tale of mutiny and assault that I was able to piece together from the girls. Three older girls - two sisters and a cousin, one sixteen, two seventeen, all recently placed in the home - had assaulted him in the laundry room. Previously that day, Terry had told them they were not allowed to see their boyfriends for a while because they had been getting high with them over the weekend in their former neighborhood. Retaliating, they jumped him, knocking him out with a blow to the head from a baseball bat. They also broke into his apartment and robbed whatever money they could find. The next thing Terry knew he woke up in the closet, his head splitting with pain, barely able to keep his eyes open, sore all over. He must have fallen in and out of sleep for a while. Finally, he got up enough energy and awareness to make some noise in the closet, hoping to alert someone to his dilemma, but all the girls in the home were away. The three mutineers had partied in the house for a while and then left to be with their boyfriends. Three other girls out of fear had gone home or stayed at a friend's house. Five other girls who were long-term placements and very respectful of Terry had been away on home visits all weekend and didn't have a clue about the supervisor's predicament, returning Sunday night, seeing the mess, finding no one home, but so tired from their travel, simply going to bed and waking up on time for school. Poor Terry! Needless to say, upon his recovery, his first act was to resign. He had considered pressing charges but then he decided just to cut all ties to the place. I had to find a replacement quickly. The three girls who had beaten him up simply never returned. I had to make all kinds of reports which basically were filed away, no real action taken by the police or agency. The Bureau of Child Welfare would do home visits and some investigative follow-ups to make sure the girls received counseling, but as the girls were all voluntarily placed by the parents, there was not much to be done. Terry had suffered a hazard of the job. It really was the most extreme case of violence against a staff member that came to my notice.

As administrator of the borough, I had to represent the agency at community board meetings whenever there was an issue that arose regarding the homes scattered among several communities on the Island. One such meeting was more like an attempted lynching of me than anything else. This was no wonder considering what prompted my "invitation" to appear before the board. Dawson Street group home was in an old-fashioned, well-established part of Staten Island where there were many long-time homeowners. It was very white, middle-class and resentful of anything that looked like it would affect the property value of their houses. The group home was a sore thumb to them. The Hispanic and black boys in the home were the frequent innocent target of shop-lifting accusations by local storeowners, and local residents seemed to think the boys were a threat to their daughters as racist slurs had been called out from passing cars as the boys sat on the front stoop of their home. Because of the sensitive nature of its location, the agency tried to steer more difficult kids into other homes, but we were not always successful. Judge Gedy loved the neighborhood of Dawson Street and sent a steady stream of boys from his Family Court to it. One boy, a troubled white kid fifteen-years-old who had been in a series of foster homes, brought enough attention to the home to place it on the second page of the Island's main newspaper for one inglorious day.

I distinctly recall the disastrous beginning of the day of the incident. I received a phone call from a counselor at another nearby boys' home. A boy had broken his arm from a spill off his bike. A bone was sticking out of it, and the counselor needed to go with the boy to the hospital in the ambulance. Someone from staff was needed to watch over the home as the supervisor was on vacation.

I answered the call, opting to accompany the child to the hospital. That was my morning, spent soothing the fears and pain of a nine-year old who had no parents, making us his legal guardian. When I checked in from the hospital, foolishly loyal, to see if anything else was popping, my counselor told me that headquarters had frantically called looking for me. When I called downtown, I got the word that the Dawson home was having a major emergency and I had to get over there as soon as possible. Arranging for someone to pick up the boy from the hospital after his arm had been set, I dashed across Island to find out what was happening. As I drove past the corner of Dawson Street, to my shock I saw the whole block had been cordoned off, local residents standing all about, and legions of police men and guys in suits running all around. Traffic was being diverted and some stores had closed. What in the world was going on?

Having parked the van, I heard calls going out for an agency representative. "Who's here from the agency? Get someone down here and fast." I was walking into a minefield. Going up to a police officer who seemed in charge, I sheepishly identified myself as the agency representative. Some locals heard me identify myself and yells instantly went out, "There he is, that's the agency guy. Get out, get out, we're closing you down for good, get out." Angry glares were all around. I saw a bomb squad dressed in protective gear wandering all over the home and yard. The police captain told me that a report of a pipe bomb had been called in from someone who claimed to be living in the home. With the home's supervisor Ted on vacation, the counselor on duty said he was sitting in the backyard when the next thing he knew police and the bomb squad were at the door. I looked past the captain to see the boys from the home standing about in the street with a look of panic. One boy Sal recognized me with relief.

"Mr. D., Mr. D., what's going on? When can we go home?"

"It's OK, Sal, don't worry. The police will check the house, and if everything's OK, you'll be in your bed tonight. If not, we'll find a place for you, maybe my house, so everything either way will be OK."

Sal was a nice fifteen-year-old kid who had had some tough breaks. His father had died of cancer, and his mother, with the strain of tending to five children, had suffered a nervous breakdown. Most of the extended family were indigent, leaving no support outside the immediate family, and Sal, his two brothers and sister had been placed while the oldest boy in the house remained with the mother, working full time and attending school. I took Sal aside who was beginning to sob.

"Mr. D., I've been trying my best since I got here six months ago but you know, you know, this is a crazy place. We get these guys from court, they come in with all kinds of fucked-up ideas and they make everyone else crazy. Sucks. Just sucks. I know this pipe-bomb thing was Johnnie's doing. He hates Mr. Ted and the counselors. He probably wants to blow the damn world up. He took off just before the police got here."

"Sal, you know you can put all this stuff aside and just mind your own future. Mr. Ted tells me you're doing OK at school and we all know how much you want to help your mom. You can do that best by helping yourself."

"Yeah but there's so much shit going down here I can't find any peace, no peace, no peace, no way. It's just one thing after another."

A surge in the crowd came our way as some angry locals tried to get at me. "What is your agency going to do about this?" "We don't want you here. Close down and get out." "Enough of these hoodlums. We want you out. Out!"

The police captain got on a loudspeaker and told everyone to go home, that all was safe, the emergency over, a false alarm. The "pipe bomb" had been found - a cannister stuffed with marbles and rocks inside a wall, a prank, or I should say, a bomb made out of human relations, a means of fragmenting a neighborhood that was already fractured by all kinds of bias and prejudice. There seemed to be no way to rise above the misery that followed these children's lives around.

Sal was a perfect example of a kid who was innocent and tortured. I remembered reading a report of a visit made by one of our social workers to his mother's home near Arthur Avenue in the Bronx. My own few experiences with Arthur Avenue jarred with the report. The *trattorie, macellerie, pasticcerie, tutti i negozietti* I recalled from my childhood. Holiday strolls there with my parents and grandparents brought a bustle of bright colors and lush smells to mind. But the report revealed a much sadder side that *turisti* don't see in tenements a few blocks down the street from Arthur Avenue. The mother's apartment door was left ajar, the report specified, with no one in sight. The worker must have knocked and called out into that eerie silence one meets when entering someone else's home with no one around. He found there was someone home but like the home itself, this person was entirely vulnerable to whatever came her way, barely occupying her own body. The worker discovered Sal's mother passed out on a couch, vomit all over her blouse, blood all over her thighs. He tried to wake her. She stirred about, eyes blood shot, knees wobbling back into life, a staggered attempt to rise. Reading the report, I imagined the words exchanged.

"What do you want? Who are you?"

"I'm here from the children's agency. We're making a visit for your son to see if he can come visit you again."

"My son? Salvatore's ok, no? Oh, yes, Sally, yes, Sally. Sure he.... he can come home to see, to see me. I'm his, his mother, Gina, yes."

The report recommended against a visit.

So there it was, another exploded scene, another kind of pipe bomb having gone off in this woman's life somewhere in the past, leaving her in tatters, unable to care for herself, her home or family. The father's death from cancer had pushed her over the edge, her alcoholism or drug abuse blossoming. And here was Sal, his eyes wide open with tears fifty miles away but his mother on a different plane of reality altogether, unable to care for herself. Somehow Sal had to find the inner strength to grow up basically on his own with whatever day to day support the agency home could give him and with the chaotic state of things, mostly caused in the home by the infusion of new forms of misery such as Johnnie's with his prank pipe bomb. There wasn't much by way of the serenity that kids need to grow. They were like flowers in an ill wind. Struggle can make people strong, ease make them soft, but problems can overwhelm too, prove stronger than the people they come to possess. One life breaks and fractures others too. Rise above the pain somehow, rise above day to day, no more distant horizon available but the now, what one does right now. But what blocks the light? The lion of anger and the she-wolf of lust impede us in the dark wood of our lives, "*selva oscura*" as the great poet Dante calls it, entering hell. We have to make our own happiness each day like a loaf of good bread. It's in the doing, not a feeling one claims but like a sunset caught in the act, an after-glow following what one does with one's hands and mind. This is the chief message I wanted to get across to the kids in my home and to Sal. And to myself, often overlooking the happiness of ordinary things.

I entered the Dawson home with the boys in a desultory fashion. They looked like they were returning to limbo, neither a home nor an exile, some difficult place between, subject to all kinds of disturbances, up-endings. The home was in turmoil from the search conducted. More important was the need to get some perspective on things for the boys who for the most part were so shaken except for Vinny who led off the discussion I insisted we all have, everyone sitting at the large kitchen table.

"So here we go, crazy house, fucking crazy all the time. And where's Mr. Ted? Off somewhere on vacation. Yeah, that's cool, real cool. Probably with his girlfriend too, not his wife and kids."

"OK, Vinny, OK. But it's where you are, where this home is that you have to make your stand. You can't depend on someone else to make your life go forward. You have to do that every day, every hour; keep to a good direction and take little steps each day towards it."

"Yeah sure. You try living here. You try having my life."

"OK, ok, this is a tough day but tomorrow can be different for you and for everyone here. It's better than what you had on Simpson Street, Vinnie, yes?"

"What about Johnnie? That's one sick kid," Ricky said.

"He'll be taken to a secure place, more able to help him than we can. Don't worry about someone else's life or problems. We all have our own."

"Yeah, like Mr. and Mrs. Ted, they're always fightin and the baby cryin all kinds of hours," Tristam said. "And I can't get no sleep in this place. Guys comin in and out of windows middle of the night, the damn baby cryin, Mrs. Ella yelling and cryin."

Ted, from what I gathered, was having some marital problems - these seemed everywhere. Word had it that he had at least two girlfriends, one of which was a policeman's wife, and that his wife had gone into a post-natal depression, triggering an apparent need for flight in the husband who was a lively man with a powerful temper.

I had no real answers for the kids. Ironically, their own homes had suffered from problems comparable to those they had entered into. There was no safe haven from the syndrome, everyone susceptible to breakdown that only real willpower, lots of communication and self-discipline could fend off or cope with if at all. Even then, what were these personal resources in the face of inner trouble that gnawed away at things? And how could children be expected to cope with such problems that the adults in their life concocted or experienced themselves? Again, day to day choices were the only control over things, the only means anywhere in sight. But some people have more choices than others. I gave my standard pep talk that rang hollow to my own ears.

"Well, guys, it's up to each one of us to find strength inside. Everyone has troubles. Everyone has to deal with them or they eat you up. For you guys, getting your education is the biggest goal, and don't lose sight of the things you have to do every day to get to where you need to go. Resist whatever would hold you back. Eyes on the prize. Time on task day after day. Just keep going ahead. Keep your own life in sight."

"Until the bomb goes off," Vinny quipped. "C'mon, Mr. D, you don't live in a group home. You guys work here. You can leave. It's just a job, but me, these guys? We don't have that option. We can't walk out of here because there ain't no place to go. And... well, you don't know what it's like. You just don't know. Trapped. Trapped. Shit. Fucked."

"Yeah, with the Johnnies coming in. That guy's a bad dream, bad ass dream," Rickie chimed in. "And how's Willie boy in your house? We all know about him. He must be going off these days from what I hear."

"What did you hear?"

"Guess you don't know. Well, not much, not much. I'm not droppin no dime on anybody, no dime. Big dots on people who drop dimes. Big dots. Zeros for 'em."

"But that's not your concern, Vinnie. The issue is here, this house and what you guys do in it. I know most of you have been here a while and it's up to you to take care of things as much as you can. Just because a new kid comes in with some real problems, it doesn't mean he takes charge. You have charge. This is your home, right? So don't let things slip out of control."

"Yeah, and the neighbors love us too," Vinny said. "They're just dying to see us take charge here. They want to burn us down even if we're taking charge, right Mr. D?"

"Look, you have food, shelter, friends, counselors who can help, a supervisor who has to care for you, some family and friends who love you, schools nearby, and this house itself, a nice yard, a park down the block. So you have a support system in place, a means to help you go forward. True, whatever happened at your own home in your own family that led to your coming here, yes, that hurts, but you can't let other people's problems drag you down. Everyone has problems. Rise above them by keeping on the path right for you and stay to it, day by day, hour by hour. I don't know what else to tell you. Time on task, t on t. Simple. It's the way the great athletes do it like Clyde Frazier or Willie Randolph."

"But it's how I feel that just... it just... I don't know...whatever, yeah, whatever, screw it all," Sal said sounding sad but then checking any display of emotion besides the acceptable cynicism and indifference. That was the code and bond among the kids wherever I went, never show hurt or sorrow or any feelings that could be seen as soft. The world was tough on them. Be tough back, and toughness meant showing no sign of vulnerability. Shut everything out, not rise above it, just lock it out, and show no way inside yourself.

Johnnie, who never returned nor was located after the pipe bomb incident, was a perfect example of self-entombment in the past, of repeating the past by raging against it, trying impossibly to change it. His case file showed he was one of five children living in a South Bronx apartment, a familiar scenario, with his mother trying to raise the family without a husband who had just lit out. She was being helped considerably by her two sisters, one of whom lived alone and was doing quite well while the other sister was married, with two children and a fully committed husband living at home. So there was an extended family helping things. But when Johnnie's father left the home, Johnnie was four-years old, the youngest of five. In the best of circumstances, the youngest child is likely to have more overlooked needs in terms of caring than the older children who need less, and in Johnnie's case, the struggle to pay bills, make ends meet, had already taken quite a toll. The father while he was there worked numerous jobs, full-time construction worker, security guard, landscaper, whatever part-time work he could find. To his credit, he had kept things afloat. The mother was just so tied up with raising children, she could not possibly work. The father's stress from nearly round the clock work, I guess, finally tipped him over the edge. He began drinking a lot and seeing a woman with a heroin habit that he had once dated before marriage. Put the two together, and the stress turned into a mess, with the father spending more and more time outside the home and finally just disappearing, apparently running off to the surprise of all including his girlfriend. The father's dereliction must have felt like a bomb going off in the house. The oldest children suddenly had to quit school and work full time, and lots of resentment set in, on top of the old one about poverty. Despite it all, the family had been fairly happy, lots of family picnics and trips to the beach, the whole family piling into the station wagon. Now there were no joint trips to knit things together and let the steam out. Johnnie ended up acting out a lot of rage probably to get attention and then to destroy the life he must have felt as suffocation or drowning. The mother reluctantly had him placed via the PINS petition process. Two months into placement, the prank pipe bomb.

I want to believe in ordinary unhappiness, as Freud put it though few people would say such a thing. It is difficult because it requires working with it rather than a daily denial of it, a contentment to work against it and not a resentment that only grows it into gross unhappiness. It is ordinary because it is through the days, not limited to any single one. It is not conspicuous and spectacular, unlike the way out and out success or failure in life can be. Joy arrives on small feet, so to speak, quietly with a sunset greeted by a modest smile acknowledging the beauty of common things, listening to a mockingbird guarding its few trees in a backyard. The bird sings and the bird flies. It does what it must. Little things can sustain if careful attention is paid, if we don't take our own territorial mocking too seriously or do it for only destructive reasons. Mocking can protect one's space but can't substitute for it. For the home kids, the cynicism and the banter were defensive strategies to fend off the turbulence and alienation that placement brought into their lives. Because of the uprootedness, however, the mocking of things, the need to be "cool" at all times, became all, nothing left behind it but pain and the need to keep others from seeing it. Pain brings weakness and vulnerability and also results from both. The cool was fake armor against detection and more hurt. On the other hand, in view of the amount of betrayal in their lives, such as Johnnie had received from his father's disappearance, the shield of cool understandably builds up over time from an acquired impulse to distrust until cool becomes cold. Who can blame such facades? What else could the kids do in a world that assaults and does so frequently from within their own families? So "tuff" guys hide the softness and the tears, growing up sometimes to forget how to cry, not accepting responsibility for their own emotions and inflicting on others their hidden pain. Self-pity fuels anger and the scapegoating of others, with all authority as the enemy. This was a very familiar psychological syndrome I encountered in many a child. It also appeared to me widespread in American men with their endless romance of power.

Late the next night I was off to another crisis. I received a call from a home a couple of miles from my own. A panicked supervisor told me that the boys had banged on his door to tell him something was on fire on the front lawn. He charged downstairs to find a large cross burning. This particular home had a large population of black kids with most of the staff also black. Two incidents that week, Mr. Keith told me, probably triggered the cross burning. One of the boys, Jerome, had been caught shoplifting in a local store. The owner had called Mr. Keith and berated him and the whole home, after having called the police. Jerome had tried to steal a cigarette lighter, that's all, but it was enough to bring the store owner to utter some slurs against "riff raff in the neighborhood." The next day, however, featured a far more disturbing event. Another boy Ollie had been accused of mugging an elderly woman in a nearby park. The police had come to the home, directed there by several neighbors who swore the "blacks" in the home were responsible. Fifteen-year-old Ollie was identified as the culprit, but anyone who knew Ollie knew the accusation had to be wrong. Ollie was a sweet, shy kid who was absolutely terrified by the allegation and by his being hauled off to the hospital where the victim was to take a look at him. Neighbors had gotten wind of the police visit and of course leaped to conclusions. Ollie, obviously shaken by the whole thing, was released by the police when the woman said he was not her assailant.

"These things happen, Ollie. Don't take it to heart. I was stopped by police once, taken out of my car at gun point, put up against the hood, and only released when someone said I was not the person who robbed the liquor store. So you see, it can happen to anybody," I told him.

"Yeah, they do but no cross was burned for you, was it? That's the thing, right in front of my own home, where I live, like right here. Feel I can't even walk down the block now. Got to turn round all the time, make sure no one's following or something. This ain't no good, no good."

"Oliver, you do live here and should feel safe. Some bad people exist everywhere and..."

"Yeah and if you're a black kid in a group home, you're in for it. C'mon, people, just line up, line up, take your best shot `cause nothing will happen to you, just shoot'em up, no problem, rattle his brain, break his world." Ollie was sobbing, shaking, when another boy Leslie, overhearing my talk with the boy, chipped in.

"C'mon, Ollie, we all know what that cross there's about. About nigger hate, and you ain't no nigger, just a kid from Brooklyn. You too low and small, too low and small, you ain't nothing to them so that's it. That's it. Lighten up. No one gonna mess with our Ollie, right Mr. D? We fuck'em up if they do."

"OK, Lester, I hear you, Ollie hears you. We can understand your wanting to help ease Ollie's fears. Just don't know if you're doing a great job of it. OK? Just let us be for a while. Yes? OK?"

"OK, Mr. D., but I just got to say, this is a black against white thing in this neighborhood. Not sure if you can feel that from this side what a cross burning feels like, looks like, on your yard, you know. I ain't standing for that bullshit. Bring it on. Tha's all. Bring it on." And he made the Black Power sign, pumping his fist in the air.

Mr. Keith came into the room and sent Lester scurrying.

"OK, Lester, you taking the big man stand again? Lose it, go head, lose it fast. I don't want to hear about your Black Panther stuff. We all brothers, all men, right, Ollie? All people just people and all's got to help out. It's not a black against white thing. It's some sick people, a few sick people, out to hurt good people. That's all and that's enough. No need to make it bigger."

"Not sure, not sure, Mr. Keith, not sure of that," Lester said, walking up the stairs on his way to bed. "I thought you knew what that cross means. Ain't you from down south, Mr. K?"

"That stuff is mostly gone even down South. This was just the work of some crazy people, that's all. I reported it to the police and they'll take the report and do some investigation. We'll all be careful from now on, but let's not talk Klu Klux Klan. This is New York City 1980's, not Montgomery, Alabama, 1920's, OK?"

Ollie was inconsolable, shivering now. Ollie was from Harlem and had seen his share of hatred and violence as well as kindness and respect, but nothing could have prepared him for the cross burning. It was a ghost out of the past, something he had read about in his American History textbook. Now it was squarely alive and coming right at him. The past so lives on in symbols and rituals that it can burn itself into being again, taking over lives, filling hearts and minds with some old terrors. What to do when it arrives at your front door? How does one get rid of a past that suddenly erupts into one's life? Then again, the neighborhood racism was not a thing of the past at all. That's what was so scary to all of us. What was next? Firebombing?

There didn't appear to be a way to serenity for anyone involved in this situation. I thought of the eight homes under my “supervision.” The word makes it sound as if one has a helicopter or something.

The nearly one hundred children, their families, interconnected with so many others, vulnerable in so many directions, linking backwards and forwards into time to so many other generations, how could these children rise up above the myriad factors holding them down, dragging them backward into the miseries they had inherited by the simple act of their coming into the world?

Chapter 9

The Gift

In the meantime, Lisa was astonished by my increasing involvement with Karrin. To her shock and mine too, as if I were observing myself, I was changing, altering inside in ways I could not fathom. "You believe in words so deeply but are at a loss for them now?" Lisa would ask me as I sat there babbling - "I'm just...just...I don't know." And what did it mean to apologize to her? But I did, often. Being sorry looks back at a wake one's already left in the sea. My strong feelings for Karrin were a following tide. The problem was I didn't know where I was going.

Karrin had far more reason to feel desperate in life, largely from the suffering imposed on her. Her mother, determined to free herself of her alcoholic husband, had married Karrin off at eighteen to a man very different from her. A gifted artist and musician, Karrin was, by marrying an engineer far more left brained than right, committing herself to a failed project of opening him up, trying to liberate him from his own passivity to join her in artistic endeavor. Mario had been her piano student, technically able but not passionate in his playing, just as he was inclined or trained to be in life. She would see the beauty of the stars at night, she told me, while her husband would count them. He also broke promises to her with blithe disregard, letting projects he vowed to take on stay in pieces all over the house. When he forgot to tell his boss of a family vacation, she drove to Disney in Florida with the kids anyway, witnessing in route a tornado touch down in Georgia on Interstate 95. But every marriage has its own blues to sing. Far from the ordinary unhappiness was the trauma the whole family suffered from taking care of a severely deformed child for eight years. Medical bills soared. He worked full and part time jobs, with Karrin delivering newspapers on weekends. But how to calculate emotional costs? The daily care of the daughter born with severe hydrocephaly fell almost entirely on Karrin, who also cared for her father in the final years of his life. The two other children in the family helped out the little they could. But who could keep up? The stories Karrin told me were harrowing. Just bathing the girl was an ordeal. Finally, she and Mario faced the hard fact that they could no longer care for the child and agreed to give up parental rights. Once ruled a ward of the state, the girl was placed in a group home where at least two adults would be assigned to care for her round the clock. The decision brought great relief and guilt. Once the pressure was off, months of depression set in. To help fend it off, she decided to fulfill her own artistic aspirations and announced she was going to college. Mario was dead set against it. She went ahead with her plan anyway.

All this suffering, when she eventually told me about it, only deepened my respect and compassion for her. In my packed class, she was too shy to speak in front of other students, but her essays on Lao-Tze, Virginia Woolf and Franz Kafka brought her mind fully to my attention. Her writings focused on the self-determining power that even the illusion of choice has in a person's life. This was an extraordinary take on the centuries-old topic of fate versus freedom. I recall reading out loud to the class one of her sentences and asking her to discuss: "The spokes of the wheel help spin the bike but not set the direction." She was embarrassed to speak at all in a class much less in one that had fifty students. As I found out more about Karrin, it made perfect sense why she would be thinking in terms of paradoxes of choice. I could see how a class in world literature had brought out feelings regarding the need for her to respect herself as an independent person and a very talented woman who for various circumstances was forced to keep herself under a bucket. I sometimes felt as if she felt I was her savior although she denied that idea, saying she saw me for what I was, a sad clown kind of dude with a twist, hiding insecurities, trying to get people to laugh and think at the same time. I told her I sometimes felt like a compulsive truth-speaker, a parrhesiast, subject to ranting and brooding. "What a fancy word," she said. "There must be a name for everything, I guess." She advised feeling compelled to speak the truth is not the same as speaking it. Despite the brooding, she told me she loved my joy. I told her it was she who made me feel it.

Lisa, when I told her Karrin's story, felt sorrow for the deformed child but little pity beyond that. "The child took a toll on her and on her marriage, but she like everyone else made her own choices. Some of her misfortunes are not her own but the others, like marrying someone you're not in sync with, that's a mistake you know from the beginning. But please. Do you really expect me to care about your girlfriend? What happened to us? I thought we were in sync. I thought you were my soul mate. To be honest, I've never felt I was yours." She struck a sympathetic chord in me when she revealed the sad truth of how she felt. My feelings for Lisa, though not the eternal ones she had wished for, were still strong and deep. So was my love for Karrin. Hard wired to be monogamous from my upbringing, I felt I was courting my own destruction. I realized part of my motivation to get involved with another woman was to look past the situation I was in, the pressures of the group home, the dissertation not going well, the scarcity of college teaching jobs awaiting me after graduation, the prospect of not leaving the group home any time soon. Karrin became my personal challenge, my protégé as Lisa put it sarcastically. At times, I caught myself feeling flattered that two women would want me, an emotional immaturity that would redden my face when I found myself feeling that way. I cherished the love I felt for Karrin but feared its intensity. I'd have to change my whole life to fit it in. By getting involved together, we were just going to hurt ourselves, I thought. Yet the love we had between us, and the incredible sex, I must say, made for exultation when together. The beauty of our connection we believed was a great gift, a once in-a-lifetime bestowal from fate, I guess, from what we could not turn down no matter how foolish and cruel we seemed. We were determined to see each other as often as we could.

My ten-year marriage with Lisa I described at the time as good but I did not know how good good could be. Lisa and I had been very good for each other in terms of what we helped each other do day to day to day. We were both happy as far as we knew, but when I less decided than discovered Karrin was in my heart, what had once been good now became dull and routine. The ordinary unhappiness I felt with Lisa was not enough. How can something tried and true but worn possibly compete with something so exciting, passionate and new? Lisa and I had not really communicated our feelings to each other for some time. She was frustrated with her job and going to school full time, and I had plenty of duties and goals on my own plate. We tended to get through the day rather than share it simply because we were hard pressed to get all the ends to meet. We were living together without being together.

Sadly, we had lost touch, and what we once had, genuine and sweet, became a memory of a romance we could not rekindle. Karrin and I met only to reach each other. The whole purpose of our meetings was to share feelings and love and to make love. We spoke so many times about our aspirations and frustrations, the pathways our lives had taken.

"So the group home is part of your beliefs in a way?"

"A belief? It's more something I identify with because of my own dysfunctional upbringing. My father beat me as a child, and, like your husband, was more into the technical side of things, with little appreciation for his liberal-arts son. Almost worse than the beatings was the daily verbal abuse. He would accuse me of being cold to him to boot and no wonder!"

"My father in contrast was silent so often, we barely knew he was there. He would drink himself into a happy stupor every night just about. My mom would pretend to conference with him in his TV room which is why he was always in agreement with what she said. I often thought he brooded about a woman he had met while a soldier during World War II overseas, a woman from Naples he fell in love with and was thinking of marrying. But her husband, thought dead, suddenly returned after a year of missing in action and that was the end of that. I don't think he ever recovered from the loss. Tragedy seemed in his blood. When his own dad was sixteen, he found his father dead from suicide, hanging from the rafters in their home in Limerick. My mom's a whole different story although there was a lot of misery in her life too. Her father was abusive and a felon. Her mother, half Sioux and Dutch, was accused of being a gypsy woman, even run out of her town church one time."

"It's like a little mirror of world history right there. Your father had a lot to be silent about, and your poor mom as a child would probably be in placement today."

"When I cared for my father the last three years of his life, he'd talk of the times we were a family. I had to tell him how weak a job he did as a father, not to hurt him, just to get him to realize it so he could open up to things rather than ignore them. The only relationship worth having is one of honesty...."

"Yes, I agree, and that's why I felt compelled, stupidly, to tell Lisa about my feelings for you right from the start, before we even kissed. Her initial shock and respect for my being upfront is now more and more given over to rage."

"But Tony, she must realize you have certain feelings for me that you do not have for her, feelings that are natural and cannot be forced into a person when they are absent from a person's life, yes? Well, I don't know what to tell you or her. In my marriage, there are few feelings that go deep. It's mostly a convenience, and I feel like a convenience. I can't go on like that."

Karrin and I made a connection with each other that was so deep and true, it was scary. It demanded acknowledgement in the basic terms of our lives. We had courted Cupid but the whole thing felt contrived by his mother Venus. I prayed to Venus, using Lucretius's hymn to the great *alma mater* of the cosmos, asking that she not destroy us. Karrin, not religious herself, was amused and a bit puzzled by my telling her this. Along with love, I also felt remorse, sorrow, and fear in every direction. She had not been raised a Catholic as I had. It also dawned on me that I felt I was liberating her from her technical-minded husband, an engineer, just as my own mother was married to an engineer who would not allow her to develop her talents in music and art, expecting her being a wife and mother of six to be enough. Karrin thought this was true too. And I was a mentor and father–figure come to rescue her, her own father having never hugged her though he was infatuated with her welfare, supporting her talent as a musician, driving her here and there for lessons and performances.

We knew all this, recognizing how our childhood's hard wiring was driving our passion for each other. The knowledge did not stop us from feeling it.

The stress of living in a group home was little compared to this new emerging personal reality that would take over our lives for many months. Karrin's husband Mario soon guessed whom she was seeing since Karrin had often mentioned my name at home, this "wonderful professor." When she told me this, I dreaded the scenario of being reported to the college, but she assured me that he would never do that. She did openly wonder with me if I had had other affairs with students. I had not though temptations were plenty.

Mario, a good man at heart, did not object though he was deeply hurt at first. Their marriage had had previous failings, such as a six-month separation. They had agreed to a divorce but to continue to live together until Karrin graduated college and could support herself fully. The child- care payment likely to be assigned by the court would be too onerous for Mario, bankrupted as the family had already been by medical bills. Karrin, not wanting to see him financially ruined and at the same time wanting to complete her education, decided to come to an agreement with him. All was basically resolved at her house. Her relationship with me had been the last straw in her marriage. It was a settled decision to leave Mario no matter what. But where was I?

This simple question was excruciating. It would go unresolved for many months, with both Lisa and Karrin urging me to make a decision. Lisa one night slammed a door on my hand after delivering an angry ultimatum.

"If this woman is in your future, fine, but you can't have it both ways. No way I'm tolerating some girlfriend on the side, some *comare*. I thought this whole nightmare would blow over but obviously you intend to keep seeing her. I can't share you with someone, and it is selfish of you to expect me to. I certainly don't want an open marriage. That is not what we vowed, buddy boy."

"I'm confused, Lisa. I didn't plan on this or hope for it. I was just, just..."

"Again lost for words, professor? There's much at stake here, us, our daughter's life."

"Her children too."

"I don't care about this person. She's not part of our equation...I thought by giving you some space to see her or whatever would be enough. I didn't want to stand in your way seeing how you told me right away, didn't hide it from me or lie. I credit you for that. But I can't do this anymore. Why don't we try marriage counseling? We can work on our relationship but you must stop seeing her. Otherwise it's out the door for me and Ariana."

"You say work on us. Well, I don't want to work on something else. I have enough of that in my life, with this job, school, teaching..."

"So then what? What, Mr. D.? You bring me to live in a group home out here and now this? What am I supposed to do? Her or us. Figure it out."

The choices were clear, a decision wrenching. Say good-bye to Karrin; lie to my wife and Karrin about my relationship with either one; or say good-bye to Lisa which would require her moving out of my live-in job. Two sets of allegiances jarred in me. The ones for Lisa were based on a long-standing loving friendship and marriage, our having a child together, and my having supported her career as well as having received her courageous support for my job; for Karrin, a shared intense joy and passionate love as well as a common bond as people of the arts. But the relationship with Lisa, even before the new person in my life, had suffered from lack of communication on my part mostly about essential things and from a growing lackadaisical attitude about intimacy. We had been taking our love for granted. Now our eyes were wide open. I was falling in love so deeply with Karrin, however, that only one direction seemed possible for me even though the emotional conflict inside me was agonizing and prospects ahead not good. The wheel was spinning me, setting the direction. Where's the brakes? I began to beat myself heavily for being stupid, foolish, a hopeless romantic, a cheater, a liar, horribly susceptible to praise of any kind, a scoundrel, and yet I also knew that Karrin and I, given our deep attraction for each and the way we were discovering things about ourselves through each other, were more than an affair. It was a life-altering event, like it or not. We were awakened to our own inner lives through each other. We were so happy when together, despite the storm around us.

And storm there was. Karrin and Lisa both saw me with increasing fear in their own severed hearts, not knowing where they stood in view of my confusion and their own. I had the strange idea that as long as I was kind to them while I was in their presence, what I was doing outside their presence should not bother them. But this was a free-love idea, "love the one you're with," as the Crosby, Stills, and Nash tune put it. But that was more of a pose and didn't suit who I was much less placate either woman. I was "hard-wired to be a family man," a college-friend of mine put it when I confided or bled all over him on the phone. His own case – devoted to his girlfriend even when she ran off to live in Vietnam with some black-market wheeler-dealer for a year – was different from mine. His girlfriend was an heiress, the girl who lived up on the hill in his Westchester town while his family struggled for the most part to make ends meet. They eventually married, with tycoons arriving at her father's palatial house for the wedding in their Bentleys, including Malcolm Forbes's brother. My case was different – isn't everyone's? This is why trying to make an ethical decision is so difficult since there's no one-size-fits-all when it comes to a dilemma. I was building a separation in my life that was threatening everything as if I had to tear apart the life I made to this point. I went around in circles in my thought and action, lost in a dark wood, hearing voices calling to me in several directions. I needed peace and sought it through Karrin and at the same time did not want to hurt Lisa but I was. How could I have peace since I was hurting her? How could I help Karrin in any way if I was so tormented inside by my heart and conscience regarding Lisa? But there I was, hurting myself, hurting them, all out of this gift of love between people, a gift that did not fit in with my current life, but one that could not be turned down. It was given us, like it or not. We could not help but feel its power and spell. The cost of it was mounting every day, and still we pursued each other, obsessed with each other.

At the same time, trouble was continuously brewing in the homes I supervised. In my own home, Willie was on the warpath again. He was desperate for attention, perhaps sensing how distant I had become from the boys. He began sneaking out at night, going out through the window in his room. He was drinking, stealing food, and basically having a whale of a time for himself. He was also torturing the counselors and the other boys. Even laconic Kevin who had grown up immured to the craziness of Bed-Stuy section-8 housing, was driven to rage. I awoke one morning to the sound of a hideous battle going on below my apartment. There was

6 foot-two Kevin hovering over Willie in the hallway, pinning him to the floor, and asking my permission to break Willie's arm.

"Please, Mr. D., let me do him. Let me shut his mouth. Let me break his arm. He keep at me all the time."

The other boys found this extremely humorous.

"Please, Mr. D., let him. He won't eat up all our food that way, a broken arm, only one to gobble stuff down with," Jimmy said.

"Yeah, Mr. D., let Kevin put the fear of God in him since you're not allowed, Mr. D. Know what I mean?" Fernando chimed in, winking. "He's such a pain in the ass."

But I insisted. "Kevin, let him go right now. You don't want to mess up your life. Think punishment, grounding. Think police. You're older and bigger and should know better. And think of your mom - what would she say?"

That was the key question. Kevin immediately relaxed his hold.

Jimmy said, "Mr.D. saving your fat taco ass, homeboy."

It was clearer and clearer that the boy had to go. He needed a more secure environment. Maybe I could go with him, I laughed to myself. I thought about all the times I had tried to reach him. I'd bring him food shopping with me, one on one. He was proud to be so picked out. I told him we'd make a special diet for him, buying things he liked but watching the fat and calorie intake. The other boys would tell him to make sure I bought this or that. He became the go-to guy when it came to coaxing me into buying some special treat or whatever. I wanted this to happen, letting Willie feel how he could be a go-between over something positive and get good results. I couldn't use sports with him as I did with the other boys to draw him in because Willie was too overweight and ashamed. So the challenge was to build some kind of personal relationship with him in some other way despite all the mischief and pranks he pulled, some of them more than pranks. Although only thirteen, he seemed bound for a life of crime, and yet one on one, this kid was sensitive, perceptive, even thoughtful. He had an incredibly winning smile that swept over his whole face and lit up his eyes. We'd have serious talks in the car on the way to shop or on the way downtown where Willie was receiving therapy.

"So how did today's session go? Anything you'd like to talk about?"

"O just stuff, you know, social worker stuff checking to see if I'm ok."

"And are you ok? Anything bothering you besides what we both know about already?"

He just shrugged his shoulders and smiled. I poked him in the side.

"Don't give me that aw shucks routine, Master Moncado. What's on that mind of yours? Something's always cookin."

"C'mon, Mr. D. You know how these people are at the office. I've heard you and Mr. Will talk about it. All concerned and all but they never come see us. Kind of phony."

"You'll find people like that in all walks of life. There's good cops and bad. Good teachers and bad. But your therapist is a really nice woman and she's always asking about you."

"Yeah well, Ms. Joanie asked me if I still wanted to go into a foster home. I told her no way. Ain't gonna happen. No one's going to adopt me now. I'm way too old. Didn't like all those foster homes I was in anyway. Plus I like our house much better. So much fun. Best place I been in."

"It can be great fun if you get your act together in school and home, and stop bugging the other guys so much and driving me and the counselors crazy. What's with the middle of the night trips outside now? That's not cool at all. You're leaving us no choice, Willie. I told you we might have to transfer you for your own good.

I like you, Willie. But listen up, please, for your own good. I'm drawing a line here. Don't cross over and out."

I held my hand out to him, and he shook it. "Here's to a better future, a great future, for Master Willie Moncado, businessman of the future."

But the bonding wouldn't hold. Once back into the mix, Willie could not control himself. It was no wonder once the case reports caught up with his current location in our agency where he was our legal ward. He had just about raised himself, left most of the times to his own resources, living in a whorehouse, basically, witnessing drug, gun and sex transactions probably on a daily basis, most of all, learning he could not trust men who often abused his aunt and her "friends," other women who came and went out of the house, a constant flow of human traffic and goods. The attempt on his life by a john who tried to drown him in the tub was the last draw, and the aunt put him in placement where he was eventually freed for adoption at eight. Three foster homes later he ended up in my group home. Each foster home saw the same behavior of petty and not so petty pilfering, disappearances, endless provocation of others, instigating any other children to go along with his schemes or harassment of them if they didn't. He was a handful, requiring as much discipline and love as three kids. I am surprised to find myself thinking of him years later now almost more than any of the other boys, even the boys I had great relations with and kept in touch with for years after I left the home. He's so often in my dreams, showing up outside the door of my childhood home on the tree-lined street in the North Bronx, so different than the home he was born into in Georgia, son of gypsy actors. He prods me in dreams to take off down the highway, go for a joy ride and fuck it all. Sit high in the saddle. Be a street-savvy mofo.

Fernando was the one who gave me the latest scoop on Willie's exploits.

"Mr. D, I don't want this guy in my room no more. I tried to help you keep him in line but no good. Now I hear he stole money from the raccoon guy down the block. You know, *mapache*, the dude who sells weed in the neighborhood. He sold some to dumbo Ray the other day and beat him with some crappy dope in the bag. I don't know where Ray got the money but it was a lot of money. Anyway, Willie got the money back and a lot more. Just telling you what I overheard from some of the guys."

The raccoon guy was an old man down the block who always wore slippers even when he walked to the corner pizzeria and whose eyes had these massive rings around them. I first heard the nickname when we made a rare trip down the long block for a group home dinner at the pizzeria on Main Street.

"Yo, there's raccoon man," José observed. "Yeah, Mr. Dooby Scooby," John said, rocking in the back seat. Everyone in the packed van laughed. "Heh, Mr. D, Mr. Al buys from him. Jesus saw him there."

"No, not true. I sent Mr. Al there to knock on his door to see if Jimmy was there."

"But I wasn't there, Mr. D," Jimmy yelled out.

"OK, OK, we'll talk about that after dinner, Jimmy."

So many things going on at any one time, it made one's head spin, and yet my job required not that I just be a custodian providing meals and getting the residents to keep the place clean but reaching as deep as they'd let me into their lives the way a parent should be connected with a child. My doing so was something of an imposture. At best the kids would allow me to be a mentor; at worst they'd see me as a dictator or chronic scold. Calling them clients, thinking in terms of a *per diem* rate of reimbursement, eighty-something dollars a night at that time for each boy sleeping overnight in my house, turned me into a janitor, warden, landlord, *lagermeister*, or plastic Jesus. "Eminence front, it's a put on," as the Who song goes.

By the time of the latest incident, Raccoon man, one Larry Dorio, had become a big problem. He had tried to hire Pedro when he heard about the "crack kid" entering the home as I learned. Now it was time to call the police again about this guy whose door they had supposedly knocked on and spoke to about being a bad influence. That was all the police did, the officer on the phone told me in a follow-up call to my complaint, because they didn't have a warrant yet to search the home. If I could get some evidence this guy was dealing, it would help get a warrant. They put me in touch with a detective assigned to the case. There was so much dealing and prostitution going on, it was no wonder raccoon man was on the backburner. I also knew a few miles from our home was Todt Hill, a very upscale area where the mafia Don, Paul "Big Paulie" Castellano, lived, in a house that looked like the White House on a smaller scale and rumored to have two or three underground stories. Who knows how many people were on his payroll ultimately with the big drug money trickling down to the street economy? The rich kids and their parents bought coke; the poor, weed and crack. Their late-night munchies fed the 7-Elevens and Jack in the Box hamburger joints that hired some of the home boys. José bragged how he saw a co-worker put a roach in a young woman's sandwich.

"Yeah, she's like at the drive-in in a Mercedes looking like rich bitch herself, nasty too. She tell us over the intercom, 'no onions - can you get it right this time?' Then at the window, she's like, 'come on, this is a drive-through, not a motel,' when she thought the order was taking too long. Her friends were all laughing in her fancy car. They should have let Dr. Drop get in and get down with them all. But they didn't know I was working that night. So anyways, Joey goes, 'here's a dried up roach I've been saving just for you, you sweet thing.' And he stuffs it in the burger. Oh shit, I almost died when she grabbed the food and sped off. Too bad we couldn't see the juice dripping out of her mouth when she took a real deep bite like this." He stuck his tongue out and was licking his lips with his eyes closed.

"Alright, José, alright, we get the point."

"Next time I'll say extra fries but hold the roaches," Fernando said.

"Yeah, they named the place Jack in the Crack for a reason. José wants his Jack in her crack but he's got no shot in hell. Tee hee, tee hee." Tony piped in. Everyone busted out laughing, even Juan who usually took offense with misogynistic humor.

"Guys, guys, enough. Let's clean up the dishes and get some homework done - unless you don't want t. v. time tonight? Plus Christmas is coming soon unless you want a dried roach in your stocking..."

"Tony wants one to smoke," José quipped.

"Look, Mr. D, be grinning now too," Jimmy said. "He's cracking the jack in his mind."

"No, I'm blowing my stack, Jimmy, and Santa ain't going bring you squat if you don't watch it."

That brought only more laughter. It was hard to rise up above the infectious craziness of it all.

Well as it turned out, Willie had clipped a lot of money from raccoon man. He didn't come home that night or the next. I called in a missing person's report but not much would be done. I was spared the misery of having to contact a parent or family member. Willie had nobody, just us.

Ray was another story. He also didn't return that night. Was he on the lam with Willie, spending up the dough? I had to call his father, the self-alleged ex-Marine, who hit the ceiling when I told him the circumstances under which his son Ray had gone AWOL.

"I'm coming over," he told me angrily.

"No need to. I'll call you if there's any developments, and of course as soon as he gets home."

"No, I'm coming over there to see for myself."

And he did, getting into my face about how I didn't know how to run the place after we'd gone downstairs for a private conference. I had been reluctant to let him in but didn't want him to make a scene for the neighbors to shake their head about.

"And where's this asshole selling weed to my boy? I'll break down his freaking house, search and destroy."

"That will only make things worse," I told him. "Let the detectives take care of it. Fact is your son is making the wrong choices he can make anywhere, but there's a lot of positive opportunities right here. Life can be pretty good in this home as you can see for yourself. Eight kids are upstairs right now but do you hear how quiet it is? They just cleaned up after dinner and are doing homework."

As I had asked her to, after five minutes, Ms. Sheila came downstairs to tell me I had a phone call.

"OK, Mr. Did-no-do, let me know when Ray gets back. I'm gonna have a little man to man with his ass."

"My last name is Danilo, Mr. Chester. Glad we spoke." And he left.

"No wonder why his kid's so screwed up," Ms. Sheila said. "Uh uh uh. Thought he was gonna break down the door he banged so hard. All the kids started asking questions. And I told'em to butt out, ain't their business. And don't you know I caught Anthony peeping upstairs again over that Valerie girl dressin in the window.

I mean what she `spect these young boys to do? I thought he was gonna fall out the window just as I seen Sergeant Chester drive up. Good Lord almighty, never a dull moment, never."

It was a particularly hectic and emotional time too with Christmas rolling around. Buying gifts for the boys was no joke as was trying to arrange things for as many kids to go visit family if they had any involved and we knew it was safe. We were having Lisa's family over, though, and any boys in the house would be welcomed to join us. Juan and John had no one. José was to be there too this Christmas when Lisa's parents and two sisters came to the home. José's mother had moved out of the country apparently, and Fernando, his half-brother, was visiting their father in the Bronx who never would acknowledge José as his son, claiming he wasn't the father. This was a real sore point for the boy as one can imagine. It distanced not only José from him but Fernando too. His chronic lack of involvement with the one son he acknowledged his made José feel like it wouldn't matter anyway.

Fernando's visit to him only made José's wound deeper. Fernando told me he had long talks with José about it and explained to him the only reason why he wanted to visit was to get him to help out his mom more. José would never say much about how he felt, committed to saying it didn't matter, shrugging his shoulders. Various social workers and my staff had tried to get him to open up a little, but it would only rattle the chain he kept around him inside. Only Ms. Sheila got him to say something once, and he was mostly flippant about it, giving her an angry glare. But he also acknowledged where he was and with whom he was making his stand:

"My dad? What dad? I don't have one. I don't need one, Ok? My people are here."

How does one bring words to the incomprehensible? We're all thrown into the world, but some more anchored than others for reasons not of a child's doing. I'd encourage José to bring up the subject himself without calling attention to my doing so. But he wouldn't go there. It was a tightrope he was walking on. I was afraid to shake the line.

I made the home visit to the alleged father Mateo Sanchez's apartment off Gun Hill Road in the Bronx without much hope. We ended up having a nice enough chat although he shut off all talk about José.

"He's not my son, period. His mother lied. She had a lot of lovers. I wasn't one of them. *Fin del cuento*."

"What about Fernando, Mr. Sanchez? He could use more contact from you. He's a great kid too."

"I do what I can, Mr. D. Like his visit coming up."

"I so hope it goes well for you both."

He told me some of his family history. His father's family had fled Nicaragua due to government-led persecution of communists, *socialistas.* He was born in Texas and came to the Bronx to join more of his family on his mother's Puerto Rican side. He was a welder now working for a fence company, just finishing up a job for the Bronx Botanical gardens. I told him I played there as a kid, and we'd ride our bikes to that spot off the parkway where we could sneak in the gardens. There was another spot my friends and I did the same with the Bronx Zoo.

"Eh, to be a boy again, eh Mr. Tony? *Joven y tonto*."

"Yes, yes. We'd find places where the miles of cyclone fencing had been cut or smashed down. The easiest way into the gardens was where the parkway bends and there's a grove of trees we'd go behind to leave our bikes, and then, pop over or through the fence."

"OK, ok. Funny but that sounds like where I work. That's still been going on there but now *no mas*. Eh, you know you help make business for my company."

We laughed. I told him he should be proud of his son who was my right-hand man among the kids, honest, caring, self-disciplined, athletic, handsome and smart.

"I'd be proud if he were my own son."

Tears welled up in the father's eyes.

"Yes, he's a gift from God. Thing was I was engaged to be married and then met Fernando's mom and fell in love. So she was my girl for a long time and when she got pregnant, you know, I did what I could. I still help out when I can, but back then I was different. I told her not to have the baby. I was wrong. *Era cosa del destino*."

He crossed himself.

"When my other son got killed in a car accident, I asked Anita where Fernando was. That's when I called you."

"Well, we're happy you stepped forward."

Fernando hadn't seen his father in eight years or so before the meeting I arranged in the downtown office. The boy was understandably nervous about the holiday visit to his house. Unfortunately, from what Fernando would tell me, the visit didn't go well. His father ended up inviting a lot of his friends and they sat around drinking, smoking and playing cards all weekend.

But to get back to Willie and the usual crisis he seemed to bring with him wherever he was. He and Ray eventually returned to the home when the money ran out. I had them both checked out for sexually transmitted diseases because I suspected that's where they went when Willie told me it was worth all the trouble he could get in.

"So you steal money from a neighbor and then go on a fling?"

"Mr. D, the raccoon man cheated Ray out of money."

"So what are you, Robin Hood now? And why is Ray buying weed at all, how about that?"

"Ask him, Mr. D. I just went there because I worked in the yard for the dude last week, throwing out some stuff he wanted me to. He didn't pay me like he was supposed to. When Ray told me the dude took his money too, I went over for our payback. That's all."

"Well, the man says you stole a lot of money from him."

"I took what he owed me and Ray. Besides, he ain't calling the cops. He's a dooba man, Mr. D. We should call the cops on him."

Willie had it all figured out. But this Larry the raccoon man was no joke, and I feared for Willie's life, depending on how much money he had clipped. I would bet Dorio a low-level mobster, some connected guy's nephew or something. He was a main source for weed in the Port Richmond area as if the cops didn't know that. But what did I really know except what Fernando had heard from a friend who lived next door to raccoon man?

"So where did you two go?" I asked Willie one on one in the counselor's room in the basement.

"Place I knew about from Julio's magazine. It's downtown."

"You mean a porno magazine?"

"Mr. D., I don't want to get no one in trouble."

"Well, you can try harder on that one, Willie. So come on, come clean with me. Where did you bring Ray?"

"Yeah, I didn't want him to come, but he told me he didn't want me to go alone."

"Isn't that sweet of him. So where did you go? And where's the money?"

Willie put his head down and started to shake it back and forth, imitating Mr. Will's laugh.

"O my God, we had some fine *chica*. We blew all the green beans."

He turned red as he looked up at me. "I couldn't help myself. I had to show Ray what to do with her. It was really funny."

"O man, Willie, geez. Did you guys at least use condoms?"

"She gave them to us, you know, it was a classy joint."

I shook my head in disbelief as much as to stop a grin from coming on. He couldn't remember the address of the place in Manhattan but he also admitted to going to another house in Queens, this time without Ray who had come home one day before Willie. As things eventually turned out, Ray went back to live with his father. He pleaded with me to convince his father not to take him back.

"I love this place, Mr. D. "

"It's not a summer camp here, Ray. Lots of kids have no one to go home to. You do. Plus you are running wilder here than you did at home. And they have the program you need in school in Eltingville near your dad's house so everything looks good."

I thanked God or Aphrodite that the boy had not tested positive for STD. When the father came to pick him up and all his stuff, including the Christmas gifts I had wrapped for the boy, he seemed a different man. He winked at me.

"That's my boy, trouble with the women."

"Thankfully he checked out in good health. No STD."

"I guess he knows what he's doing," the father laughed. Then he tensed up. "But that pot shit, that's the last draw. I ain't going to let him slip that way. Saw too many of my friends get hooked on all kinds of shit after Nam."

"You were a soldier in the war?"

"Yeah I did a tour of duty. Saw a lot of guys do stupid shit stoned out. Just carried on over here when they got back, so much of it here too anyway, you know, you know." He cleared his throat. "You look like someone who knows people too doing that crap. You work with them or join them?"

He looked at my longish hair, little round gold glasses and worn-out bell-bottom jeans. Not that I had specially dressed for his visit to pick up his son. I disregarded his slur against me.

"Yes, it's about making the right choices. Everything is everywhere nowadays. Ray needs a lot of guidance but also love. He's not a mean or bad kid. He wants to do good. He wants to make people laugh too much and that gets him into mischief. Let our agency know if there is anything else we can do."

"Thanks for the gifts, Mr. D," Ray said. I gave Ray a little hug.

"Don't open them until Christmas, Ray. Heh, stay out of trouble, ok?"

"Ok."

And they left. I don't know how things turned out for Ray when he got home. His father had taken up with a new girlfriend who worked at his print shop. So there was a family business, I guess. With so many kids in and out of our lives at the home, it was hard enough to understand where they were coming from. Keeping up with where they went after they left our home was not really part of my work. We had our hands filled anyway. For every boy that left at any time, another boy or ten of them could be waiting to get in, depending on what was happening in the city. Typically, wintertime saw more kids needing placement. And when crack hit the streets in the eighties, there was a tidal wave of kids seeking a home. It made me think that we are all living in a wilderness together, a human wilderness. Who'd let someone lost in the wilderness go hungry if we could offer them some food? Imagine being out there in the woods. Maybe we have a whole satchel of food or a truck load of it with us, and a weak and tired person comes upon our campfire and there we are, stuffed and bloated with sausages and cheeses from all over the world, and we have so much more to come, like a Venetian hour in our fridge, and this one person lost for days without much water and no food staggers out of nowhere. Would we not offer the person food even if we had only a granola bar to share? And yet, down the block from supermarkets, there are thousands of kids going hungry every day. This is a human wildness, a type of meanness, never seen in the wild. No need to walk some trail in God's country.

But Willie proved a different story in terms of finding out what happened to him years after he left the home. The question at the time was what to do about him with raccoon man sure to seek revenge. Plus, to tell truth, I longed for peaceful days and nights again. As crazy as these could get especially during full moons, I kid you not, when the boys in the home would go nuts, nothing could compare in my mind to the guilty bliss of a life without Willie again. He was driving us all crazy. Ever notice that? One truly disturbed person can overtake all the more or less sane people in the house who spend a lot of their time trying to figure out what's wrong with the one person. It was clear as day. Willie had to go to a more secure environment but as a ward of the state with our agency his legal guardian, there were complications we had to figure out. I urged the social worker to help my home get back on its feet, that Willie was just too much to handle and his own safety now in the neighborhood was a real issue. His therapist also agreed Willie was at risk and was putting other boys in the home at risk. Arrangements were made with a more secure environment in an upstate facility, a reformatory – a lock-up - for delinquent youths. The earliest the transfer could be done was the second week of December. It was agreed not to tell Willie who would just run away as his routine in several foster homes showed.

When I told Mr. Al, he said "Hallelujah. Tony, I was ready to choke him the other day. I actually had him in a bear hug, telling him I wasn't fooling around. He kept kicking at my chair when I was helping Jimmy with homework last night. He kept doing it and doing it. I'm thinking ok so that's all I need, to be investigated now for child abuse or something."

"Well, I know what you mean. Been down that road as you know. This is why he's got to go. We're in over our heads with him. Be sure to write down all the details. Did Willie put his hands on you first?"

"No, but it was like I had to restrain myself from hitting him so I put him in a bear hug. He just would not stop kicking the chair every other minute coming by even after I walked him to his room and told him to stay in it. Tony, he kept coming out like it was a joke. "

Al and I had become friends. Fortunately, he remained a good counselor as our friendship grew. He would listen when I had to play boss, and we both knew I was playing boss but I had to be serious. He could laugh out of sight, but I had to hide my mirth when I played the role I would rehearse with Al prior to confronting one of the boys. O the lies the boys would tell to cover their antics! I'd go along for a while so they could sink deeper, making up stuff at the spur of the moment while I would see Al holding his hands over his eyes and shaking his head. Kind of a tightrope to walk but that was how the whole place was, living with our so-called clients and staff, working for the children really and not just with them, acting like a father but far from assuming I could take that role especially the way some of the boys' fathers were. The older boys would say once in a while it was only a job for me. It was life for them. Al helped us all relax. He worked hard at taking life easy. He was thus great in a crisis. Even the kids tried to get a rise out of him but would fail. One night, José came running up to him when he was sitting alone on the couch eating popcorn and watching t.v.

"Yo yo, Mr. Al, Mr. Al, Adam set the couch on fire downstairs."

"OK, get a pitcher of water and put it out. I'll be down next advertisement."

"No really, don't you smell it?"

"O that smell? Well, like I say, I'll be right down."

Then there was a long silence. Finally, the kids in the hallway couldn't take it anymore and busted out laughing. It was a prank.

"Damn," Adam said. "Dude don't budge."

"OK, ok, so what's with the smell?" Al finally would say.

"Well, we burnt a whole set of matches in the hall thinking to fool you."

"Adam did that, Mr. Al, I had nothing to do with it," Jimmy said.

Juan came downstairs asking what's that smell, and when José told me the story of how they tried to get Mr. Al excited, Juan said, "No, you'd have to lock the fridge to do that."

And everybody laughed. Then Al sent Adam to his room for the night for burning matches. He told me he knew what they were doing all along.

"But when you smelt the matches..."

"Tony, I could see what they were doing in the mirror."

I had strategically hung a large mirror so we could see down the hallway while we sat in the living room to watch TV. Adam went to his room, saying it was worth it. It was the kids' way of testing Mr. Al. He had passed this test and others, and had earned the boys' admiration and, usually, their obedience.

"Mr. Al's cool," José told me." "I'd have dropped those fools with just my jab but he just gives that weird look of his and they chill 'cept for Willie boy."

Al helped increase my level of tolerance too, helping me to lower my expectations and relax more. We did manage to get silly often enough to keep sanity although my superiors may not have seen it that way. One time, we were expecting a new boy to come so I had to assign Al morning hours to cover the house. I had to go downtown to turn in a budget. When I went to tell him I was leaving, I couldn't find him so I went through four bedrooms, finally coming to Juan's room upstairs. There was all six-foot-plus of Al stuffed into Juan's bunk bed, wearing Juan's doo-rag and resting his head on Juan's teddy bear, pretending to sleep, snoring away. I nearly doubled over in stitches. He gave me a hard time waking up though I kept shaking him by his shoulder, saying, "Juan, Juan, you're late for school. And when did your bulbous nose grow hairs that way?" He finally pretended to wake up.

"I'm the new placement Felipe, and I want a free room juz like dis."

When we stopped laughing, he said, "what did you say about my nose? What word did you use, professor?"

"Could you imagine if the social worker found you sleeping like that?"

Another time we didn't have to imagine. Again the boys were all away at school that morning. The day before I had bought a load of Christmas gifts, left them in the counselor's room, and asked Al to wrap some of them, following my long list of who got what. When I went to look for him to see if he had any questions before I got ready to go downtown for a meeting, I couldn't find him. "O boy, here we go again," I called out.

When I got to the basement, he jumped out at me with a water pistol in his hand, drenching me. He also had placed a dart with a suction cup on his forehead.

"I told you to wrap the gifts, not wear them."

The chase was on as he dashed up the stairs. I filled another water gun and went hunting after him. As I passed the front door, I heard someone knock lightly and figured it must be him. I turned the knob so that the door would swing open a little. I hid behind it in the stairwell. The door creaked open slowly. There was a long moment of silence. I lunged out with my pistol in hand firing away. But it wasn't Al. It was a supervisor from the Bureau of Child Welfare. I stood there aghast in my bathrobe. My aim had been dead on. The man wiped the water from his face after having instinctively held his hand up.

"Who's in charge here? I want to speak with the supervisor."

"I am the supervisor."

Al peered down above us on the staircase with the dart stilled suctioned on his forehead.

"And that's a counselor."

"I could have guessed that. Looks like you've both worked a few too many hours.""

Thank God the guy had a sense of humor although the way he opened his eyes and mouth when I identified myself was a textbook example of how the negative sublime registers on a face.

"All the kids are at school and it's just our way of relieving stress."

"And then some," he said. "Sure got my heart pumping."

"Anyway, how can I help you? Excuse my appearance but I've got a meeting to go and was just about to get dressed."

"Water pistol in hand."

"Yeah, that's agency issue. In case we have to get rough with the kids. Al and I were just keeping ourselves sharp for that critical moment."

"Well, I didn't mean to barge in on your game. I was next door looking for Mr. Byars but his wife told me he's not home. I figured I'd introduce myself to you. Mr. Danilo, yes?"

"Yes."

"I've heard good things about this house from our workers."

"Sorry to disappoint you."

"No problem, no offense. Do you know where Mr. Byars is?"

"He's going to the same meeting downtown I am. He's probably in route there now in his own car."

The supervisor from BCW left, saying he'd get back to me soon. I didn't know why he was looking for Ronnie but I'm sure I'd find out from our supervisor Walter. It didn't sound good. In truth, there was no telling where Ronnie might be even at that time, long before he went missing for good. But the code was that we group home supervisors covered for each other, and so I did.

But the big issue this Christmas was Willie and how we'd transfer him upstate without his running away and somehow without being cruel about it, springing it on him two weeks before Christmas. While I looked forward to peace without him in the house, I knew transfer out would hurt this boy who had been so unfortunate his entire life. I decided to buy him a whole new wardrobe along with other items and put them all in the agency car, wrapped as gifts and hidden in lawn and leaf bags so he wouldn't notice.

"Willie, for your own safety, until things cool down, we're going to bring you to another home for a week or so. It's just a visit there. So bring a few changes of clothes and whatever you want for the week. On our end, we'll take care of Raccoon man and get the cops to warn him away from you. At the same time, we'll figure out how to pay him back if that's the real case."

"I took only what he owed me and what he took from Ray."

"Whatever. The truth will come out, Willie. But for now, you're much safer upstate. Mr. Al will drive you this afternoon."

"Today? But I got things to do."

"Well, it's for your own good. Get some things together for your trip, and then we'll have a nice lunch. I ordered a pizza."

When Al and Willie arrived upstate and it dawned on Willie it was a lockup, he tried to bolt but Al grabbed him by the wrist and brought him through the buzzing door.

"Don't worry. It's not for good, Willie. You'll be alright. It's the best thing for you right now. You're safe here."

When Al returned with the bags filled with gifts, Willie knew.

"I'm here for Christmas? No, no, you're leaving me here for good. I don't want that crap. Fuck the gifts. I want to go back."

"Mr. D said to call him when you got here."

"What for? He's nobody to me now. Nobody. Fuck you all."

I checked on Willie's progress for a while, but he wouldn't talk to me. A couple of years or so went by before I heard anything about him. One day I received a phone call from Staten Island criminal court to appear at Willie's hearing. Our agency was still his legal guardian, and when the social worker called my agency's director, he gave my number as the agency representative. As I waited in a private room at the courthouse, Willie was brought in by a court officer. He was in handcuffs and was seated in a chair opposite mine. We sat there with our heads down in silence. Willie began to sob.

"I screwed up, Mr. D. I screwed up."

Willie had gone AWOL from the upstate lockup a few months after Al dropped him off. He wandered his way back to Staten Island and took to a street life, stealing what he could, hanging out with a gang of fellow Latinos, some of whom he had met in the high school he had been attending until his transfer. Somewhere along the line, he had turned vicious. He was under arrest for having robbed and assaulted an old woman on the Staten Island ferry where he had been selling loose joints. The woman had said she was going to call the police when she saw him selling a joint to a kid.

"I don't know what to say to you, Willie, except what I always said. Get your act together. It's a first offense. You're young and so intelligent. Cut the violence out. That's no part of your life."

"Sorry, Mr. D. I fucked up. You gave me chances but that was a long time ago."

"Yes, we had some good times together, man. There can be good ones ahead too for you. Stay strong for yourself, Willie."

He gave me a puzzled look and then narrowed his eyes into mine.

"Yeah, got no one else. You got rid of me too. Whatever."

He was taken away to Rikers. I wrote to the judge for leniency, providing the sad details of Willie's background, the gypsy parents who abandoned him, the prostitute Aunt, the john who tried to drown him. Willie would have his eighteenth birthday in prison, receiving a sentence of one to two years for assault, robbery and possession with intent to sell. A sobbing young man in manacles was the last I'd see of him. More than two decades later, he's still in my dreams, ageless, laughing that infectious laugh of his while staring in my eyes.

I knew his whole world had failed him, and I was part of that world. I hated it.

Chapter 10

Free For All

With Willie out of our home's life, our lives got much quieter. The raccoon man disappeared too from the neighborhood, leaving a few months later, his house just left there, subject to a few parties when some of the kids in my home and the neighborhood found out it was vacated. As usual it was Fernando who told me about it. Eventually, the house was bordered up and the partying stopped, at least down the block. Anthony got a girl in the neighborhood pregnant, and her family went on the warpath against our house for a while. Anthony's girlfriend stood by him as did I. He and I went to the family's house, and he apologized. That cooled tempers off a bit. The girl had an abortion. Anthony and his girlfriend soon afterwards moved into an apartment together in Brooklyn where he had an uncle and aunt living. When he moved out of the group home, it was like the end of an era. He had lived in the home next door for a few years but his last two were spent in my house. He had done well in school, and once graduated from high school, found a job in a local gas station, moving into a basement apartment of his own. He was quickly overwhelmed with bills. This time around, however, his second leaving was on surer ground. His uncle had arranged for a full-time gig with a construction company the uncle's friend owned. Anthony always had made funny wisecracks, but when it came time to leaving, we embraced and he broke down.

"Gonna miss all the good times, even the crazy ones."

"Think you can live without nine other kids to tease?"

"I'll call on the phone to get the latest craziness."

"Sure hope you keep in touch. We're all going to miss you."

I never heard from him again.

Two days later, another boy was placed in the home. Luis was an older quiet kid whom I put in Juan's room after little Sammie had been sent to live with an aunt in Pennsylvania that the agency social worker had been talking to for several months, arranging home visits for Sammie. When Jimmy had found out from Sammie that Juan had sodomized him – what Sammie called "sticking me down there"- he understandably wanted to beat Juan up. I had to have long talks with him, some more with Juan and with the two together. Sammie's transfer cooled things down between them a bit. In my private talks with Juan, I reiterated how I expected much better behavior from him and also had several sessions with Juan and his social worker. Juan said he didn't really think about what he was doing. He just had natural feelings towards little Sammie and when he sat on his lap, one thing led to another.

"But that was a while ago. I've changed. Are you still disappointed in me, Mr. D?"

"What you did then was a big letdown, I do have to say. But Juan, Lisa and I both know how capable you are of being a great person. We've enjoyed your help, your offers to help, so many times. Just last week you saw Lisa struggling up the stairs with all those packages and you rushed out to help her. You've got that spirit of compassion in you. We're both fond of you, Juan, and you know that. That's one of the reasons why your room is right next to our apartment. We trust you. We want to see you prosper. But you must absolutely promise never to do anything again like you did to Sammie in our house or you'll have to leave."

I spoke to the new kid Luis too, but at sixteen he was pretty savvy.

"Heh, I got no problem with gay if he's that way as long as he has no ideas because the answer is no. I got a girl in Queens. You know I have a friend who is gay, actually, a friend of my girl's in Queens. He kind of protects her when guys hit on her and I'm not there."

Juan and I continued to have talks about sexuality. He would bring it up to me after his downtown sessions with the social worker.

"Am I gay, Mr. D?"

"Why do you have to decide that all at once, Juan? Whatever your orientation, be patient with yourself. When you're an adult, you'll have a chance to find out who you are, especially if you live in the New York City area. It's about freedom of choice, Juan. It's also about consent, about consenting adults, Juan. Remember that. Consenting adults. That is absolutely key. And so will be protected sex, wearing a condom always."

"But am I weird? I don't know anyone like me at school. I get made fun of all the time because I like things guys aren't supposed to like."

"Like what, Juan?"

"I don't know. Well, like fashion. I love clothes, fancy clothes. And I love to dance, not with anybody, just with myself in my room. I hate sports. And to tell the truth, all my friends are girls at school, and guys make fun of me for that."

"Maybe they're jealous? You have an outgoing personality and make friends easily with girls if not guys. What's wrong with that? As for making guy friends, you can bet there's a lot of guys just like you, maybe not so much in our area but in Manhattan. Guys who love fashion, dance, the arts. Did you ever hear of Baryshnikov and Ralph Lauren?"

"No. Are they famous or something?"

"One's a famous ballet dancer, the other a famous fashion designer. They show you that a man can have cultural interests beyond the typical low-end dude culture. And those people are famous because they excel at what they do. You too could succeed once you decide what field you want to pursue."

"But I'm this black orphan kid."

"Heh, ever hear of Alvin Ailey?"

"No."

"He's the founder of a black dance theater that goes all over the world. We can find out more about him at the library. Check your school library first and ask the librarian there."

"Ok, Mr. D. I feel more than normal already. I'm on the way to worldwide fame."

"Screw normal to the wall. It's boring."

We laughed and I gave him a little hug.

Before the episode with Sammie, Juan's world had been rocked pretty badly. He and his younger sister Tabby, who was in placement at one of our girl's group homes, had been asking about who their parents had been. Both were freed for adoption at an early age. Juan begged me to let him see his birth certificate. He said the social worker said it was ok. When I asked our agency social worker, she said I should delay that until he was eighteen. But his requests grew urgent.

"It really bothers me that I don't know anything about my dad at all. I've heard the rumors about my mom but nothing about him. Mr. D, can you imagine how that feels?"

"No, Juan, I can't. But listen. You know my father, Juan. Sure, he's so nice when he came here for Christmas dinner and all. And I love him. But did I often wish he'd disappear when I was growing up? He'd lose his temper and beat me up physically and verbally. Even when he wasn't in a rage over something, he would say mean things sometimes. Other times, he could be really nice. But when he went overboard with anger, it was horrible. One time, he picked me up by the neck and pinned me against the wall. He said, 'I gave you life and I can take it away.' He convinced me right there that he could strangle me. And what had I done? Probably mouthed off again but who deserves that? So maybe you're better off in some ways. Know what I mean?"

"Wow, Mr. D. that sucks what your dad did to you. That nice old man? Wow. I can't imagine it. He is a big guy. Maybe he didn't realize how strong he was?"

"No need to make excuses for him, Juan. It was a long time ago when I was, like, ten. My dad and I are cool now. But the point is you might be better off not knowing. Concentrate on all the good things ahead. Your grades are good. You have real talent in art, dancing, writing, and you love those things. Imagine getting a job in something you love to do?"

"I really need to know something about my dad, anything. I mean come on. No one is going to adopt me at my age. I'm this old black kid now. So why can't I at least see my birth certificate?"

I gave in, obtaining the document as representative of his legal guardian. The father was identified as Carlos Williams. We knew who the mother was all along. Juan suspected he was half Latin from his own first name. His father was probably half-Hispanic, half-black. That is all I would tell Juan who wanted to see the certificate for himself. But I held it back, saying when he turned eighteen, I'd give it to him. In truth, I would not relish giving him the document under any circumstances, even if he were fifty years old. The spelling of his name on the birth certificate was Wand. Juan took my not letting him see the certificate as a betrayal.

"You said you'd let me see. That's not right. You get to see it. I don't? Hello, it's my life."

"Juan, I sympathize, I really do. But I said I'd get it for you, not give it to you. Again, when you're of legal age as an independent person, it's yours. Concentrate on the future."

A month or so later, a different side of Juan came into the picture. I received a phone call early one morning from a woman in the neighborhood.

"Hello, can I speak to Juan?"

"Who's this? This is his supervisor here at the home."

"O, I didn't know he lived in a home. Well, he was supposed to drop by with the meat this morning but I'm running out the door."

"The meat?"

"Yes, the leg of lamb I ordered. He says he's working for a butcher?"

"Er, no. He lives in the group home here."

"O sorry." And she hung up.

It dawned on me right then why we seemed to be running out of meat so quickly. I suspected Al's friend for a while but had pulled up short of actually saying that to Al. "Your friend's welcome to eat here but we're not a free bodega if you know what I mean. Keep him out of the pantry."

"Tony, he's cheap but he wouldn't steal. You don't think I'd let him?"

So that had been a moment of tension between us but the revelation about Juan instantly clarified things. When I told Al, he couldn't believe his ears.

"Juan? He's taking stuff right out of the freezer and selling it? No shit. What does he think this is, the Cow Palace?"

"Actually, it was a leg of lamb he was selling, the one I ordered for Christmas."

"O man. Wait till he gets home. He's got some explaining to do. Should be interesting to hear what he's got to say with his gift for gab."

"Let's play him along a bit, ok? Take the leg of lamb out of the freezer and hide it somewhere."

A little later he arrived from school in his usual merry mood.

"Heh guys, I'm back. How's your sunny day going? I'm liking it after all that cold."

"Good to feel some sun, I hear that, Juan," I said. "O you got a phone call right after you left for school this morning. I hope you got the message already?"

"Phone call?"

"Yes, a woman said not to drop off the package just yet. She said bring it later in the afternoon."

"A package?"

Juan was trying so hard to play dumb but his eyes opened wide with terror as if he had seen a ghost. From the corner of my eye, I saw Al leave us in the kitchen. When I heard Al's attempt to stifle a fit of laughter, a grin lit across my face involuntarily.

"Mr. D, what? You playing a joke on me!"

"No, Juan, I'm not. I'd have to be as cold as ice, as cold as a frozen piece of meat to do such a thing to you. Make you think you did something wrong and you didn't, right?"

"I hope you think well of me. I'd hate to think you don't." Juan raised his arms as if he was going to dance. Al busted out laughing in the next room.

"What's so funny, Mr. Al?" Juan called out. "Yes, I like to dance. Get over it."

"No, he's laughing because he knows you want to cook for us tonight, and he's so happy because he knows you're the best cook of all the guys. Yes, take out that leg of lamb from the freezer here, would you, Juan?"

"The freezer?" Juan scrunched his eyebrows together,

"Yeah, look in the freezer and take the leg of lamb out. We'll put it in a big pot of cold water to defrost it. It will take a while."

Juan opened the freezer and shuffled the packages around.

"O it's not there, Juan? Maybe you have to run down the block to get it?"

Juan started to tremble and then started balling.

"Mr. D, I'm sorry, so sorry, I don't know why."

Long talk later revealed why he was stealing meat.

"I was trying to get some money together so I could get my own place soon. I want to start my independent life as soon as I can."

"And that's the way to do it? Stealing? Stealing from us?"

"It's not you, Mr. D. I'd never take anything from you or Miss L. It's the agency meat, and I hate that place for not doing more for me."

"Well, this is your home right now, our house, where we all live together. And the agency is providing it for you, for us all. I'm disappointed, Juan. This is not who you are or want to be. A thief? You feel good about that?"

And he cried some more. He was willing to do the extra chores we assigned him as a reminder he had to show respect for the home. He could renew his pledge to do so by helping to clean it that weekend. And he did, offering apologies to me every chance he got.

As I mentioned a few pages back, before I got entwined in so many stories, Lisa's family came for one Christmas. Juan, John, and José were delighted to partake in our Italian feast. Lisa's two younger adult sisters spent a lot of time downstairs in the group home kitchen talking to John and José about what chores they did and how they liked school. John swayed back and forth happy to receive such attention from two young women who were fascinated by how the house was run and felt sympathy for the boys with no one of their own family to have Christmas with.

John was proud to announce he was the maintenance man in the home. He pointed out the behavior chart on the fridge and the star next to his name for that month.

"Mr. D told me I'm the only guy without a fixed chore because I do everything, the go-to guy when the house needs something done. Like I helped Mr. D put the lights on the tree."

"Yeah you're good at going round and round," José laughed, jealous of the attention he was getting. John was so often the butt of jokes because of his rocking back and forth when he spoke, he was eager to shine in a stranger's eyes, and especially a woman's. He had no recollection of his own mother at all, who had abandoned him at two years old. He was raised by his father for a while until the father too disappeared under investigation by the IRS. He lived with an aunt for a while but she was too sickly to care for him and called the Bureau of Child Welfare for help finding a home for him. She agreed to free him for adoption. Despite these setbacks, he was almost always a pleasant kid, happy go-lucky until one time he blew up at Willie when Willie poured hot sauce on his stomach after he fell asleep watching TV on the couch. He flew up in a rage but his glasses went crooked on his face, stopping him in his tracks. Willie just laughed as did all the guys in the room.

For the feast, we all gathered together in the group home dining room, large enough to fit a dozen people. I shopped for a week to get everything together. Lisa did most of the cooking, and her mother had brought a ton of food for the boys which they would eat for the next week. First we had appetizers, *soppressata*, stuffed mushroom and liver wrapped with bacon as well as several types of cheeses. Then *manicotti* and *braciola*, followed by the main course, a roast beef, all kinds of vegetables, scalloped potatoes and mashed sweet yams, and breads, and then pastries, pies, fruits, nuts. "O my God, this is like a free for all," said Juan. "I'm so happy you all came!"

We ate for three hours – had it been my own Neapolitan family, it would have been four hours. My side too would eventually come for Easter to celebrate with the boys. After dinner, I found myself alone with Lisa's mother Victoria who was helping me wash dishes downstairs while the rest of the family was up in our apartment. She was a short vivacious woman whose little chuckle of a laugh accompanied her frequent teasing me for being her liberal son-in-law. "Ah *mio genero*," she'd greet me, "*il mio professore liberale*." This time she took my arm and looked me in the eye to say, "You're hurting my daughter. You're hurting yourself. Be the wise man I know you are. That's all I have to say. OK. I'll bring these plates upstairs. What nice china your grandmother gave you. Nice you let the boys use them today." And she left.

I stood there stunned. It was as if the Grand Canyon had opened at my feet. The fact that my wife had confided in her mother put a new light on the whole thing, and I imagined the impact on my own parents. I didn't realize it but tears were coming down my face. John walked in the kitchen and asked me if everything was ok. He had never seen me cry before and looked really worried.

"You ok? Should I get Mrs. D?"

"No, John, just feeling a little down, that's all. I miss my own folks. That's all. Thanks for asking."

"When I get that way, I just look in the mirror and make a stupid face and I laugh."

I made a stupid face.

"See, it works, Mr. D." And he ran upstairs.

What right did I have to cry in the face of this boy and his own misfortunes all inherited? My dilemma was caused by choices I made. On the other hand, I had not chosen to cry just now and would not have in front of others, aware of the need to hold back. When I was alone, the tears came of their own accord. I was unaware I was crying. Oh what of love? Does one choose to fall in or out of love? Yet I had made choices after having acknowledged these feelings, acting upon them of my own will after I recognized the fact of their existence. In my head played out an endless choreography of fate and choice. Who can say what boundary holds them distinct? As the poet Yeats asked, "how can we know the dancer from the dance?" I thought too of a phrase from Virgil describing Dido – "Fate's willing follower." And his riddle of a question – "is one's own longing a god to each person?" I was half-exonerating, half-blaming myself, but there was no doubt about the difficult choice ahead I faced.

When I went back upstairs with the last dishes, I found Lisa making espresso and everyone else sitting in our living room watching a Christmas rock concert with Karen Carpenter. José was sitting a little too close to Paulina, Lisa's sister, who was oblivious on the couch to his hand held down next to her legs. He looked at me with a wild grin.

"Don't get too happy, José. Give Paulina a little more room there." I should have been more discrete in my choice of words.

Paulina laughed and said it was fine. José turned a bit red in the face. Everyone else just kept watching tv, sleepy from all the food. The espresso was to wake up my father-in-law a bit for the two-hour ride home back to the Bronx where I had met Lisa some dozen blocks away from my own childhood home.

I went back in our kitchen and said to Lisa, "Wow, one big happy family in there."

"Yes, great to see my family here. The boys are having fun too."

Then she turned from the sink to face me directly. "What about you? Are you here with us?"

"I am."

And she kissed me lightly on the lips.

Later that night, after her family went home, I went to buy Juan some acetaminophen for a toothache, hoping I could find a drug store open and only too glad to escape, gathering my own thoughts a bit. Maybe I'd call Karrin from the phone booth outside the supermarket. I ran into Ronnie.

"Tony, Merry Christmas, my main man. Where you been?"

"No - where have *you* been?" I asked.

"O, I settled all that with Leo downtown and the wife downstairs. I had some personal business, you know what I mean?" He winked at me. "I went for one of Will's two-week haircuts. No, seriously though – I know you covered for me and my house a couple of nights and I want to thank you for that."

"No problem." I lied to avoid a confrontation.

"Why you look so sad, bro? It's Christmas." He put his arm around me.

For some reason, I felt I had to bleed on him of all people.

"Wow, ok, ok, that's a crossroads, man. You're on one and ain't no one to tell you what to do but yourself. Been there a few times. Can't say I made the right choices but they felt right at the time.

And that's all you got. Go with a gut feeling even if later on you get indigestion."

He chuckled, and I just had to laugh.

"Seriously though, is this other woman worth all that? I mean you don't fool around much like me so you fell in love or think you have...Heh, why buy the cow if you're getting the milk for free, know what I mean?"

I gave him a wry smile.

"Ok, ok, T, I guess you're a follow your heart kind of guy. You will in the long run anyway. We all do. You probably drifting out to call her now?"

"Well, I don't know, I have to buy some medication for Juan and..."

"Come on, drug store open on Christmas? I don't think so. Tell Juan to gargle with warm salt water and then shake his little heinie to bed. What, are you going to call her on that phone in the parking lot I saw you at last week? Yeah, I saw you there 'bout 9 or so and I was thinking what the hell is he doing there, is everything alright. Did his car breakdown? But when I came out of the store, you were gone so I figured you were ok."

"Well, yes, that was me," I laughed.

"Heh man, you can make that call from my house if you want. Use the counselor's room. No one's home but me and my family."

"O, it's alright. Thanks, man."

"You gotta do what you gotta do."

"I know what you mean," I said and jumped in my car, driving directly to the parking lot phone and called Karrin who was hoping I'd call. We spoke for about thirty minutes, with her talking most of the time, telling me about the amazing decorations she had put up and how she so wished I could see them. She was sitting in front of her fireplace. I was freezing without giving it much thought. I was thinking of her, wanting to be with her. But she sensed something in my voice. She always could, so aware of tone as a musician.

"What's wrong? Somebody say something?"

"Well, Lisa's mother knows about us. She was discreet about it but I felt her pain, her puzzlement over how could I do such a thing."

There was a long pause.

"Follow your heart, my Tony. You're free to do that."

"It's not that simple. My head's in my heart too. Is it want or need going on here?"

She thought for a while and then said, "If it's need, I don't want it."

"If it's need, we don't have a choice."

"Maybe we need not to want it."

"Or we want to need it and we're kidding ourselves."

We laughed but we hurt. I was feeling the confusion my desire for her created in me despite my situation, hers, and the best of my intentions and plans. Do we make of desire a little god as if we had no choice? As if. We're blind, not love.

"Good night, my love, until we meet again," I told Karrin.

"If we don't, I will still love you."

And we hung up. Mine was the only car in the parking lot a few hundred yards from my home. The snow that had stopped falling was swirling up from the sidewalks in a little fandango. I could see the heavy flow of cars on the highway in the distance as they streamed past the biggest landfill in human history, visible from outer space I had read, like the Great Wall of China.

When I got home, Lisa knew where I had gone and gave me an ultimatum.

"After a day like this, and you go call her?"

"Please Ariana will hear. Juan too."

"Oh like she's not going to find out when we move out. What am I supposed to tell her? You're sleeping in the counselor's room from now on because that's where you're sleeping tonight."

"I understand how you feel. And I apologize."

"You understand but are not going to stop seeing her? How is the marriage therapy going to help? But you know what? I'm done talking, you're making your choice. If she's the soul mate I don't want to stand in your way. We'll move out but you'll move out of my bed first."

"I'm sure the agency can make arrangements if you want me to go that route."

"O the agency, the agency. You're acting like Byars next door or how about one of the fathers of the kids downstairs? No, one better – like one of the kids."

"Please lower your voice. Juan's right behind the wall here, sleeping I hope. Lisa, it's just I..."

"Did you find a drug store or was that just bull?"

"I looked. It wasn't bull. I saw two closed."

"Well, I made him gargle with salt and water."

"Thanks...I don't really know what I'm doing. I'm lost."

"O please. If you're in some kind of identity crisis, not a great idea to get involved with a girlfriend, wrecking your marriage, impacting so many lives. Isn't that what the therapist said? But I don't know what's in your heart."

"Well, it's not like knowing what's in your pocket."

She smirked at me.

"Lisa, I have been pretty open from the start. I told you though you hadn't really suspected."

"You were talking a lot about her. She's like your protégé and you're her hero rescuing her or she's like your mom, the artist who married an engineer. But I don't care about all that. What about us? I love you so much but if you have to go, go. Don't hang in the middle. I can't take it."

She cried for a bit and then looked out the window. It was snowing again and would throughout the night.

"OK, I'll sleep in the counselor's room as you want."

"No, come to our bed. It's Christmas night."

At this point, I wanted to sleep in the hall, on the roof or in the woods and let the night have its way with me. I still couldn't feel my feet they were so numb from my phone call. I wished I couldn't feel my heart since I didn't know what following it meant, what direction, what path. Something like a cage door had opened, one that I didn't know was there until it opened. I was standing there inside, looking out at an unknown world, afraid, but exhilarated by the freedom of it as if I were on a mountain top. I also knew I had not even begun to climb the mountain ahead, if that's where I was going, and it appeared a tough route, to leave my wife and mother of our child, because of my newfound love for a woman herself married with children. And was Karrin herself doing the right thing, still suffering from the trauma of having to give up her daughter? We must be out of our minds to think it could possibly work. But Karrin was definite about leaving Mario who half-expected the news that she had found another. And when I considered how many people would be impacted by such an attempt on our parts to be free for each other, in my mind it felt like I was at a bumper-car ride with too many cars and all of them going in different directions. A free for all but not free from all. Laws of motion and emotion were in place, like it or not. In a way, God does play billiard balls with the universe. Even he has to play by the rules. One body cannot be in two places at once no matter what the heart or head says or doesn't say. Yet I was split. The emotional intelligence I was struggling for sounded like a contradiction in terms. I needed an out.

"Let's take a cruise or something," I said to my wife and daughter the next morning.

"Yeah, let's get away from all this cold. We're overdo."

"O my God, are you serious?"

"Yeah, let's go to St. Maarten like we were supposed to last year. I disappointed you then with the job creep and all. But you know what? We both need a break."

My daughter and wife jumped up and down. Even Juan came out of his room and looked in our open door.

"Wow, that's exciting!" he said, folding his arms and leaning on the threshold. "Of course, you wouldn't even think about leaving me here, no, not Juan, he's so useful to have around. He can watch Ariana while you go out to dance at this nice little place on the beach."

"Nice try, Juan. Don't worry. I'll make sure the counselors bring you guys to do fun things while we're away."

"O you know for sure the guys are going to have some fun. Good thing Willie's not here."

"Well, ok, Juan, go and gargle again. I'll get that anti-inflammatory for you and call the dentist right away."

"OK, I get the picture. I'll go back to my boring life," he said, rolling his eyes and spinning down the stairs. But then he stopped and called up to us. "You deserve a good time Mr. D. and so do you, Mrs. D. My advice? Stay together. O and it was so nice to meet your family yesterday!" He scampered down the stairs.

"He's a nice kid," Lisa said. "My family really liked him. He was telling stories like crazy to my sisters about how it feels to live here."

"Yes, I bet. He told Sheila her last shift here that he wants to be transferred into a Jewish group home."

"What?" Lisa said in disbelief. "Juan's Jewish now?"

"No, no." I laughed. "He's got it in his head they have more to give the kids and the kids aren't so hard core."

"Really? Is that true?"

"Well, he's right. They are more funded, but leave it to Juan. He's a piece of work. Heh why not? I told him to talk to the social worker about that. I told him I didn't take it as rejection although I'd miss him. He said he liked us and his room upstairs and all, but he couldn't take the hounding and insults all the time, and that's what most kids do, just bug him. He wouldn't say it but there's that tension between him and Jimmy."

We went on our trip. Karrin was crushed when I told her. "Well I hope you can make your marriage work."

I said it was just a vacation, and Ariana would be with us in the hotel room, not exactly a romantic setting.

"And meanwhile, you're still with your husband."

"Well, we're not going to the Caribbean anytime soon or even out dancing. Tony, Tony. I have no problem. Go in the direction you want."

But the cruise wasn't a direction. It was my response to not wanting to sleep on the roof. My emotions had not clarified. I was keeping them to myself but they kept held of me. I was a buoy in the ocean of love. How stupid that sounds unless you have had that obsession when it comes to a passion that feels like fated attraction. *Dira cupido, deus meus.* Boing boing, ding dong, green and red lights. No matter what, Lisa would enjoy the trip and so would Ariana and I. If this was the last hooray, might as well go out in style. Willie's voice crept in my head a little: "Sometimes you just gotta go for a ride."

I arranged for coverage at the home and off we went. Our hotel was on the Dutch side of St. Maarten, but which side we were on didn't matter when we arrived. The big news was a hurricane veering down on the island some two hundred miles away. Would it hit the island? Had we rushed off to greet it there, to arrive just in time as if by fate? Thinking this way is sure to lead to insanity. What does the universe know of snow on our birthdate or a beautiful sky on a divorce?

"You no worry, monsieur," the maid told us. "Last big storm rose only to the top of de first floor. It no hit this second floor." Her eyes lit up when I asked if we could fish in the lobby. "Throw out nets and see what you get."

Somehow we did not find this comforting. But the storm suddenly veered and the island was spared. We walked far out on the beach to see the massive waves pounding the coral reef. On the way out, we stumbled onto a nude beach. Our six-year-old was pretty observant so I distracted her by giving her some of the local currency, telling her she can buy some special treat later. We were right in the middle of the nude section when she called out, "Heh, he's got a flappy thing hanging out." Though that did not exactly narrow the field, the closest guy to us said "sorry" and covered himself. People were laughing, and we felt embarrassed. "What's that all about, Mommy? Why is it out?" We shuffled her along.

"It was in fact prodigious," I said to Lisa.

"Yeah makes me wonder why I'm with you, " and she jabbed me in the ribs a little. I asked her how many had she seen, and she asked if this was a multiple-choice test. She asked how many I had seen, and I assumed she meant women and said four. She said, "Really?"

"And I married almost everyone except three got away."

"Ha, ha," she laughed sarcastically. "So which of us has more experience?"

"OK, is this your multiple-choice test? You mean the women I've been with?"

"No, why would I care about the others? There's only you or me, A or B on this one."

"Experience, hmmm. Does it have to be about intercourse? People could be holding hands."

"Wha? Not sure I follow you, Mr. Tony. I never said intercourse."

"I mean experiences would be hard to count if we included, say, dancing with people."

"So dancing is a form of sex now? Wow, is that why you love to dance so much?"

Karrin and I had a very similar conversation, and she said to me, "Sometimes, a cigar is just a cigar. Isn't that what you said to me on my paper about Kafka?" But the point was it seemed none of us had much experience with other people compared to the people I knew or what I had read or heard. But then what if we changed the terms for what we mean by experience to any intimate contact? Eye contact can be the most intimate of acts, which is why I always feel awkward looking into people's eyes whether they are close to me or strangers. It's like peering down a well or off into a desert or out over a cliff or at the pounding ocean or an overgrown parking lot or a barn door left open with all the animals escaped or roadkill. One glance is an adventure, a risk of involuntary disclosure of what is in one's soul which is nothing but contact between people. The soul lives through free interchange. The ego charges a toll. That's why one learns to wear a poker face, inscrutable and shielded.

At the bustling open-air market in St. Maarten, we saw the women of the island wearing their bright flowery colors and selling their wares. There was some swapping of goods going on too in what looked like a barter system. Everything was grown or made there on the island. Some tourists taking pictures of the women kept waiting for them to smile at the camera, but they didn't pay attention unless you were there to buy. There was no time for posing or other nonsense. Imagine someone walking into a supermarket in New York waiting for the store manager to smile. It was all hectic negotiations driven by a need to sell and make money or not be able to pay one's bills. A lot of the women had blank or hard looks in contrast to the gay clothes they wore. Outside such markets run by the islanders, I noticed that most of the natives worked for the white foreigners who owned the hotels and restaurants. *Per diem* rates like fate everywhere we go. *O dio, dio*? No. O history, history. Lisa agreed that it was sad to see but there was nothing we could do about it. In fact, we were helping the present economy whatever the exploitive past.

Lisa took Ariana to stroll the tourist trap stores where the cruise ships left people off on the wharf. I headed to the beach for a swim. It was still blustery but there had been some calm after the storm. The beach I had spotted on the taxi ride on the way to our hotel was just too tempting and within walking distance of a mile or so.

When I arrived, the beach was empty except for a couple of people holding on to their hats at the far end of the beach near the parking lot. I had fins, a mask with a snorkel and was dying to see some coral. The water was cool and inviting, transparent down to its depths, luring me on and on. I saw a pool of blue and yellow fish up ahead drifting back and forth in the tide out towards the reef. I swam with my head down in the water scanning the living coral rising below me, the many colors of the darting fish and swaying flora spellbinding like a whole new world that could only be seen in noiseless splendor. The rhythms of the sea have a secret code in which the mystery of life is concealed. We see only a third of our world and that not clearly, everything in motion, a step ahead of chaos, a step ahead back into it, life that rare moment where a head lifts up out of its supporting envelope to fall out of oneness with it, growing aware of itself. Even then, how much do we see beyond our own fishbowl? Something told me to look up. When I did, I was shocked. I had thought I knew where I was. I didn't. I had swum directly out from the beach about hundred feet and turned right to follow the fish out to the coral reef. The tide had taken me further out beyond the beach so that directly across now was no beach but high bluffs running a long way, with the waves crashing into them. Hotels looked down from the bluffs, and I could see several groups of people looking out from balconies and terraces, but they were just moving tiny figures high up above me and far away. It was going to take a prolonged effort to swim parallel to the bluffs and get out of the current driving me into them. The maid had warned me about swimming. "Our beaches are most beautiful but de waters will fool you, I tell you, good sir. People have drowned. Don't swim alone." Now I was in real trouble. Although I swam hard for a while, when I looked up, I had barely made any progress away from the bluffs so I decided to swim directly out and then swim parallel although going further out felt counter-intuitive. I slowed my pace, gained some distance from the bluffs, and then I just stopped. For some reason, I just stopped swimming, allowing myself to go still and drift as if I was giving up or giving myself to the tide, free with it to go where it would, to take me where it would, free because of it. I could see the people in the hotel holding drinks and going in and out of rooms. I thought I could hear some music drifting out over the waters but it was sporadic, merging with the lapping of the waves and then distinct for a moment. Then I heard myself say, "You can't do this, you can't do this," and I turned away and swam directly out again with a slow and steady pace. It was as if once I realized I would probably not drown, I toyed with the sensation of being on the edge of death, taking a risk I need not take. It took tremendous effort to reverse the course I had allowed.

When I finally got to the beach, I kissed the sand and fell down exhausted on my back, arms extended like I was signaling a plane to land. It seemed like forever for me to regain my breath, but when I did, I sat up and embraced my knees. I felt how close I had come, and that was scary but more scary was the part of me that almost let it happen. I had had to fight against that part or voice or whatever it was that makes someone not care, just stop and drift. Maybe I sensed deep down I still had a mountain to climb.

I didn't tell Lisa about the incident. I just said I had a tough time getting back to the beach. She said she had seen Christie Brinkley walking through the shops with an entourage behind her. A cruise ship had just arrived in port, and the shops suddenly filled up while she and Ariana were there. "You were drowning in people," I said to her. "Ship's probably in port only overnight so it's shop, shop, shop."

When we got back to the group home late one Sunday night, the counselor gave me the bad news. To help hold things together while I was away, I had given some staffing hours during the week to the former group home supervisor's wife Ann. She was to cook dinner a few weekdays in the house. She knew some of the boys, and her own husband had been a child in the agency's care and then became a supervisor in the same house I had taken over. She had asked if it was ok to bring her three and a half-year-old daughter and I said sure. While Ann went to the bathroom, one of the newer boys, sixteen-year-old Charlie had taken the girl into his room where another boy found him holding her hand to his exposed penis. Ann had to be restrained by a couple of the boys from attacking Charlie. It must have been a dreadful scene. Thankfully, Ann's husband Mark had been away on a business trip although he had already called repeatedly by the time I arrived back, wanting to speak to the boy face to face, saying he'd show up Monday when I was back. So I knew it was going to be a bad time all around the next day. The vacation was over.

In a demented way, though, I almost welcomed the traumatic events I was returning to because they would allow me to drown myself in my job for a while. I could stop thinking about how to break the news as much to myself as to Karrin. I found myself thinking more and more that the way forward for me was to stop seeing Karrin, doing my best for my family to resist these powerful feelings that had been visited upon us and that we both had flamed into a fire. "It was not possible, not possible," I kept saying to myself. "Too much heartache and grief for my family." I would make a noble sacrifice, at least I spun it that way to myself knowing that I was spinning, trying to convince myself. I also felt like a coward, afraid of the deepest love I had ever felt for another human being. Should one allow such a love to change the course of one's life and most of all to hurt one's family? I was looking for the words to persuade myself. In the literature I searched I stumbled upon the philosopher Bertrand Russell's affirmation that one could love two people in the fullest of ways. Of course, he was a philanderer, justifying his own betrayals and amusements. I thought I was hard wired for monogamy, but my circuitry had fried somewhere along the way. The passion Karrin and I shared for each other had already altered our understanding of others and ourselves. But how could our lives catch up to what we had discovered?

The next day I woke up early, fearing Mark would barge into the house looking for Charlie. Most of the boys were very happy to see me back.

"Some peace now for everyone now that you're back, Mr. D," Fernando said.

"I know you're happy to see me as much as I am to see you, Mr. D. I feel safer already," Juan said, spinning by me in the hallway.

That morning I made arrangements with the social worker downtown to have Charlie transferred for his own protection from an understandably enraged Mark. The girl's father did not show up and did not answer the phone when I called. So there was some respite there for a while at least. I knew I still had a very difficult time ahead the next day. I had resolved to tell Karrin face to face that our affair was over. We planned to meet at Riis Park in Queens. I had to be in Queens that morning to pay John's uncle a visit. Out of nowhere, he had contacted the agency upon his return from Germany to ask about the boy, long since freed for adoption and at sixteen for all purposes on his own after the group home until this paternal uncle showed up.

"Nice of you to get involved with John, Mr. Doering. He has really enjoyed the phone calls and was shocked when he found out he had an uncle. What made you contact the agency about him?"

"Well, my wife passed away in Germany just before we were to return to New York. She had always wanted to take John in after my sister, John's aunt, told us she couldn't do it anymore but things just didn't work out. My company transferred me to Germany and that was that."

Besides the cigarette smoke Doering blew in my face just about the entire visit, there was something about him that made me uneasy. He fidgeted the whole time and seemed depressed. He was unable or unwilling to look me in the eyes for more than a second and then would nervously look away, glancing out a window at the ceaseless flow of traffic on Queens Boulevard as if he were waiting for a cab.

"Can't get those days back but you know John deserves better than his lot has allowed. He'd be like the son we lost."

"You lost a son?"

"Yes, my son died at two years old from encephalitis ten years ago. Well, at least I loved him like a son."

"He wasn't your son then?"

"No, he was a stepchild. My wife was already a couple of months pregnant with another man's baby at the time I met her. She was in a bad way. Her parents didn't want anything to do with her. They were Lebanese who believed in arranged marriages. They had set her up with some rich guy coming over from Beirut or something like that. They disowned her when she decided to move in with her boyfriend. He turned out to be a junkie and took off. She found herself pregnant, living on her own, holding two part-time jobs. That's when I came along and got her a job with the company I was with back then. We kind of fell in love at first sight, decided to get married and have the baby. But then he died. And now she's gone too. Life's a trip, isn't it? Well, John would be that son now."

"Does John know you have plans for him to come and stay?"

"No, that would be too fast. I want to make sure he wants to stay."

"John told me he loves that he has an uncle and has enjoyed your phone calls. He's excited to visit. But let's go slow here, first things first. I wouldn't mention about his staying just yet. Let's see how you two get along, yes? That's a big question."

"Sure, I wouldn't have it any other way."

"Where would John sleep on a visit?"

"On the pull-out couch I'm sitting on. If things work out, I'll get a two-bedroom place. Already have my eye on a building down the block where I know the super. But like you say, first things first."

Although I had the authority to give clearance to a visit, I still resolved to ask our social worker to pay Doering a visit, and I told Doering that it was just routine.

"Ok, ok, I get it, Mr. Danilo, but you know you'll find I'm a good guy and have only the best intentions here."

Fact was John was doing pretty well in the group home, and I didn't want some family member who suddenly shows up wanting a big commitment to screw things up for the boy. Who knows whom to trust in any situation? When it comes to entrusting the care of a child to someone, the decision staggers the mind. Evidence of abuse is always too late to avoid it from happening. As I left Doering's apartment, I wasn't even sure I could trust myself anymore. Was I making the right choice in telling Karrin goodbye? Would I be looking backwards for a long, long time with inconsolable grief?

Chapter 11

Rapture

Karrin and I were fooling ourselves into saying good-bye. When she first came into my car, she looked at me as if I were a dead man. "Thanks for the memories, Tony. How could you have died to us?" Ashamed, I looked down at my hands as if they could answer. Then we kissed. We flew into the backseat, expert as we were in negotiating my Honda. The cold weather near the ocean and the parking lot would not deter us from stripping. While we were making love, two boys on bikes went by my lone car parked at the far end of the lot. They giggled and sped off. That sudden moment of unease broke the zone we had fallen in. We worried, laughed and cried into each other's eyes. As we were getting dressed, a police car appeared out of nowhere and drove directly to us. The boys must have snitched. We scrambled half-dressed into the front seat.

"Everything ok, miss?"

"Yes, officer," Karrin said.

Then he looked hard at me.

"This your wife, sir?"

Karrin answered, "we're not married yet, officer."

Then he left.

"Could have been worse if a cop had showed up that time on the ballfield."

"O my God, K, remember how the lights suddenly came on? We were on the pitcher's mound."

"The what?"

"The grass and the moon were so soft. Who could resist?"

"Well, I'm learning to, Tony."

She looked away into the sunlight. We both heard the hard silence. Then she sobbed a bit, shook her head and turned on me, summoning up anger.

"Really? A cruise? You go on a cruise in the middle of all this? Well, how was it?"

"I called you twice. I left messages."

"I have to move on, Tony. Drown these feelings in the ocean where they belong now."

"I came here to say the same thing."

"For different reasons."

"Yes, and the same big one. It's impossible."

"It could have been a possible impossible. O whatever."

"You say different reasons. How different?"

"You're holding on to the past. I'm moving on to the future."

"Glad you're taking the higher road. Maybe I'll join you there one day."

"Life's too short to wait for what I can't make happen. Besides, that's not what I mean. Why do you think that way, always making it like a competition or something? That's your childhood speaking, the way you were brought up, your father setting one against the other. You should do some individual therapy, and yes, Tony, work on the marriage. It needs it."

And with that, she left my car and drove off. I was stunned. As I drove out of the lot, I made eye contact with the two boys and flipped them the bird. They looked at each other and smirked.

The ride home felt like the wrong direction. The traffic on the Belt Parkway prolonged that uncanny sense. As I limped past the exit for Kennedy Airport, I thought of jumping on a plane to anywhere.

I arrived back just in time or too soon for more trauma, considering how out of body I felt, as if I were watching myself fade away. I had just picked up Ariana from Mimi's house, Will's wife who had been taking care of my daughter during the day whenever I couldn't. Miss Sheila gave me the lowdown as we entered the front door.

"Sorry to greet you with this, T, but Mark Sawyer's going to be here any second to speak to Charlie. He called the house, told Jimmy to tell you and hung up before I could speak to him." Should I let him in?"

"Holy shit. Let me get her upstairs and then I'll come down."

No sooner had I locked Ariana in her room when the front doorbell rang. Ms. Sheila and I together answered the door and went outside, closing the door behind us. Mark at least appeared calm.

"Tony, I want to speak to Charlie about what he did to my daughter."

"Mark, we don't think that's a good idea just yet. I know Ann filed a police report, and we made a report to BCW..."

"Tony, I don't care about your report. I want to look him in the eye and tell him what I think of him, of what he did."

What worked in our favor was that Mark himself had grown up in one of the agency's group homes in the Bronx. He had gone on to become a supervisor and then a social worker for the agency.

"Mark, you're a fellow professional. You must know we can't let you see him this way. Let's arrange for a meeting in the downtown office this week."

Mark pulled me aside. I nodded to Ms. Sheila that it was ok. We stepped away from the doorway into the little garden the boys had planted as a springtime project. Mark looked up at me and put his arm on my shoulder.

"Tony, trust me. I have no intention of going off on him. The boy is sick. When does he get to know he's hurt someone? You really think you're helping him by protecting him?"

I almost gave in but snapped out of it.

"Mark, it's just not the right way to do this. I can't risk it."

"Sure, cover your ass. I know the score. You're going to transfer him out of here. The whole thing's going to get pushed under the rug."

"No, it's not. He'll be transferred to a detention home to get the counseling treatment he needs. You know..."

"Spofford's just another holding tank."

"But he will be held, Mark. He will lose a lot of freedom because of what he did, and he knows that. He's been told that too. Believe me. You know he's had a sad history of child abuse himself."

"Yes, I read his file downtown. That's what I want to tell him. Think about how he felt when that happened to him. Why would he do that to someone else? It's not just wrong. It's evil."

"Yes, that will no doubt be a main focus of his therapy..."

"Sure, sure, and we're supposed to think there's no such thing as a bad kid like it's a fucking Boys Town movie or something. He's just going to do it to some other child."

"Mark, we do what we can."

"Well, that's not enough. Not good enough, Tony. Put that in your damn log."

He walked back towards the door and stood before the imposing figure of Miss Sheila who loomed above him on the stairs. She said she was sorry for what happened and then put her arms on her hips.

"Just know, you ain't getting in here tonight. I just cooked a big meal for the boys and no one is going to mess it up. There's nine other boys in here besides that damn fool upstairs. Don't you worry though. Charlie's gonna know who's on duty tonight. He gonna know exactly what I think about what he done. Yes, sir. Lord have mercy. The nerve of that damn kid. Ahun, ahun. He gonna know something from me. That's for sure."

Mark shook his head, adding, "He's going to find out what I've got to say too."

He drove off. I stood there on the side of the house for a little while, staring in disbelief.

Sheila came outside again, calling out to me.

"You coming in, T? Don't be stepping on those flowers now. We just had the boys plant them too."

I laughed at how she said this to me, supposedly her boss, though we both knew she'd make a much better supervisor of the boys than I was. In fact, I had asked her if she'd like to take over one of the group homes. Rumor had it that Rosie was leaving her job as a girls group home supervisor. This was no surprise to me, given how badly she needed to rehabilitate from her coke habit. She had been great the first year or so at the job but then she succumbed to the stress and an old habit came back. Byars's ready supply of the stuff had not helped her situation, to say the least.

Sheila had laughed at the idea.

"Girls home? You must think I'm crazy. Rather move into the Staten Island Zoo and feed the bears a Whopper with my own hand. Now a boys home, I might consider, maybe think about it twice but then I'd come to my right mind. Please. I like to sleep at night, know what I'm saying?"

When I came into the house, I thanked her.

"For what? No way I'd leave you on a limb outside with that man. Turned out alright but you never know. You needed backup."

"I like the way you handled that, Sheila. Showed Mark you were on his side and yet made it clear we wouldn't let him in."

"Is that what I did? Well, it sure helps to look the way I do too. Don't mind my weight so much when I can throw it around for a good cause."

"Well, if Mark was thinking he'd force his way in, you gave him a lot to think about."

"Same way with the boys. And you know I got some words for Charlie up there. I don't want to see him down here eating with the other boys. Fernando says he won't sit at the same table and I have to respect that. So I hope you don't mind but I told Charlie I'd bring him his supper in his room after we all ate. For his own protection. Creep us all out. Know what I'm saying?"

"Yes, good idea. He's gone tomorrow. BCW will send someone to pick him up at the agency downtown. I'll drive him in."

"Go see your daughter, T. I got everything covered down here."

When Lisa got back from work, she was upset over my having left Ariana for so long in our apartment.

"Mark wasn't here that long. It felt like he was but only because it was intense for all of us, the whole situation."

"You have that right. It's more than intense. It's not safe. Tony, that boy's still here and you leave her alone?"

"I locked our door and the door to her room. Do we really want to raise our daughter here anymore? Most of the boys would never do such a thing but the new ones scare me. That arsonist kid two months ago. Now this horror show."

Lisa was referring to a boy who had set fires in his last two foster homes. He came to us at a last minute on a Friday. When I saw the case-history which finally came down the pike to me, I raised the red flag and brought him down to the BCW office. We were never to take children with a history of arson. They needed a more secure setting.

The next day I drove Charlie to the office. He knew the score.

"Guess I'm getting transferred today, Mr. D."

"It's for your own good, Charlie. I can't guarantee your safety anymore. And I worry about future incidents with you. You need some help, some rehab too from what I hear."

"That's the thing, Mr. D. I was pretty high when that little girl walked into my room and I was just laying there in my bed with my headphones on and she just came over and started touching me. Then José walked in and told Mrs. Sawyer."

"I doubt if that's true. That's not what José told Mrs. Sawyer. She asked José to look for her daughter because she was at the stove cooking when she noticed the girl wandered off. You're going to tell me she went right to your bedroom and closed the door behind her and came over to you, touching you there?"

"Mr. D, I don't know. I'll be honest. I had just smoked up on the way home from school and I was tired so I went straight to bed. Next thing I know she's standing there."

"You're were so stoned out, you didn't know what was happening?"

"Literally, Mr. D."

"Sounds more like crack you did, not weed. But whatever the case, you definitely need to be in a rehab program. Plus it's not safe for you at our place anymore so you'll be better off."

Charlie started to sob.

"I fucked up again. Mr. D, what's wrong with me? Why can't shit go right?"

"Charlie, I know you're dealing with some bad memories, stuff that happened to you when you were little, through no fault of your own. But now you've got to make the right choices. You're a young man, your whole life ahead of you. You love to draw and you love music. Keep drawing every chance you get. Take up an instrument and you can play the Kiss tunes you so love. Wouldn't that be cool, Charlie?"

Despite numerous attempts, he didn't answer me, shutting down into an angry silence the rest of the drive. As soon as we stopped at a red light once we were off the East River drive, he bolted out the door, running across 1st Avenue and almost getting hit by a car. By the time the light changed, he had disappeared. I cruised around the area for a while. Gone. Another disturbed teen on the streets of New York. I went to the agency office and made the necessary calls and reports. I told Mark who was there what happened when he asked me where the boy was. He just shook his head.

"I'm not going to wish him ill. As long as he doesn't show up at your house again. Ann wants to kill him."

"Well, she says that. She'd never. But you have no worries there, Mark. He'd not come back our way. He's got some relatives in Queens he'll probably drop in on."

"I'll let be, let be. It's just so sad. The whole damn thing, the whole system really. Bandaid on cancer."

"It helped you."

"I survived because I was determined. God helps those who help themselves."

"So does the devil. It should be God helps those who help others."

We laughed.

"I'd like to see that in my paycheck. Well, whatever, Tony. It's just depressing right now."

I left the office and figured I drop in to visit my parents, my sister and my brother who were still living in our childhood home in the north Bronx. They were all sitting there in the living room watching tv. After a warm greeting from everyone, the conversation took a wrong turn very quickly. My father started it off.

"Heard about those animals in Central Park who raped that woman? Terrible."

"They're not sure she's going to make it. So sad," my mother said.

"They should hang the little bastards from the trees, set an example," my sister said.

I was appalled.

"Really, sister? Is that what they're teaching you in your college, a Catholic college? You want strange fruit in Central Park?"

"What are you talking about? What the hell is strange fruit?"

"It's a Billie Holiday song about lynching down south," my mother said.

"They're a bunch of wild kids probably from broken homes," I said.

"O my bleeding heart of a son. Why not have them move into your group home there with you?" my father berated.

"Yeah, maybe have them move in with you and Lisa. I'm sure she'd love that," my brother added.

"Your sister's right, string'em up. They're animals," my father concurred.

I could see all but my mother were in a kind of rapture of hate that had taken away any sense of rationality.

"It's called due process, dad. Well, everyone have a nice day."

I kissed my mom and left. Anger and grief took over me. I drove like a madman for a while, hitting eighty miles an hour on Pelham Parkway until I had to slam on the brakes at a red light. A police car came racing towards me, and I took off right through the red light, down a side block and up someone's alleyway. The police car zipped by. I waited a while and got back on the road. I felt like an empty shell, lost somewhere between rage and mourning. Next thing I knew I was in Manhattan on 125th street. I parked the car and walked around, not knowing where I was going. I felt out of destinations. I passed the apartment building where I had once visited Eddie's father and just stood outside the lobby for a while. A big guy came over to me and signaled if I wanted to buy coke, putting a finger to his nose. I guessed when a white dude hung out there, it was probably what he wanted. I walked off to find a bar a few blocks away. When I walked into the place, it went silent for a moment. It was so dark I could barely see the few heads that looked my way. Then people went back to their thing, and I felt ok with being the one strange white guy in the place. It was a local bar but because it was in Harlem, anyone from the world could walk in. New York City. Manhattan. Mannahatta. Welcome, citizens of the universe. We embrace multitudes.

The bartender seemed to know why I was there. He kept pouring shots of bourbon after I knocked down the first one. There were so many people I was trying not to think about. It felt great to be among strangers. I wanted to become organism, creature, animal, orphan of the cosmos, bare life, anything but what's called human. Perhaps a newt or any bird. I had to debrief myself with alcohol, de-brain myself a bit to get there. Turn the alarm clock off. Find where it's plugged into my mind, into my soul. Our souls. The darkness outside grew darker than the one in the bar. I embraced numbness until I could barely walk to the men's room. When I came spinning out, somebody called out to me.

"Mistah, sit over here, man. You need to sit. Come. Join us. Ya?"

He laughed and waved his hand to me. There were two women at his table. They were smiling. I sat down.

"Forget the drink. You need some water, man. I'll get some for you."

I smiled at the women and slumped onto the bench in the booth. When he came back, he told me he could get me anything I wanted but I had to sober up from the alcohol first.

"Yes, ever try some peyote, my man? We just did some."

"Never did that. Nope. Thanks for the water."

"Yes, you should try it with a clean head for the first time. You will love it. It makes you drunk with life. Just ask Dina here. Her first time too. Heh, man, what's your name?"

"T is good."

"You will love it," Dina said.

I started to blurt out how I had played bongos with Tito Puente on Orchard Beach when he'd show up there with a busload of drummers. The women were Hispanic so I figured to impress a little.

"Do you like to dance?" Dina asked me.

"There a salsa club not far from here, T. Maybe later. Yeah man. I'm Ramón."

I took the peyote he gave me and offered him a twenty. My wallet was bulging with group home money.

"No man. That's for later. You can run up a tab. This is Lourdes here. She's from the Bronx like you."

"O Orchard Beach. I love it. I'd go there with my family on the number six," Lourdes said.

"Let's go there now," I said.

"Ah, too cold, too cold," Ramón said.

Soon enough I ran to the bathroom to throw up, the alcohol and the bitter fruit of the cactus foaming in the toilet. I was purged.

"Now you will enjoy the pure ride," Ramón said.

Next thing I knew we were outside, swaying down the street and into Ramón's car. Lourdes knew someone throwing a party but we had to bring our own food and drink. I bought a whole bunch of stuff at the bodega and a couple of bottles of Pedron.

"My man," Ramón said.

"One hand washes the other. You spill on me so I spill back."

I watched everything turn into a moving silhouette now and then, and then it would all turn back.

"*Madre de dio*," I said quite a few times in the car ride.

"O now T thinks he's Latino."

"Everyone should be!" I shouted.

When we got to the apartment building where the party was, rainbows appeared in the lights. People were coming and going as I sat there on the couch, dazed, confused and happy.

Lourdes kept checking on me.

"You ok, T?"

I'd smile and shake my head no. I went to the bathroom. When I came out, two guys pushed me in a room and put me on the floor. I was too out of it to resist. They did what they wanted. I woke up to find Lourdes hovering over me.

"*Estas bien*? You ok?"

My wallet, watch and ring were gone.

"At least they left me my keys. *Mis dientes tambien*," I said, checking for my teeth, and I smiled. I mean, it was Lourdes waking me up. What could be better? She was beautiful. I didn't feel the black eye and bloody bump on my head yet. We were at Orchard

Beach. No, wait. We had just come back. Who cared? I was with Lourdes. The peyote was still working its magic.

She snuck me out of the building and told me to wait for her outside.

"I'll be back. T. Just let me tell Dina."

We got on the train, and she took me to her apartment. I think we made love but I can't be sure. I regret to this day not remembering if we did. But everything was like making love at the time, I was so high. Just looking into her green eyes was enough. Then I saw Karrin in there dancing somewhere alone, cursing me. "How could you let us die?"

I saw myself in a coffin floating down the East River, Hell's Gate ahead, the fire coming out of me. There was debris everywhere, planks of wood I couldn't steer the coffin from. My father was yelling, "throw the line, throw the line," but the dock was too far away. The line kept falling into the water. My death boat smashed into the Statue of Liberty where Lisa was having this party on the island and I hadn't helped her at all. My whole family was there. I was in black face.

"What is this, Halloween?" my brother asked.

I panicked. I had to run downstairs to attend to the inmates but I was only a child myself. What could they expect of me? Who gave me the keys? Do they open or shut? The locks have rusted. I hear shouts. Who's there? Help. Stop. Chill. Get away. Check the log book. The pages are stuck together. Whose handwriting? What? There's an out somewhere. It has no entry. Where's it hiding? To what does it open? To the sky? In the way it looks back? Not down or up? Do we disappear forever now? Is she? Was she?

In the morning, I awoke to find Lourdes hovering over me on the fire escape a couple of flights up from her apartment. I had watched there for the sunrise, an unseen glory beyond the high tenements.

"*Ahí tienes.* You ok? *Entra conmigo ahora. Baja.*"

I followed her through the window into her apartment. She made me coffee and told me I had to leave soon. Ramón was coming over.

"He's going to want money and you have none."

As I came round with the coffee, I realized Ramón had pimped Lourdes out with me.

"I didn't know you worked for him. But you were just nice to me. I didn't ask to put you to work."

"It's going to be trouble for me."

There was a knock on the door.

"Too late," she said to me. "Go hide in the bedroom." And she opened the door.

"Ah *mi hermano pequeño.*"

And she gave him a kiss.

"Another customer. I hate that."

"No. no. I helped this man."

As I entered the kitchen, I was stunned to recognize who it was. It was Pedro. He looked at me equally astonished.

"Mr. D? *Que mierda.*"

"*Lo conosces?*"

"He's the guy from that group home in Staten Island. He...you put me out, Mr. D."

"Pedro, I had to. You had a bad habit then. I hope you're better now."

He told me what had happened after I dropped him off at the BCW downtown office.

He was sent upstate to a lock-up. He did his time for a while to clean himself up and then lit out, ending up back in Manhattan, hooking up with the gang again who took care of him. He had his own place now a few blocks away shared with a cousin. His sister had left her abusive boyfriend in the Bronx and, working for Ramón, managed to support herself. He found out where she was through a *pandillero* who knew Ramón.

"We're family. I don't want her working for that creep no more. I be making enough soon so she don't have to. But what are you doing here?"

Lourdes told him the story of how we met up in the bar, how I was beat up and robbed at the party house by two of Ramón's associates. Another knock on the door. It was Ramón demanding to be let in.

"That *cabron*. I'll kill him."

"*Salir ahora. Ve rápido.*"

She opened the window to the fire escape. Pedro wanted to confront Ramón who was now pounding on the door. I grabbed him by the arm.

"Your sister's going to get hurt if you try something. Let's go. There's a better way to help her. Let's go, man."

We ducked out and walked down the street, with my holding Pedro who wanted to go back.

"Let go of me. Don't tell me what to do. You don't give a shit."

We noticed a few guys hanging out on the corner, one of whom was alerting the others to us.

"Better walk the other way. Stay away from my sister or I'll fuck you up next time I see you."

He said this not with anger but with a pained look as if he was required to say it.

"Go, Mr. D. Go while you still can. It's your turn now to leave. I live here. Like you said to me, 'Best of luck.'"

And he ran down an alleyway. I could see the group of men had started to come down the block but when I headed fast towards Broadway, they stopped. Or had they been after Pedro? My heart was pounding in my chest. I wondered how Lourdes was making out with Ramón. It was most likely his own guys who rolled me so what more could he want out of her? Maybe he was angry she had helped me. She had given me a free ride when she could have been making money. I didn't know. These thoughts were running through my head until I felt the keys in my pocket. I fell back into my own life. I had to get home.

Chapter 12

Division and Union

A frantic search led to my car on 125th street. I drove to the downtown office and waited for it to open. I called our home and left a message for Lisa. Then I called her at work.

"Thank God. What happened?"

"I got mugged in Manhattan and had to find shelter overnight. But I'm ok."

"What? Were you hurt? Where are you?"

"No, except for a bump on the head and what feels like a black eye or two. Don't worry. I'm in the office downtown. As soon as it opened, I went to call you. I'll borrow some money so I can pay the toll for the bridge. I'm ok."

"Your mom called looking for you last night. She was worried. You left the house in a rush after some kind of argument and flew out of the driveway. When I told her I hadn't heard from you, she was really upset. So was I. What happened? You got mugged? God. Did you call the police?"

"I'll tell you all about it when I get home. Ariana's ok?"

"Yes, I dropped her off at Mimi's. Now she's worried too. You better call the home. I heard all kinds of commotion next door early this morning. Woke me up. I saw a lot of cars parked outside. Looked like detectives going in and out when I left this morning."

"Our boys ok?"

"Yes, all's ok, I think. I told Al to leave last night. He offered to stay overnight when we saw you weren't back by 11. But the boys were all in bed and the house was quiet. So I had no problem. Al came in early to cover the house before I left to drop Ariana off. I went to work sick with worry. Why didn't you call?"

"I couldn't. I will tell you all about it when I get back."

"You, you, didn't go to see her, did you?"

"Lisa, no. No. We'll talk when we're home."

"You're able to drive?"

"Yes, just a little bump and some bruises. They took my wallet, watch and ring too. I've got some phone calls to make, cancelling credit cards and all that crap."

"Your ring too? Lucky you weren't killed. Where were you?"

"Making a home visit on 123rd St. I went to see if Eddie was doing ok. I'll tell you all about it. Don't worry. I'll pick up Ariana and see you home."

When I called the group home, Al gave me the lowdown. Next door was raided by detectives and police early in the morning. The boys told them no one was on duty. They broke the door downstairs into Byars' apartment. No one was there. They spent a long time searching through the whole house, waking up all the kids and searching their rooms. Beyond a small amount of pot they found in two of the boys' rooms, they found nothing. The police had called the downtown agency, and when Byars couldn't be located, the agency director Leo contacted our home, looking for me. Al covered for me, saying I was visiting relatives in the Bronx.

Al asked me, "What happened to you, T?"

"Had a wild night in Manhattan. Got drunk, stoned, went to a party, got mugged, woke up in some woman's apartment and had to run out when her pimp came by. You know. Typical night."

"Damn. Mugged? You ok?"

"Yeah, ok. Be home soon. Everything cool there in the house?"

"Ok here. Next door's the big deal. All the guys are talking about it. Looks like we're going have to pull double duty here and next door."

"Let me see what they know down here if anything. They got to help us out."

I went to see director Leo, but he had already left his office for the island. It would be bad publicity for the agency if word got out. And what about the boys? What must they be thinking?

When I got back, after picking up my daughter and telling Mimi I was ok, a detective called me and asked me a lot of questions about Byars. He wanted me to come down to the precinct, but I told him I was on duty and couldn't leave. It was true. I sent Al home, not wanting to use up all the staffing hours my house had been assigned especially if we had to cover next door. Leo knocked on the door to my apartment.

"Tony, what the hell is going on out here? You know detectives are looking for your friend Ronnie. Do you know where he is?"

"Last time I spoke to him was about a week ago."

"And?"

"All was ok then. You're more of a friend than I am. You knew him before he worked here. You hired him. You'd be more likely to know, Leo, than I would.

"You live right next door. I don't."

"I've got my own house to run, my own ten boys here. I'll make some phone calls to my counselors to arrange for coverage until things shake out. Maybe some of the other supervisors have staff who'd like to pick up a few more hours too."

"Great for the time being. But what are we going to do about a supervisor?"

"Ronnie's out of the picture."

"You can say that. You know what the detective told me?"

"I can guess."

"Really?"

"He's probably using coke again just like before he rehabbed. Maybe dealing now."

"You knew he was using?"

"Leo, come on. He was high when he gave that anti-drug presentation in front of you. We all knew that. I am surprised you didn't."

He got into my face a little.

"Do you think I'd ask him to give a talk on how to spot drug abuse if I knew he was using again?"

"Am I supposed to answer that? I don't know what you knew. Ronnie certainly knew what he was talking about."

He glared at me.

"That's a moot point now. He's doing more than that, Tony. The detective told me there's a warrant for his arrest for drug dealing and gun running. He told me out of respect for the kids under his care. That woman counselor he hired – what's her name?"

"Charlene."

"Yes, Charlene, Charlene Brown. Her brother's connected to some mob in Newark. Ronnie's in with that crowd. He's been dealing right out of the house here apparently. Some of the boys must know something. The one kid home from school here – what's his name? I wrote it down – Reuben Alamas - is not talking much to me. Find out something. Also, I want all the boys in the home downtown for a group talk. And where are Ronnie's wife and kids? We're going to need that apartment."

"From what I've heard, Leo, they haven't been here for a week or so. The kids told my counselor Al they last saw Ronnie couple of nights ago. He was packing up stuff in his car. Told them he had to drop it off. I doubt if they have seen any staff person since then either. I know he was giving a lot of hours to Charlene. I think the counselor Joe left a couple of weeks ago, and the other counselor – his name is Frank – works alternate weekends next door and in my house. Ronnie's wife had some hours too. If Newark is involved, I'm surprised the FBI's not here."

"They might show up. I don't have to tell you this is not good for the agency.

"Ya think? Imagine its impact on the kids."

"That's why I want to speak to the boys as a group downtown. Let them see all the good things we can do for them. We'll bring them to lunch after we talk. You can bring them out to shop for some clothes. We got to keep this quiet as much as possible. If the neighbors find out...well, I told the one boy to tell the other the boys not to go around yapping about it. It's about pride, their pride in where they live."

"That's a hard case to sell them at this point in time, Leo. Your group talk with lunch idea? I don't know about that. They'd have to miss school. Heh, why not come here on a Saturday to do it? You can help cover too that way. That's a great idea, Leo, yes?"

His face went blank.

"Look, Leo. I'll talk to them. Miguel's a great kid here. I'll start with him and then one by one. We'll do a group talk too. Maybe I can get that counselor over in New Dorp. He's working on a psych degree at Columbia."

"Well, if you hear anything, keep me informed right away no matter the hour of the day. We've got to stay ahead of this as much as possible. If Ronnie shows, you've got to call the detective, understand? Otherwise, you're implicated. Here's his number."

"Got ya. He already left me a message to call him. What Saturday or Sunday do you want to come visit us?"

"I'll let you know. Keep me posted."

And he left. I had a lot on my plate. I rushed upstairs to check on Ariana locked in her room and started to make calls, cancelling credit cards, looking for staff willing to work. Thankfully, all the boys in both houses were at school except for Reuben, Miguel's younger brother who was ill. I went next door to have him stay in my house and located the keys to the house in the counselor's room. The whole house was in shambles from the search that had been conducted. Byars's apartment was roped off.

Reuben looked at me with desperation. I gave him a hug and walked him to a couch.

"Mr. D, what's going on? All these detectives. What did Mr. B do? Where's the counselors? Where's Mrs. Byars?"

"We're not sure, Reuben, just yet. Just you worry about getting better. Stay with us for the time being. It's going to be ok. Things will pan out sooner or later. We've got your back."

I managed to contact the counselor John who was pursuing a graduate degree in psych. He was willing to cover. I told him some of the sorry tale and asked him just to calm the boys down.

"Tell them to stick to the daily routine. If they ask about Byars, tell them he's sick and had to go to the hospital but we're not sure which one just yet.

"Wow, I feel bad for the kids. Sure, I'll help out. I have some time during this week."

"Great. You're just the guy, John. Think of what Freud would do in this situation. No, better. Think of what your friend Woody would do. Use some humor to lighten things up maybe."

"Laughing in the dark puts a light on or something like that," he said. "Just unbelievable what these kids have been exposed to in their young lives. Now this. I'll do my best."

John, who lived in Manhattan, had Diane Keaton for a good friend. I had occasions to speak to him in the past but he was mostly mum's the word about the circle he travelled in. He could stay a couple of days and overnights too. When he arrived, he knocked on my door. I filled him in some more and handed him the keys.

"So glad you could help out. Anything you need, just knock on my door. I'm not sure how up to date the house log is. Just be sure to write a sentence or two about each boy as they come home today. You can also write in it what I told you about Byars. Yeah, we're not covering up anything. There's plenty of food in the freezer but not much in the fridge. Please feel free to take from here what you need to make dinner. O and when Miguel comes home, let him know I'd like to speak to him."

Miguel knocked on my door, the first back from school.

"What's up, Mr. D. Am I in trouble or something?"

"No, not at all. I'm sure you are wondering what's going on."

"I don't know much. Yeah, what is going on? We have a new supervisor now? Where's Mr. B.?"

I brought Miguel into my apartment where I could tend to Ariana. He said all the guys knew something weird was up, with all the cars coming and going and people going in and out of Mr. B.'s apartment downstairs. This traffic has been going for a few weeks. He also heard a lot of yelling between Mr. and Mrs. B. Everyone knew he was fucking Ms. Charlene. He'd sleep upstairs in the counselor's room whenever she was on duty. But he was buying stuff for the boys. Big things like a new stereo or a tv for their room.

"Yeah, he bought me this cool boom box. So we all thought whatever was going on, it was none of our business. We were getting stuff. Still, I felt bad for Mrs. B. And Mr. B. You know, I like Mr. B whatever shit he's got going on. Always treated me right. Helped me a few times."

"Miguel, there's a lot of good things about him. He gave me some advice too. He cares for people whatever his problems are."

"I'm worried, Mr. D. You're staying right?"

"Sure. Why do you think I'm not?"

"I don't know. I hear from Jimmy you never got back last night and they didn't know where you were. You got a black eye, Mr. D."

The boys always had a way of finding out things. There was no privacy with twenty boys sharing walls and finding out what no child should know or hear. I got Miguel to open up a little.

"I know you like to do the right thing, Miguel. Keep on, keep on. Don't let anything turn your head from what you have to do."

"Mr. D., I don't like all this stuff going on here. I wish my parents would get it straight and I could go home."

"Your mom's a great person but she has her hands full as you know, Miguel. Your dad's a different story. He's got to get his act together more before she'll take him back. You are making your mom proud, though, with those good grades. And I hear you scored a touchdown last game?"

"No, I made an interception. Then we scored and won the game." He beamed for a moment and then shook his head.

"Yeah that felt good, Mr. D. Now this shit."

"We all have to do what we can. Do the right thing for yourself just like you're doing. And don't worry about Mr. and Mrs. B. That's not your life. Your life is in here and you've got plenty of it."

I pointed to his heart. He looked at me straight in the eye.

"Need more than that, Mr. D. But whatever."

I put an arm on his shoulder.

"Hang in there, Miguel. We've got your back. Trust me. Help Mr. John. Mr. Frank will be here this weekend. Everything's going back to normal the way you like it. You're a good young man, Miguel. I know we can trust you to help out."

"Sure, Mr. D."

He went back next door. The detective called me. I told him I didn't know much about Byars except that he and his wife were on the outs. As I did with Leo, I held back the incident about Byars's blowing coke in the diner and the massive bag of coke I had seen on his table which he was selling to supervisor Rosie. Rumor had it that Leo also copped from Byars so that was a dead end to tell what I knew to Leo. Telling the detective would implicate me immediately because I should have told the authorities at the agency right then and there. But I didn't. Like Miguel, I too liked Ronnie who at one time was excellent with the boys. When Charlene was hired, things changed quickly. Also, there was the betrayal factor. If I snitched on Ronnie, I'd break the code supervisors had. Our private lives were exactly that. Because we lived where we worked, it was important to close our doors as much as we could. The stress of the job we shared was also a bond. We covered each other's back. The downtown people had no idea what it was like to do what we did though they pretended to be experts and have all this compassion for the kids. That was a key thing to maintain, though, compassion. The kids knew the staff members who were just putting in time from the ones who genuinely gave a damn. It was crucial to everything we did to gain their trust in that way and to keep trust in each other too as supervisors. If we shared marital, drug or alcohol problems with each other, as long as they were not impacting our ability to care for the boys, they were confidential matters. But Byars had crossed the line as even if he must have known, the reason why he was basically bribing his boys to keep quiet. I had enough problems of my own to worry about, in my own life and with the boys, not to complicate things even more by spilling the beans on Ronnie's coke habit and dealing. I just wanted to keep my own nose clean and out of his business. But now he was way overboard. The magnitude of his problems alone spilled out on all of us in both group homes. It forced him out into the open. His was a tragic turnaround because of the magical effect he first had on the boys under his care. Their grades almost to a child had gone up along with sports participation at the high school. Three of the boys joined the junior and varsity football teams, became standouts and were mostly humble about it. When congratulated, two of the boys would put their head down, and they'd say "thanks." Their attitude alone if not their play on the field would shine anywhere in the world. There's a universal clarity in sports too, an assuring certainty about it. In a race, there's usually no doubt about who came in first, who last. A clock doesn't lie. A body cannot be in two places at once or nowhere at all although there are claims otherwise. The body is its own proof, living our life, so to speak, like it or not. Sometimes its natural abilities do go recognized. A combination of fate and human bias takes a lucky turn. In the boys' case, if they felt in exile from their family, they were heroic nomads on the field. Fernando too in my house had the same humble pride. We had spoken about this and agreed that one cannot take pride in one's humility, but one can be humble and still be proud of accomplishments. He struck the right balance, I told him, impressive at any age. Maybe children in their innocence are more likely to get this right than adults. Any vanity, secret or otherwise, that clings to pride, even one based upon genuine accomplishment, turns one vapid. The shine of success turns lurid.

A transformation in this darker direction through a return to what he had been had occurred with Ronnie. Now the task was to keep the boys believing in the light, even if the bearer of it no longer did.

When Lisa returned from work, she looked bewildered but glad to see me. I had lies to tell about last night if we were to keep sane, focused on what we had to do. It was true that Karrin and I had said good-bye yesterday in a way that convinced both of us it was for good. At least I did not have to lie about that although I told Lisa we broke up over the phone.

"I'm glad you say that's over, but I can't say it didn't take a toll on me, on us, on how I feel about us, about you, my trust in you. If you stay true to me, then you gain more and more trust back. I still can't believe you were mugged. You sure you don't have a concussion?"

"I was lucky I wasn't stabbed or something. Not so lucky now, though, with what's going on next door."

"What's that all about?"

"The detectives have search and arrest warrants for Ronnie. He's apparently involved with some gangsters in Newark through his girlfriend Charlene's brother.

"Charlene? The counselor? She's his girlfriend? My God."

"Yeah, apparently that's been going on for a while which explains why his wife was so stressed all the time. Remember you said how pale and nervous she was when you ran into her at the store?"

"Well, now I know why she feels that way. I hate to say it but I do know the feeling myself. So what's he done now with these gangsters?"

"Looks like he was running drugs and guns out of the house next door."

"O my God. From the house? What the hell's next here? A shootout? And what about Ariana? This is no good. No good."

We sat in silence for a good long while, my head between my hands, Lisa looking out the window, her arms folded.

"Ariana and I can't live here anymore, Tony. We need to rent an apartment. I've been looking through the paper for one near the hospital. It's just not safe here anymore. I didn't mind it so much before. But now that she's older, I have to worry every day to see what I'm coming home to. And frankly, this job of yours has not helped our marriage, the stress, the boys club you supervisors seem to have. I don't want this. I was willing to move in and I am fond of some of the boys. You know I admire the work you're doing, I mean what could be better and harder than caring for these kids. But this is too much. It really is."

"I will be applying for full-time teaching once I finish the Ph. D."

"I can't wait for that to happen. I know you'll finish it but with all that's going on in this job of yours, I mean, when? A year or two from now? And you have doubts you will even find a full-time job with the market the way it is for English professors. No. I don't feel safe. Our daughter's not safe. Let's get an apartment. I mean I'm assuming you will join us?"

As I considered what was beyond life in the group home, the full impact of having said goodbye to Karrin hit me. A future without her, with anyone else but her, seemed long and dreary, heavy with duty, little by way of joy. I spoke like a machine.

"Of course, I will join you. What do you mean, join? We're a family."

And we kissed.

Chapter 13

Wilderness

Lisa and Ariana moved out in a few weeks into a two-bedroom pied à terre near the hospital, a more gentrified section of Staten Island. With the staff shortage caused by next door, I didn't get to sleep there often in the weeks ahead. The old widow who rented out the place knew Lisa from her own volunteer work at the hospital and made a point of telling me how she felt such pity for the boys.

"They're behind the eight ball point right from the start. You have to feel sorry for them."

"You'd be surprised at how strong they are, determined to get ahead. They feel uncomfortable if they sense pity for them. It's a lean meal at any rate, like hope."

"Tony, she's only being nice. Yes, I feel the same way. Sorry for them," Lisa added, giving me a look.

The exodus of my family was to be followed by three of the boys who had been with me for years, as if what Byars had done set off a chain reaction. John was going to try to live with his uncle in Queens. The weekend visits had gone well, and he was looking forward to a new life. Fernando, now 18 and about to graduate from high school, was preparing to live with his mom, who had moved into a new apartment off Jerome Avenue in the Bronx, having been awarded some of the funds due her from the father. Juan too was busy making arrangements through his social worker to move into a Jewish group home.

"Mr. D., just know it's not about you. I'm fond of you and Mrs. D too."

"Well, I will definitely miss you, Juan, if and when you do get accepted."

"I'm hoping for that one in Queens. It's the best one. Their kids get so many more opportunities from what I hear."

"The social worker told me there's a good high school there too."

"Anything would be better than the one here."

"That's not true, Juan. It's an ok public school."

"But just know I will always miss you, Mr. D."

And he kissed me on the cheek. We both teared up a bit.

"But heh, this may never happen."

It did. Within the month, Juan was gone, as soon as he graduated sophomore year. We had a going-away party, both houses attending. Juan smiled throughout his speech about how "wonderful" he felt about me and Mrs. D and some of the boys.

"It's a crazy house but we've had a lot of good times here. Weird times but fun. Like that guy who was going to the bathroom in the plants. O my God. Or the time James ran around in his underwear, saying he'd bomb the place. And Mr. Al and Ms. Sheila. I'm going miss our talks, Ms. Sheila. And all our laughs, Mr. Al. You saved my teddy from Willie."

Everyone laughed.

"Mr. D., though. What can I say?'

And he came over and we hugged. He was gone two days later. I'd never see him again.

A new supervisor was hired for next door. He was a minister newly engaged. His fiancée would move in after they married, he told me.

"Tell her to visit often before she does. Maybe have supper with the kids a few times. Can she cook? The guys would love that," I told him.

Some of the boys next door complained to me right away. The supervisor immediately had enforced a set of rules, with behavioral charts hung up on a board in the kitchen. I cautioned him about coming on too heavy or the kids would run, not mentioning they had already complained, or I'd break their trust not to say anything.

"They need discipline and the love of God in their lives. I work towards both."

"I hope you can tell jokes and be silly too, David. Play sports often. Let them beat you without their knowing it."

I didn't know how much Leo had told him about Byars. I didn't want to scare him away. I had been running both houses in the interim, arranging coverage, shopping like crazy, making sure all the boys ate well. In times of crisis, let them eat steak with plenty of cake too. It would keep them coming to the table. It would keep them coming back home.

A new boy replaced Juan. I let him take Juan's room though it was right next to my apartment. With Lisa and Ariana gone, I didn't have much to worry about. He was a big kid, a young adult really transferred from one of our Bronx group homes so he could be closer to his aunt. Jorge was a quiet one, even somber, who quickly proved I had nothing to fear. He would always call me "Sir" and nod his head. The other boys would look at me when he said and did that, as if they were seeing me in a new light, as if I were a public figure, a stranger with authority over their lives, not one of them. I had worked to become one with them, a pseudo-family.

Jorge would have none of that, always civil but distant, keeping at more than arm's length. He was that way with the other boys too, never unpleasant but poker-faced. He kept his room immaculate and would press his dungarees and t-shirts. As I read his file, I knew why. Freed for adoption at ten, he had run away from a foster home and gone off the radar screen for years. Then, at the instigation of one of the boys in the Bronx home, he knocked on the supervisor's door, asking if he could stay. He was sixteen and very ill. He had forced himself into independence for all those years. He had worked with a landscape company and as a carpenter's helper, busboy, and cashier, among other jobs, making ends meet somehow until his luck ran out when he developed appendicitis. After a stint in the hospital, he moved into the Bronx home and began attending preparatory GED summer classes. An agency social worker located an aunt in Staten Island who said she was thrilled to hear he was found. He told me he wanted to move in with his aunt to help her out once she was ready to get a bigger apartment. He wanted to join the police or the Coast Guard. He studied harder than any of the other boys except for Fernando who was usually the last to leave the table with his books.

"Need help, Jorge, with that biology project?" I'd ask.

"No, sir. Thank you."

Fernando would look at me and smile.

"The other guys can take a lesson from him," Fernando said to me.

And Jorge smiled a little.

"Take a lesson from birds too. They know how to survive," he said and went back to his studies.

Summer was in full swing. Most of the boys went to day camp or had part-time jobs, one at Rita's Ices down the block, another at the pizzeria, another at the supermarket. One boy Ricardo, who didn't have anything lined up, didn't want to do anything except stay in bed until noon or so, have a massive breakfast and then back to bed. He had sabotaged the one job we got for him at the bread bakery just up the street. He had to show up at 6am, work three hours or so packaging the loaves, and then he was done for the day. Al told me the only way to wake him up was to throw him out of the bed, and he wasn't going to do it. Ricky had been with us about eight months or so, coming from his grandmother's apartment. His parents were mostly out of the picture, the mother drifting in and out of contact over the years and the father barely known. At first, Ricky was happy to move in. I brought him out to buy some new clothes as I always did with new placements. José welcomed him into his room. It was a good time for an overhaul in that room, which had access to a half bath, a real plus I pointed out to Ricky, the only room that had one. I let them choose a paint color together, allowing black as an accent wall but not the whole room as they wanted. They painted along with counselor Frank over a weekend and did a decent job of it. They had to keep it neat. I promised to have the opaque window fixed in the bathroom, which presently had a Q-Tip stuck in mid pane to keep the bugs out. Little story there. One evening, after I took the garbage out, I thought I smelled pot. When I went to the back of the house, I saw a joint glowing out a window. Someone had somehow drilled a hole through it just big enough to insert a joint from outside the window which they would close, puffing on the joint from inside the bathroom, with no smell in the house if the smoke was kept inside the lungs long enough. I marveled at the cleverness of the whole thing and then grabbed the lit joint. The window flew open and there was Tony, astonished to see me there.

"Looking for something?"

Tony could be a wild kid at times, but he always took care of his business, with decent grades in school and a lot of friends in the neighborhood. One of his friends who lived just down the block had a father who owned a construction company. Tony regularly worked for him, earning double the minimum hourly wage which was about three dollars at the time. Senior year was his big party year. He had a place lined up to move into after he graduated and would be able to pay modest rent, working full time in construction and part-time at the deli. He had a lot of hustle and connections. He was bound to succeed.

I did a quick search of his room and found a dime or two of weed.

"Yo, Mr. D. I was just holding it for a friend. I'll give it back."

"Sure, you will. And you were holding that joint for him he was smoking out your window."

"Tee hee, tee hee. Sorry, Mr. D."

"Clever, Tony, clever. How did you make the hole? Now you can pay for a new window too."

"Tee he. Tee he. I borrowed a drill with a diamond tip from work."

"Not funny, Tony. Not. Your curfew the next few weekends is 9 pm now, not 11. Tee hee to you."

José, his roommate at the time, covered his head with a pillow to smother his laughter.

"Mr. D., but my girl has a birthday next Saturday."

"Let her mom talk to me or a counselor. No parent there, you're not going. If there is one, 10 o'clock latest. Yeah, you lost some of your freedom for a while."

"You taking the weed?"

"No, I'm flushing it down the toilet."

"O man, it's Gold, Mr. D. At least keep it for yourself. Tee hee, tee hee."

He always laughed that way. Mr Al called him the "tee hee kid," as if he was a sidekick in a Western. I went into the bathroom and pretended to flush the weed.

We helped Tony move out on his own that summer. He'd come back often for a while, mostly to visit José and Mr. Al. We'd force him to take some food despite his protests that he didn't need it. He always gave me a big greeting whenever he'd come back. Then we lost track. José felt a bit betrayed, missing him. I half-missed his shenanigans and silly little laugh. I admired him, how he prepared for and now had made his independence stick. I told him that the last time I saw him. The window with the hole was like a memento of his presence in the house for two years.

The honeymoon period with Ricky did not last long. He started cutting out of school. It was a struggle for us and him but somehow he managed to pass his classes barely to avoid summer school. He didn't keep the appointments we made for him for job interviews in the neighborhood. The bakery job was his last chance. Nobody else wanted it because of the 6am start-time. At least it was something. But Ricky just wanted to chill all summer. We weren't going to allow that. Every day was a big to-do just to get him out of bed and stay out of bed. And then he started to peel the latex paint from the wall behind his bed that he had just painted. Morning after morning that was his routine. Mr. Will threw water in his face one morning and Ricky went for him. Mr. Will just put his massive stomach out and Ricky bounced to the floor. He just went back to bed, cursing at Will.

"Kid's like a rattlesnake, Tony," Mr Will told me. "He just recoiled and went back to curl up in his lair, spitting out curses at me in Spanish."

When I would speak to Ricky one on one, he was for a while a happy boy glad to be with us. But when he started his lethargic routine, our talks went nowhere. He was sullen and obviously depressed. He wouldn't say why. He had a million reasons given his background. I arranged for therapy at the office but he refused to go. I had the social worker talk to him in the house several times. She told me he had a lot of anger directed at his mother whom we couldn't locate at present and also at his grandmother. He had a history of truancy and late hours in Brooklyn where he had lived with his grandmother. He'd hang out in Prospect Park, getting high and shoplifting. Unable to rein him in, she took out a PINS petition.

One morning, after he again refused to get out of bed for Mr. Al, I went in to give him the lowdown.

"Ricky, looks like things are not working out for you here. Do you see you're the only guy in the house still in bed? No one does that in this house. We're all out doing things we need to day after day. Mr. Al asked you to help him with the food shopping. I have to go out. You can't stay in the house alone."

He just turned away in his bed.

"Ricky, this can't go on. Get out of the bed. If you don't, like Mr. Will told you, we're going to have to call BCW and have you transferred to a lock-down. You know this is a good place. Why mess it up for yourself?"

I turned him towards me in the bed and he took a fit.

"Don't be touching me, man, *gran jefe*. And Mr. Will, *gran mierda. Follarlo.*"

"We don't talk that way in this place. You leave us no choice if you don't cooperate."

"So transfer me. I don't give a shit."

I walked out and staged a phone call, pulling the cord down the hallway from the kitchen so Ricky could overhear. Next thing I knew he bolted out of the house with a bag full of clothes.

"Fuck you all," he screamed outside the house back at me when I followed him out the door. And he ran down the street. Ten minutes later, a rock came flying through the front window.

By the time Al got to the front door, whoever did it was gone. It had to be Ricky. I made the phone calls to the social worker and his grandmother. The police wouldn't take a missing person's report until the next day when the boy had gone missing twenty-four hours. That was the last time I saw Ricky or heard about him. Another lost teen wandering the streets of NYC.

What bugged me when things like this happened was that I had to give so much time to the kids not doing well while the ones doing well received less and less attention depending on the crisis we were tending to. One of these boys who did well was Bobby. He had arrived in the group home with his younger brother from the Bronx. The mom they had been living with off Arthur Avenue was suffering from mental illness while their dad had remarried and moved to Italy. He claimed he'd take the two boys back when he returned to New York with his new bride and her two children. He had pleaded with his ex-wife to take a PINS petition out when the boys stopped going to school and would wander around the city for days. She finally was forced to when she had to be hospitalized for a longer period. Bobby and his brother Lenny started the same routine when they first came to my house, getting on the ferry and traipsing around Manhattan. They would jump turnstiles and ride the subways. The police picked them up in the middle of the night and they were returned to the home. They were trying to find their maternal uncle in the city and they had different addresses for where he might be. At least that's what Lenny told me. Although younger, Lenny did most of the talking.

"You can't do that anymore. You're here now. We'll see if we can get in touch with your uncle. That will take some time. If you keep going on these wild rides, you force us to transfer both of you to a more secure setting. Give your new home a chance, guys. You might really like it here. We can help you out."

Lenny proved incorrigible about going to the local grammar school. He just wanted to go back with his mom. His starting a new school felt like a betrayal of her. Bobby turned things around quickly. He hated to make trouble. Lenny eventually went to live with his mom when she returned from the hospital. Bobby stayed on. He liked the boys, and it would make things easier for his mom if she had to care for only one of them. At least, that's what his mom had told him.

"I can visit her on weekends to help out," he told me.

"Sure, the social worker or I will make another home visit now that your mom is feeling better. Let's see how Lenny does."

Bobby proved a really nice kid, happy to be in our home, off the streets of the Bronx, playing sports a bit, doing well in school. He was a bit shy but knew how to laugh at a good joke or prank. He'd never start one himself. The boys liked the way he laughed, clapping his hands together and shaking his head. He quickly earned a nickname, "Eggie Toes."

When I asked Jimmy why he was called that, Jimmy explained.

"He dances like a chicken when he laughs."

"Yeah and he's got weird skin between his toes," José added.

Bobby didn't mind the nickname. It meant he had become one of them. We were all fond of him. He was thriving.

I was not. Because I had to sleep several nights a week in the group home, Lisa and I were seeing less and less of each other. It did give me time to work on my dissertation because it gave me a lot of alone time. Any spare moment I had, however, I found myself wondering what Karrin was doing. I was falling into despair though more fighting against than allowing it, which only made me sink deeper. Music was helping me accept it. Coltrane, Miles, Stan Getz, Satie, Ella, Nina Simone, any blues ballad helped ease the pain a bit. Under its spell, I felt camaraderie with the singer, a beauty in shared sadness. Heartbreak proves a source of song. Outside music, I felt self-pity and self-loathing, now indulging in my grief, now scowling at my weakness, considering the much worse plight of so many people I knew. On the other hand, Lisa seemed happy in the new apartment. Ariana was being cared for by an older woman who was a friend of Lisa's and who lived down the block from the hospital.

"I feel so relieved, Tony, not living there anymore. I didn't realize how stressful it was until I moved in here. I can sleep at night. Ariana's safe. We do miss you, though, but I know you're getting your writing done, right?"

I had only more stress ahead of me with John and Fernando now planning to leave the house. Who knew what new boy would show up, with what fear of the future and anger over being rejected, shadowed by troubles they were too young to understand? I also knew I'd miss those two who had lived with me for years now. I decided to have more than a party for them. Why not a hiking trip together for a few days to celebrate Fernando's graduation from high school and their moving back to family? It would do us all good to close that chapter in their lives in a positive way. I had some difficult emotions to let go of too. Wilderness, even more than music, had always helped me with that. In some weird way, they were connected or my brain was wired to receive them in that way, music occurring against and working with a silence it could not contain, wilderness immersing one in it. I don't know why but somehow both got the tears out.

Fernando loved the idea of a hiking trip. We cleared it with the social worker, Fernando's mother, and his boss whom he worked for this summer at the hardware store. John wanted to go too but didn't want to disappoint his uncle whom he was helping with the new apartment in Queens, getting it ready for his moving in. Bobby heard about the trip from Fernando and came up to me quietly and asked if he could come.

"You think you'd take me too, Mr. D? I'd love to see some mountains. My dad's always talking about them in Italy. Never seen any myself."

"Let me have the social worker check with your dad and mom. If they say yes, then why not?"

Things had to be cleared because the trip I planned was out of state to Shenandoah National Park in Virginia, an asylum I knew well. Our request for Bobby to go was approved.

Lisa wasn't too happy with the idea.

"So you're taking a vacation without us, your own family?"

"It's just a short trip. You can't get off work anyway."

"I might have had you let me know earlier."

"I hadn't planned this out. It's kind of spur of the moment. You're not exactly into sleeping in the woods anyway."

"You're right on that one. I'm not a girl-scout type. Well, have a good time. Be safe out there. Don't take any chances. Yes, I'll worry about you. Let me know the phone number to the park. Tell the ranger where you're hiking."

"I always do."

I arranged for coverage at the home, and the two boys and I headed off to Virginia. On the six-hour drive down, I asked Fernando if he was looking forward to moving in with his mom.

"Sure, I'm looking forward to it and starting college too. My mom says she has some part-time job leads for me already. It's time to help her and time for me to go forward. She told me last night to thank you again for all you've done. I thank you too, Mr. D."

"Well, I'm sure going miss you in the house but you know what? Thank you for all the help, for the sanity you bring with you wherever you go. I hope we'll keep in touch. I really do. Heh, your plan sounds great. Bronx Community College is a good place to begin. Maybe think about Lehman College after your two years there or even sooner, depending on your major. Like BCC, it's not too far from your mom's apartment. I know she's looking forward to your moving in."

"She says Jesus answered her prayers. She was lighting candles in the church every week for the last year."

"O wow. Well, she can stop the campfires there. Her big son's going home."

"Yeah, she's very religious."

"Yes, she must be, all those novenas. Catholic?"

"O yes. Very Catholic. She's got statues and pictures all over the place. She prays the rosary in her room every night."

"I know you pray too at night. You told me."

"Yeah, but I'm not so into it like she is. That's one thing I never understood about the group home."

"What's that?"

"I mean it's Catholic and all but outside the one cross in the hallway, I never saw anything else religious about the place. My mom was disappointed when I told her we never went to mass.

I guess she'll want me to go."

"I always encouraged the boys to walk the two blocks if they wanted to go to mass on Sunday. I'm not traditional myself, and I did not want to force them to go."

"I remember we had this big talk one time about God. Most of the guys just laughed."

"I remember. You were upset."

"Yeah, they were just laughing, saying it was all bull."

"Juan said he prays," I said.

. "Yeah, then he said he wonders what clothes God wears," Bobby quipped. "Tony said God just walks around naked. Jimmy said he's like an animal, just fur."

"Ok, ok. They just don't get it," Fernando retorted. "Neither does my brother."

"I agree with you, Fernando. It's a serious thing everyone has to think about their whole life. It's about the sacredness of life to me. To me God is love. We create God in our lives through love. I wanted the guys to think about it at least. That's why after that talk, I invited the parish priest to come round. He asked me if I brought them to mass and I said I left it up to them. He said come to church with them. I told him if he visited us, we'd make a nice dinner for him and he could have a chat, you know, show his interest. But all he said was, 'Come to mass.' I invited him a few times after that too, leaving messages. He didn't return the call. I mean, we're a couple of blocks away."

"Yeah, he should have dropped in. He seemed like a good guy from the few times I went to church."

"You were the only one to go," Bobby said.

"Yeah, and we're a Catholic group home. What's up with that, Mr. D?"

"The work the agency does helping kids out could not be more spiritual, Fernando, whether the priest came or not, whether people are forced to go to mass or not. The boys know if they wanted to go to church, we'd take them. Mr. Will and Mr. Frank or whoever the weekend counselor would offer. We should have more talks about it, about what they believe in. I will try. Got to find those right moments when they can be a little serious."

"Seems like a lot of people downtown don't really care that much about the kids," Fernando said.

I asked Bobby if he felt that way too.

"Yeah, really, like how many times did we see someone visit our house from downtown? They don't even know who we are," he said.

" All they care about is the money they get," Fernando said.

"Not true, Fernando. It's like any profession. For every bad cop or doctor, there's twenty good ones. Same with priests, counselors, teachers, whoever. The work they're trained to do is what's important and how well they do it. You can't blame the water for the dirt in it, know what I mean?" I asked.

"That's why whatever I end up doing, I'm going to be the best I can. I know God is watching if no one else is."

"You've got a conscience, Fernando. That's good. You've got a good inner voice inside. It's like a gift. You are kind. You care. Don't lose that."

"What about you, Mr. D? Do you believe in God?"

I sighed and thought about how honest I should be with him. I went philosophical rather than personal.

"You know what I tell my students the few times I've been asked that? I say I'm still stuck on the word exists."

"What do you mean?"

"You know when people ask, 'do you believe God exists?' I try to say something that will keep people thinking, including myself. So I'll say something like, 'God is so great, God doesn't need to exist.' Or "I know I love the feeling I feel when I believe God exists but I can't answer your question. It goes beyond what anyone can know."

"That's just weird, Mr. D."

"Well, it's not a multiple-choice question to me, yes, no, maybe so, don't know. It's a paradoxical question, Fernando. The Bible is full of paradox, full of poetry. God died on the cross. Right there. Mind-blowing story. What to make of it? I was raised a Catholic, grammar school through college. I went from just reciting the prayers I was told to memorize to questioning everything, full of doubt. There are some really puzzling things. You know what? It's good to be puzzled about such things. Keep the puzzle going. No clear picture ahead."

"Well, God is just love. Isn't that enough? What's so puzzling about that?"

"Sure, we need more love in our lives. The whole world does. If there's any center or circle, any thought for me I hold onto when I need it, that's it. Love's the best of what we humans make. But let me ask. If God is the source of all that is good, why did God create the devil? Why did he allow his only son to die for sins he didn't commit? Why was Abraham asked by God to kill his son Isaac as a test of faith? Why did Abraham say ok? I don't have answers but I am deeply disturbed by those stories. Deeply puzzled."

"My mom says it's about faith and forgiveness."

"Yes, she has her heart in the right place there, Fernando. Forgiveness."

"All that studying you do, Mr. D. I would think you can see that."

"Yes, reading, reflecting. I've thought a lot about what one of the fathers of the Church wrote. He had a saying, 'faith seeks understanding.' For me, it's more like understanding seeking faith."

"What about seek and you will find, Mr. D?"

"I'm still seeking, Fernando. Your faith is a gift. If it gives you strength to do the right thing, it's a great thing."

"My mom tells me that all the time. It gives her strength."

"What about your dad?"

"Mr. D. Let's not go there, please."

He paused and put his thoughts together.

"It just hasn't worked out. My mom hates him. Any contact I have with him, I can't tell her about. So I got to hold on to what I have. I love her. She needs my help. My dad? He hasn't been there for me. Or for José."

I could see he was getting upset so I dropped the subject. I had spoken to José many times about how he felt about Fernando's leaving. The social worker did too. José acted as if it was all ok with him.

"That's his mom. Not mine. It's cool."

"We'll arrange visits for you there if you like, if his mom's ok with it."

"I don't really know her that much, and she doesn't know me. That's ok. We're brothers, will always be, no matter what."

We had not been able to locate José's own mom in Puerto Rico which was the last place the social worker said she was reported to be. The dad was just out of the picture, probably for the better at any rate from what Fernando had told me about the Christmas visit. I had been thinking about bringing José on the hiking trip but without a parent to consent to it, I was leery of doing so. I didn't tell him that, though, to avoid rubbing salt in a wound. I did tell him I was taking only older boys and only two this time. I'd take him when he got older and maybe Fernando would come then too. He said he understood. "Sleep in the woods? Nah. I don't like bugs, Mr. D" was all he'd say and laughed.

I wanted to get Bobby into our conversation in the car more. He was sitting in the backseat, taking the ride in, the rest of the country like a revelation to him the way he kept turning his head and looking back.

"Bobby, you ok, back there? You hungry?"

"I'm good. Yeah, food sounds good."

"We'll stop soon. First time out of New York, Bobby?"

"I used to go to a beach in Jersey sometimes."

"Which beach?"

"I can't remember the name but it had a big jetty. I used to climb out on the rocks and get yelled at."

"I guess your parents took you?"

"Yeah. We'd go in this old station wagon. We didn't think it would make it."

"So you've seen the ocean now but never the mountains before?"

"No, never. This will be the first time."

"I think you told me your dad was talking about the mountains in Italy. Not the Alps?"

"No, it's the...it begins with A."

"The Apennines?"

"Yeah, that's it maybe. He lives in a town outside Boloney."

"It's pronounced Bologna."

"Yeah, his girlfriend's family's from there and has a shoe business, I think. He works for them."

"How did he meet his new wife, your stepmom? They are married, I think – yes?"

"I'm not sure about that. I think they met in the Bronx. She was visiting or something."

"Did you like living over there on Arthur Avenue?"

"It's on 179th St. My mom's still there."

"That's right. The social worker visited her there."

"I don't miss all the craziness. Lots of people hanging out. Lots of cars coming and going all the time."

"O yeah. It's kind of a legendary neighborhood, all those Italian restaurants and stores, Dino and the Belmonts."

"Who?"

"Dino and the Belmonts named after Belmont Avenue. I guess you wouldn't know a doo-whop band."

I started singing "I Wonder Why": "*Don't know why I love you, don't know why I care.* Yeah. Big hit in the fifties."

"Never heard of them. I've been on Belmont Avenue plenty of times. Had lots of friends there. Right down the block from where we lived."

Bobby turned away and looked out the window. I could sense he didn't really want to talk about it.

"You're going to love the mountains, Bobby. They're not that big as far as mountains go but they are older than the Rockies. Probably as old as the Apennines. The road goes right up to the top with awesome views. We'll hike down the trail. Kind of unusual. Usually you have to hike up from a road. You've seen mountains, Fernando?"

"Yeah once. Upstate New York. I think it was Bear Mountain. I was little. Went there with my dad. Don't remember too much."

I was looking forward to seeing their reaction to a place I so loved. I had often gone solo hiking there. It was a treat to have these guys coming along. I just hoped the weather held.

After a dinner stop at the town of Warrenton, active like a little city with all the cars and chain stores, we entered the park as the sun was setting. Up and up I drove until we reached Skyline Drive. Even in the car, you could feel the peace of the woods on all sides. The boys had never seen so many trees. Our destination was Betty's rock, an outcropping of stone that had a summit's view of the wide valley below. I knew a short walk-in there off the parking lot to a flat grassy area where we could make a tent site just above the Appalachian trail. We threw our sleeping stuff together and loaded it all into one pack. As we approached the area where I wanted to pitch, we could see a shadow rise fifty feet ahead up the trail, silhouetted against the last light of day. We stopped dead in our tracks. It was a rival claimant to the bedstead, a large stag. He had risen to his feet when he heard us and now stood a little above us. The trail we were on was the only way in.

"Let's get out of here, Mr. D.," Fernando said.

"Yeah, let's go to that motel we saw," Bobby pleaded.

"Just back away. Give him a way out," I said.

But the stag turned around and leapt off the outcropping into the forest just below on the other side.

"OK, the vacancy sign just went on, guys. We good."

The valley was lit up below us. The stars had already rushed into the sky. Fernando and then Bobby ran to the top of the rock to get the full glory of the scene. Their fear instantly melted. They were amazed. As I worked alone to pitch the tent, I felt at home in this little nook where I had slept on so many solo trips. Thoughts of Karrin flooded me. I could hear her calling out, "where are you? I can't see you." The boys came off the little summit and I snapped back.

"Mr. D, this is awesome," Fernando said.

"It really is," Robby added. "Think that deer will come back?"

"Only if he smells a doe around," I replied. "That was a big boy, no doubt. This must be his throne room, the king of the forest."

"Where did he go? Where did he jump off?"

"He probably jumped down to the Appalachian trail just below us about twenty feet."

"Damn. I didn't see no way down. It looks like a cliff."

"Yeah, for us, it would be a little work to climb straight down. For the stag, just a quick jump or two. That's how it is out here.

We're just another creature who have to hoof it, and we're pretty slow and clumsy."

The boys went to sleep almost instantly. I went up to the summit and let the night empty me of thought. I loved getting puny. How vast the space and yet how intimate the silence. I felt able to rest, put in my place like an ant climbing a blade of grass.

The next day we woke early and drove down to Big Meadows where we had a large breakfast in the restaurant and lodge there. We wandered out to a deck.

"Why not stay here tonight? It's a really cool place," Bobby asked.

"Yeah, that deer scared you last night, I guess. I'll protect you," Fernando ribbed.

"It's not that. It's just the woods and all. Pretty wild here. Plus it looks like it's going to rain."

"Bobby, don't worry. We'll take a short hike to some waterfalls I know after we drive down to the southern section. Bit more secluded there, more chance to see animals. We'll camp near the falls. You'll love it. If it rains that bad today, we can always head back to the car just a mile or so away."

The weather held. The falls were flowing even at this time in late June because of recent torrential rain. Fernando climbed to the top of the falls and yelled down for us to follow.

Bobby was uneasy about climbing on the slippery rocks so I stayed with him at the base of the falls.

"Wow, this is awesome. Never seen anything so beautiful, Mr. D. I'm good right here, taking it all in," Bobby said.

"Anywhere is beautiful here. I hear ya. Do what you're comfortable with. I won't press you to do more."

Fernando came down all excited.

"It's freaking beautiful up there. There's a little open space in the forest and the water's just flowing like crazy. I was standing right where it falls off. Must be really cool at night. We're staying here, right?"

"Yes, just a little past where we put our stuff."

I cooked the first dinner they ever had in the woods. Just some packaged dehydrated foods I had bought which they thought the best they ever tasted.

"Out here, anything would taste good. Just like when you're out in a boat too. Suddenly you're not so picky," I said. "Wilderness does that. Kind of levels us to where we stand."

"Yeah, if I had four legs, no problem out here."

"Two's just as good, Bobby. I had no problem climbing to the top of the falls. Just gotta be careful."

"Exactly. I'm gonna be careful."

As soon as the sun set, the skies opened up, a deluge in the complete dark. We scampered to the tent, our packs after dinner hung on some rope we tied as high as we could, tossing it between two trees about 100 feet from our tent. I had almost crowned myself with the rock I had tied to the rope so I could throw it to an overhanging branch. The end of the rope where the rock was tied came sailing down from the branch which the rope had fallen over and whistled just past my head, a close one.

"Damn, Mr. D. Out here, can't take no chances," Bobby said.

"Not that different from the city really. I mean we wait to cross a street with a dump truck speeding past three feet away with the driver fighting sleep and don't think of it for a second."

The rain poured down like the waterfall. We were dry inside the tent in our sleeping bags, laid out like sardines in a can. I lit a candle inside a little lantern and hung it down from the roof of the tent.

"Feel safe, Bobby? See it's warm and dry. See what a little light will do."

"Yeah, yeah. As long as the rain keeps out. The tent is pretty thin."

"The rain jacket will do the trick. And I waxed all the seams before we left. Amazing what a little nylon will do. Keeps us warm and dry. Just chill, Bobby."

"This is cool. What's the plan for tomorrow, Mr. D?" Fernando asked.

"We'll do Big Run just across the highway. It's a good hike down like three thousand feet or so. We'll do about a few almost all downhill. Nice trail, easy walk for the most part."

"Why that trail?"

"It's very quiet and wild especially at the bottom, Fernando. Biggest water run in the park. Goes right to the boundary of the park. You go down into this canyon, some water crossings, but not hard ones. Then at the bottom, it just opens up to a wide mostly shallow creek. Some old rail tracks down there too. Story goes that General Stonewall Jackson hid his confederate army down there during the civil war and had supplies trained in from the valley. He was a holy terror in battle. Maybe we'll find a cannonball or a bullet."

Fernando looked stunned and shook his head.

"The canyon. That's holy. Fighting for slavery? Not holy. Messed up. History's friggin weird."

"Sounds steep to me. Lot of wet rocks too, I bet."

"Bobby, the trail winds its way down, never really steep. I walked it a few years ago doing a solo. I loved the peace and quiet, the water running, the big scree overhead, very secluded. You can see how they could hide an army down there."

"Who cares."

"A scree?"

"It's a big pile of fallen rocks a few hundred feet high. We won't have to climb it or anything. We'll pitch camp along the creek a bit past the base of the scree."

The rain and wind picked up a lot, pushing at the walls of our tent, threatening to lift our little house into the trees. I started humming the song "Magic Carpet Ride." They didn't know the tune or didn't get the joke. Bobby looked more worried than usual. I asked him if this was how he pictured mountains.

"I guess so from what my dad told me. Just didn't think it would get so dark."

The sway of the lantern inside the tent flickered our shadows in a wild dance.

"So he's done some hiking, I guess. Where? In Italy?"

"Yeah, a little bit. Not sure if he slept in the woods."

"Well now you can tell him you have. Does he like Italy?"

"He says he loves it there."

"Do you think you would?"

"I don't know. Doesn't sound like it from what I read."

"What were you reading?"

"We did World War 2 in history class. Italy was the enemy."

"Crazy Mussolini and the fascists."

"Yeah but he was popular like Hitler. Still is my dad says."

"Really? He met Italians who like Mussolini?"

"He says he likes Mussolini."

"Why?"

"My dad says he was a strong leader. Got things done. Wouldn't allow a train strike like my dad says was going on there."

"Mussolini was a lunatic. Wanted the Roman empire to come back. It was his fantasy to conquer the world as it was Hirohito and Hitler's. The three emperors joined and almost destroyed the world."

"That's what I learned too, Mr. D.", Fernando said.

"My dad says Mussolini wanted all the foreigners out of Italy. He put a lot of criminals in jail. He says Italy needs someone like him again with all the crime now."

"*Il Duce, Duce.* Yeah, fall in line behind the great leader and blame someone else for all your problems, some scapegoat like immigrants. Well, it didn't end well for him or for Italy. The Italians beat Mussolini to a pulp and then hung him in the street. They strung up his girlfriend right next to him. Talk about a one-night stand. Sorry, bad joke."

"That's some wild shit. From leader to lynched like a slave," Fernando said. "Let's just be here in the woods."

"We are," Bobby said as if this was in doubt.

"I mean enough. All this craziness. I almost wish you hadn't told us about that Confederate general. Kind of spoils things a bit."

"Well when we see those few rail tracks down there almost totally disappeared in the woods, we'll see what happens in the end to big schemes of conquest. Dust to dust. The river runs clean."

"That's God's way. God," Fernando insisted.

"As long as He doesn't flood the tent," Bobby said.

We all laughed. The wind subsided.

"See? He answered our prayer," Fernando insisted.

"Well, they call the wilderness God's country for a reason."

"That's because it's so beautiful, Mr. D. The way God made it. Unspoiled. What happens out here is the way it's supposed to. Not like all the crap we do to ourselves for no reason really. Crazy."

In the drizzly morning, we lit down Big Run. The sun began flashing now and then through the trees above. Bobby had this huge stick with him that impeded his balance and raised a blister on his hand. He dropped it a mile down the trail. At a trail juncture where we rested, someone had left a walking stick perfect for Bobby.

"See, the wilderness provides," I reassured Bobby.

"No, Mr. D. God left it there for him so we don't have to carry him back," Fernando ribbed.

The waters were running high in all the streams. We all got wet at one of the crossings further down the mountain. I told Bobby it was better to get wet than take a spill on a rock trying to keep his boots dry. When we finally made it all the way down, the afternoon sun was beaming on Big Run, glistening in the early summer rain and headstrong to reach the Shenandoah River. We found some flat stones and began to dry out our clothes and Bobby's sopping wet boots and socks. He had refused at our last resting spot just before the crossings got deep, to put on the strap-on sandals I urged him to wear and had bought the boys just for this occasion. He was afraid they wouldn't give him enough grip on the slippery rocks. O well, there's only so much one can do. Learning from someone else's experience is genius; only from one's own, folly. Perhaps the sun would be merciful and dry Bobby's boots. Fernando and I went further downstream to find a place to pitch. We had to go aways. The banks of the run were rocky and the canyon walls steep though the trees had found abundant places to make a stand, growing tall off ledges and slopes precariously perched. We finally found the place I had camped the last time I was there, a few hundred feet or so not far from where Big Run takes a turn close to the boundary of the park. I recalled to Fernando how stunned I was that earlier trip alone, coming out of the woods at dusk to find a gate closed to cars and just beyond it, a dirt road and a mud-cracked house. I ran back into the woods like a wild animal getting its first view of man, but I was more surprised by my reaction than I was stumbling on a house in the middle of nowhere as if it were some sneering demon. I felt more protected inside wilderness than out. I hadn't seen anyone for three days nor even heard the sound of an engine. How loud we are in the world!

"Mr. D, I'm surprised you don't carry a gun," Fernando said. "You'd feel safer if nothing else especially when you're alone out here."

"Maybe you're right. I don't know. Just one more thing to carry you probably won't need. People are much scarier than animals."

"Yeah, but the animals don't have guns. People do."

"Exactly."

We headed back to Bobby a few hundred yards up the run. He was basking in the sun and was much relieved to see us back. When I told him to watch out because he seemed to be enjoying himself, he shook his head.

"Mr. D, yes, I like this place in the daytime and when it's not raining. Night's a different thing. And all these damn bugs all the time."

"We're like a walking supermarket to them," I chuckled.

"We're hamburgers and we deliver," Fernando quipped, scratching his butt.

We lingered in the sun and the glistening waters. Fernando and I went for a swim in a large pool, joining some trout we saw flash by. Bobby was a bit leery and stayed next to the packs, sunning himself on a large rock. I asked him to pick our trail back the next day, giving him the topo map and showing him how to read it.

The quiet in the woods is always astonishing. It drowns out the waters of the run if you wander a few hundred feet away from them. I wanted Bobby to hear it.

"Bobby, when was the last time you didn't hear cars going by?"

He thought a while.

"I guess at the beach last summer."

"Yes, the ocean takes over there. Here the stream is loud but take a little walk into the woods and it's funny how quickly silent things get."

"Kind of spooky."

"Yeah but it shows us how loud we are, always caught up in our stream. It's good to get out of it. Feel how restful the world can be. Trust that feeling. Let the silence grow a bit. Save a piece of it in your mind for those times when things don't go well. It's like a little shelter you can go to inside. Listen to the creek flow or the wind through the trees. I know it works for me."

Fernando had come out of the water and heard the last bit of what I was saying.

"Yeah, it is so quiet. Makes you want to whisper as if you were in a church or something."

"It is my church. The stream's my preacher."

"Yeah and the clouds are telling me it's going to rain again."

We laughed at Bobby's joke. He laughed too. The day was rushing off with the waters, heading for the night the way the run flowed west to the river. Down this canyon, light arrives late and is quick to leave. We carried our packs across to the flat spot where we had decided to pitch the tent and set up camp for an overnight. Fernando insisted on taking over the cooking, setting up the little white-gas stove. I pitched the tent and went to hang up the packs, asking Bobby to pump some water from the run, a bushwhack away a couple of hundred feet. His face went blank with fear at the thought, so I had him help me launch the packs up trees to keep them off the floor. Then we wandered our way to the run together and filled our canteens. We ate the rehydrated food as if it were the nectar of the gods and watched the woods go from dim to black. We lit a fire for a while in the small firepit Fernando had made.

"You're already a good woodsman," I told him.

"Have to be out here. Still got a lot to learn like organize my damn pack better and put stuff back where I can find it again."

"That's a law of the nomad. Travel light. Leave no trace."

"Damn it's dark," Bobby noticed again.

"Amazing how this little flame lights up the place," Fernando observed. "Keep the bears off."

"Black bears here are pretty shy compared to the ones in the Smokies."

"Mr. D, I wish we had a gun," Bobby said.

"I really doubt if we'll see a bear much less have one bother our tent. Just clang a pot and pan together if one does come around. It'll run like hell."

"Love to see that," Fernando said.

Fernando and I hung outside. Bobby headed for his sleeping bag. In silence, we watched our little fire go out in a bed of glowing embers. When Fernando turned in, I sat there alone in near absolute dark that I paid no attention to, fearing the sorrow I felt welling up inside. I wandered down to the run, following it aways so I couldn't be heard or seen by the boys. The tears came of their own accord. I'd never see Karrin again.

An hour or so of light rain passed. Some stars appeared. I shook my head at my reaction to them, loving the beauty of this place while feeling so lost. I put my ear to where the waters were spinning round a stone. I told it my sorrow and feel asleep on some bankside moss, listening to the run, giving myself to the woods and the night. A voice called out. "Mr. D, Mr. D." It was Fernando.

"Mr. D, you ok?"

He had woken to find no one else at the camp site and began to worry. After a brief search, he found me asleep down river.

"But where's Bobby?"

We went back to the camp and called out for him. No answer. We walked further away from the run and ended up on a trail. After we had walked it a while, he answered our call. He told us he had gotten up in the middle of the night to pee and was worried when he didn't see me. He stumbled around in the woods a while but couldn't find the tent again. Then he heard something in the woods. At first he thought it was a bear but then saw a couple of guys walking in the woods. He knew it wasn't us. When they started to walk towards him, he lit off into the woods, ran down the trail and hid in the woods.

"Scared the shit out of me. Who the fuck are they?"

"Maybe hobos or just hikers. Who knows?" I said.

"Maybe ghosts."

"No, I know what I seen, Fernando."

"They could be the people who live in that house right outside the park boundary. We must be a few hundred feet from it."

We walked back to the tent, put some large sticks in it, and eventually dozed off. I woke up just before dawn to see from under the rain jacket two feet standing just outside the tent. I didn't want to wake the guys up so I just waited to see what this person wanted. Whoever it was wandered off. After a quick breakfast, we hiked out of the canyon. I never told them. Why spoil the rest of the trip? It made no sense worrying about what didn't happen. We certainly had enough wildness of a different sort waiting for us back home as my phone call to Lisa revealed.

Chapter 14

Solitaire

As soon as we got back to civilization in the form of Skyline Drive, I phoned Lisa who told me all was well with her and Ariana, but the counselor Frank had called her asking if she had heard from me yet. He explained to her everything was under control by that time, no need to worry. He just didn't want to hit me with all the news at once when I walked in the door. Apparently there was a fire at the house. None of the boys were hurt and not much damage done. That's all Frank would tell her. When I called the house, Ms. Sheila answered the phone and gave me the lowdown. First of all, José had run off the day after we left. A missing person's report had been filed with the police the next day. With a bed open in my house, downtown had allowed a new boy Jason to be placed temporarily over the weekend, awaiting a Family-Court hearing on the Island. Jimmy and the new kid got into a fight over the TV and had to be separated. Jason had also hit Frank when he tried to break them up, opening a cut over his eye. He needed stitches so arranged for next door's counselor to cover both houses for a while, with the new supervisor next door also away for the weekend. Frank came back to a quiet house with all the boys asleep. What happened next was not very clear. Frank awoke to someone knocking on the window outside the counselor's room. When he looked out, he saw flames and ran outside. The garbage pails and some bushes right next to the agency van were up in flames that were also beginning to reach the side of the house. Way too big for him to put out. He got all the kids out of the house except for Jason. Luis said he saw Jason running down the block. Frank managed to drive the van out into the street. From next door, he called the Fire Department which came and put the fire out. It took a while. Some of the trees in the empty lot next door had caught fire. Thankfully, no one was hurt. Only the side of the house was a little charred. It was quite a scene. A lot of neighbors came out. Everyone went back to bed. Jason never returned. The next day, they found out why. It looked like Jason had robbed the place. The cash in the tin box in the counselor's room was missing, Jimmy's money from the work check he just cashed was gone, and my apartment had been broken into. Frank found my door open. Apparently, Jason had set the fire to cover his theft.

"Poor Mr. Frank been through hell this weekend," Sheila said. "Why they put that boy in this house like that? Had no business doing that. Well, you take it easy driving home, Tony. I got it all covered here. Don't you worry."

Fernando and Bobby were fresh from the coin showers, washed up for the second part of the hike down to White Oak Canyon and still a bit sore from the strenuous hike up from Big Run. They could see from my face something was wrong. I told them what had happened back home.

"That's bat shit crazy right there," Bobby said.

"Yeah, I can't wait to be clean of it. Too wild all the time but not like this good wild out here. All these messed up new kids. Damn," Fernando yelled. "Setting a fire like that."

"You're not worried about José?" I asked.

"Not really."

"Why not?"

"I promised him I wouldn't say anything until we got back but he told me he was going to stay out one night to be with this girl."

"What girl? Where does she live?"

"You met her once, Mr. D. She came to my birthday party. She's my old girlfriend María's younger sister Juana."

"You had so many friends at the party I can't recall. Nice girl, I hope?"

"Yeah, she's alright. Little boy crazy like her sister which is why I broke up with her. Always flirting."

"I remember you told me that. You liked her too."

"She fooled me into thinking she stopped seeing other guys."

"She can fool me anytime. She was hot," Bobby joined in.

"Ok, Bobby. Hot or not is not the point. When you're fond of someone, it hurts when you break up," I said.

"I can't say it hurt that much. More relieved than anything. She had guys fighting over her."

"That's because the guys lust after her. Their desire for her gives her power, you know, social power. How she handles that..."

"Yeah, a power to lie and cheat, Mr. D."

"That's something else. That's not fair whether a man or woman does it. And let's face it. Guys do it a lot, probably more than women."

"You know I wouldn't have minded if she told me she was going to see other guys. OK. Cool. Then I decide if I'm chill with that. But to pretend there's no one else and get me to buy these gifts for her and make me think it's only me she's with."

"Messed up," Bobby said.

"Well, don't let that one time make you think bad of feeling love for someone."

“I didn’t love her, Mr. D. I said liked,” Fernando said a bit angrily.

I sensed some hidden pain there and dropped the subject, perhaps the fundamental one to growing up. How to come to terms with a broken heart that begins with grieving the loss of one’s childhood? One’s attitude towards that primal loss connects with how one loves someone else as one would love oneself, if that’s the right way to put it, a deeply ambiguous though common phrasing. I thought for a while what to say to Fernando who was looking out the window as we drove to our next campsite in Big Meadows. Each bend in the road revealed a staggering view. We stopped at an overlook and sat there in silence a while, taking it in. I risked offering some advice.

“Fernando, whatever the relationship you have with another person, no matter if it lasts forever or a second, you can learn something, take away a lesson about yourself and others for the next person you meet, a lesson about trust and honesty, about what to keep private and what to share. My best advice is keep loving but with your eyes open. Know what I mean?”

“Yeah, I was a damn fool.”

“Don’t feel bad. It’s a crowded boat, Fernando.”

“That’s for sure.”

He thought for a while.

“Look at all these new kids from messed up homes. Fathers and mothers hating each other or cheating on each other, screwing up their kids or leaving them behind. What’s up with that?”

“I wish I knew, I wish. Great question. People make mistakes for a hundred reasons, almost always with their eyes closed. Then there are the unavoidable consequences.”

I knew Fernando was including his own family’s scenario in his puzzlement and Bobby’s also who was intently listening as we rested there on a ledge. There was also my own version of broken faith in love with two women in my life. I had to say something, Fernando's question too important to let it just hang in the air.

"I don't know, Fernando. We need a big view of ourselves, I think, kind of like the one we're getting here. It's not often we look at ourselves from on high. Know what I mean? We're a speck in the ocean, just another creature in the woods, with no certain home. Each living thing is a nomad in the universe, a unique form of life. Yet we're all connected."

"You got that right. I'm still scratching from all the bugs," Bobby chimed in.

We all laughed.

I told them we'd stay only one more night and head home, too much going on there. I had to get back. No more waterfalls or canyons, just a quick walk-in into Big Meadows where we could pitch and walk to a nearby restaurant if they wanted. Fernando was disappointed, Bobby relieved, sick of the bugs and sore from the hike up that day. We pitched a little back from the edge where the forest and meadow meet and waited for the sunset. The golden slant light through the clouds made the valley and mountains miraculous to behold. A few deer came close to our camp to graze in the high grass. A fawn tugged at the doe's breast. For how many centuries in this meadow, this rhythm of the sky and all the life depending on it?

Farewell, wilderness.

When we got back to the house, no one was there. I called Lisa who was relieved I was back. I read the log, noting all the boys at work. There were long entries Frank and Sheila had made to try to make sense of the weekend's bedlam. Frank always wrote big paragraphs in a nervous hand, Sheila brief phrases in block letters for each boy. I always read her logs first for their concision and humor.

A typical log from her would read something like one boy "moped around all day – Nuttin new honey like the cereal he ate." Another, "Said he cleaned room but mostly fidgeted in there. Gotta do better. Poppa don't like no mess." Another – "Home all day a little too happy. Why?" For Jason today, she wrote, "No sign of him – he come back be dealing with me first, then the cops." The mess in my apartment showed he'd been in there, cabinets opened, some drawers on the floor, couple of hundred in cash gone from the nightstand. José was still missing. Now Fernando was worried because his brother had said he'd spend overnight with the girl, not the whole weekend, and now he was not at work Monday. A missing person report had been filed on him and on Jason. Frank had also reported the fire and break-in to the police who came to talk to Frank and took a report. With no eyewitness to the fire setting or burglary, Jason was a suspect, but no warrant was issued for his arrest. We had never pressed charges against any of the boys, even against Ricardo for his attempted murder of Marcos. We left it in the hands of BCW, Family Court judges, and the downtown agency whose priority was always to avoid bad publicity.

I waited for the all the boys to come home from their summer jobs to have a talk with them and assure them everything was ok. I told Jimmy we'd reimburse him for his stolen money. With Al arriving to stay for the night as had been arranged for coverage before I left for the hiking trip, I drove to Lisa's apartment to stay the night. When I gave her all the sorry details of what had happened at the home, she again urged me to quit the job, with anything better than the chaos and stress.

"You won't know how stressful it is until you leave the house," she told me. "I can't tell you how relieved I am that Ariana is not there anymore."

"I'll be finished the dissertation this summer. I've already applied for quite a few jobs. But the job market is flooded right now with applications, and there aren't that many tenure-track positions."

"Didn't that administrator for the city tell you you'd get a lot of field credits towards a master's in social work? You'd only have to take a handful of courses and you'd have your MSW degree. You could go work for the city. The administrator would pull some strings for you."

"If no professor job pans out this year, I just might go that route in January and register for some courses."

"More waiting, Tony. I kind of feel we're in limbo here. I hardly see you now and even when you are here, it's almost as if you're paying a visit. We're not really together. It's almost as if...I don't want to say it."

"What? Tell me."

"It's almost as if you married to the group home and the boys are your family. Ariana and I are like an afterthought or like one of those home visits you have to make. Ariana needs a father you know."

"That is so not true."

"That's how I'm feeling."

"But that's not true."

"I feel that way, Tony. I have a right to my feelings. And you know I have to say ever since you broke up with that woman if you really did break up, you haven't really come back to me, to us."

I had to hold back my tears.

"So you're going to cry for her now right in front of me? Or are you crying for us?"

"I'm sorry. I'm sorry. I know I messed up, lost my way. But I'm struggling..."

"With what? What? Go ahead and say it. You still love her."

"I'm not going to say that. It's over. Things will be better between us."

"When? We haven't made love once since I moved out."

"Not true. What about..."

"O that time three months ago when you came here drunk or stoned or whatever?"

"Yeah, ok, I stopped at the bar after work. It was a really tough day. I forget what was going on. But you understood and we made love."

"And you fell asleep right after. Things have to change, Tony. They really have to. Please listen to me."

"I've got a lot on my plate, Lisa. Once the dissertation's finished and I get a teaching job, we'll have a better life, with a lot less stress for me and for you."

Now she was sobbing. We hugged, kissed, and fell asleep on the couch.

The next morning Fernando's father called me. A very drunk José had come to his apartment building in the Bronx and waited for him in the lobby. When he got off the elevator, José confronted him, accusing him of having been so bad to his mother that she left the country. He called him all kinds of names and had to be forcefully restrained by him and another man when he went to assault him with a knife. Then he broke free and left. This was late last night.

"I'm thinking of calling the cops, Mr. Tony. No telling what that kid has in mind. *Está loco. Loco.*"

"He's upset because Fernando's going home to his mom's house next week."

"I know that. I've paid her money. I help her out. Fernando's my son. But this kid, I'm nothing to him. I've told that to the judge and social worker. And I never hurt his mother. She went back to Puerto Rico. Maybe he should go there, you know?"

"Do you have an address for her? We've tried to locate her whereabouts."

"Last I heard, somewhere in Puerto Rico maybe. I'm not sure. But this boy, he stays away from me or else. He pulled a knife on me. I still have it. He dropped it when we grabbed him."

"I'm sorry, Mr. Sanchez. He did not have our permission to stay out all night, certainly not to visit you. If he does show up again, call the police and let us know right away too, please. We'll come and get him."

Fernando took the news hard. He called his father and pleaded with him not to press charges. He had not spoken to his father in months when Fernando had told him that he planned to move in with his mother and help her. He needed to understand how José felt about the whole situation, with a missing mom, a father not to speak of, and a brother moving out of the home they had shared for years. José would come to his senses once Fernando spoke to him, he told his father. At least that is what Fernando first told me of the phone call. I had allowed him privacy for the call but heard a lot of yelling from Fernando. What was that about?

"I called him *tacaño*, Mr. D, you know, cheap, cheap with my mother. And he can't blame José for being mad. He's been holding it in a long time. Not that it's right that he got attacked or anything."

A tired José turned up after supper and told me and Fernando that he didn't want to talk about it. Fernando yelled at him, and José went up into Fernando's face.

"What you gonna do about it? You don't give a shit."

I had to get in between them, no easy task in a narrow hallway. Adam and Jorge got up to watch from the living room. John and Luis looked on from the stairs. Unlike most arguments in the house that seemed to intensify the bigger audience they had, this one did not. José backed off, turned and walked into his room, closing the door behind him as if he had been caught naked. I felt immensely relieved. Fernando stood there stunned. I took him by the side, out of earshot. He couldn't believe José had threatened him. He must be high or something. I told him the three of us will talk when things cool down. I also asked the rest of the boys to go back to what they were doing and give José some space. He's been through a rough time. Al showed up for his tour of duty, lucky for me, much needed back-up. I had asked him to sleep over a weekday night that I usually covered, not wanting to use up the allotted staff hours that way, saving them for when the boys were up and about. But given what Lisa had said to me the day before, I figured it was best to do so at least for this one night. Who knew it was going to be a wild one? I filled Al in on what was going on with José.

Later, with the house quiet and Fernando shut in his own room, I lightly knocked on José's door a few times rather than just barging in. I announced myself and waited, standing there less than a minute that felt like an hour. If I opened the door, what would happen? What would I find? Al waited down the hallway out of sight in case I needed help. Then much welcomed words.

"Come in."

I opened the door. José was curled up in a ball on his bed, facing the wall. To my own surprise, I automatically asked him if he wanted something to eat as if nothing had happened. I told him there was leftover meatloaf from supper still on the stove. It had been left there for him in case he came home. There were also caramelized onions on the side the way he liked it. I closed the door.

"What's going on in there? Everything ok?" Al asked me.

"He's laying in bed. I asked him if he wanted some meatloaf."

Al chuckled a bit.

"That's it? You're not going to talk to him? Should I go in with you?"

"No. no. Let him stew a bit in there and think about or not think about what he did. The meatloaf and onions will lure him out eventually."

"Lure?" he asked, grinning. "Like a wild animal."

"Yeah, we all need to be trained," I said. Woof, woof."

José's roommate Jimmy walked in, hungry after his part-time stint at the supermarket. As he devoured his dinner, Al and I spoke to him about letting José have his space as much as possible. If he wants to talk, great. If not, that's fine too. I asked Jimmy if he wanted to sleep in Marcos's room upstairs and just let José be alone for the night. Marcos's room had an empty bed.

"That kid's a slob. No. I'm good. I ain't worried about José. He's my homie. We good."

As we stood just down the hall, Jimmy went into the room and came back to tell us he had asked José if he was hungry as I had asked him to ask. José just said no and that he just wanted to sleep. With all apparently quiet for the night, I told Al I was going to see Lisa and would be back the next morning to relieve him of duty. Anything pops, I'm a phone call away.

As I drove, I thought of my childhood home and how we all could eat no matter what the circumstance. Of course, food like music, a forest or a beach brings people together the world over, and with my Italian upbringing, we could eat several courses anywhere no matter what, rain or shine, sinking rowboat or cruise line. My father could remember a meal he had twenty years ago. He'd reminisce about the eggplant parmigiana he ate after a wake at some restaurant he wanted to go back to. But he couldn't recall the name of the person whose funeral it was. My mom and more so my Neapolitan grandmother on my father's side insisted on giving anyone who walked into the house a sfogliatelle or some manicotti or whatever. "*Mangia, mangia*" was a chant good times and bad. Even Lisa's Sicilian grandmother, a great cook, did not take up the chant as much as my family did. One always was made to feel a bit impolite or even uncaring if food was turned down. So we ate. In the group home, I saw that food had crowd-control potential, the reason why I'd cook a huge pot of meat sauce for the boys a couple of times a month to last several days. It helped calm things down. I guess that's what Marie Antoinette had in mind when she said let them eat cake. Her mistake was she didn't say let them eat lasagna. Had she, an entire revolution would never have happened or at least been delayed long enough for her to have gotten out of town. I hoped meatloaf would work for José. Home is wherever the belly's full. If it's happy, the heart's sure to follow although, as I knew, that didn't always happen.

The next few weeks of the summer felt like a revolution. The one positive was that José did come round, asking for forgiveness of Fernando and me after a long talk. He refused, however, to apologize to his alleged father and thank him for not pressing charges. When the day arrived for Fernando to move out, José helped him carry everything into the van and then accompanied me and Fernando on the drive to the Bronx. That went much better than we all hoped. John also moved out to live with his uncle. Three new boys arrived to fill the beds. I would miss Fernando and John badly while feeling apprehensive about the new ones considering what had happened with arsonist Jason, who remained at large in the city somewhere. Al, my friend and counselor, left for a full-time job at a nursing home with good benefits. There were hardly any benefits afforded by the agency. We couldn't compete.

But the biggest turnover was with Lisa, who told me one night that summer she had feelings she didn't know what to do with as I had once told her. She had been good friends with this doctor at the hospital since her first day at the medical library. Now the friendship had become something more to them, and she was afraid of her feelings for him. They were very strong. The doctor, single since a divorce, had professed affection for her, and she didn't know what to do because she wanted to say yes to him. She felt confused. At first, egotistically I thought she was making this up to make me jealous, but after a while, I realized she was serious. She kept bringing him up. Finally, she told me she wanted to begin seeing him. I had to respect her honesty as she had once respected mine, at least in the beginning of my affair with Karrin. What can one say in view of such courage and vulnerability? I did feel angry and betrayed though I also felt hypocritical for feeling that way. It more than anything made me feel despair over how I had wrecked the marriage and led Lisa to this. Who could blame her really, given how she had agreed to move into a group home, dealing with all that stress from what was not her job, while I had over time sought love elsewhere? Even my grief felt duplicitous because in truth I knew I had been sleepwalking through my marriage for a long time. Had I performed something rather than felt it? What is the difference if there is one? I thought of some lines from a favorite poem, "See Naples and Die," by Anthony Hecht, where the speaker ponders why love has left his marriage if it was ever really there or just a "well intentioned" illusion –

The cold, envenoming spirit of Despair,
turning what was the nectar of the world
to ashes in our mouths.

In our case, honey into guilt. Lisa apologized to me, and I to her after my initial anger. I told Lisa I'd sleep at the group home to avoid seeing her and to give her the space she obviously needed. She told me that deep down she always felt I was her soulmate but she was never mine, even before anyone else had entered my life. I told her that sounds more stalemate than soulmate. She told me I was very witty. We sobbed a bit, then straightened up. We were freeing ourselves of each other's version of each other and also grieving the pain of a failing marriage. Most of all, we did not want to have any of our separation to impact Ariana whom I would still see every day so that little would change there. What would an eight-year-old understand of estrangement between parents without thinking she was not in some way being rejected or was the cause of it? I had heard so many versions of this damaging misunderstanding from so many of the boys.

Of course, Karrin was on my mind. She had never left it, although she had left me. I was still very much under her emotional sway like a wake in water. Her absence only made more apparent how strong she remained in me. She had passed through my life and changed its course, no matter where I was headed. I recalled what I had told Fernando, about how every person we love teaches us something about ourselves. She showed me I wasn't being who I needed to be. Or should I say that my love for her and for what she saw in me made me want to become that person she thought I could be? I think I had the same effect on her. But I was having these thoughts to what end? Does she even think of me, I wondered. Maybe she cringes when she remembers me. Who can know what another thinks? The acidic clarity of Hecht's poem came to mind again:

> An accord essentially self-flattering,
> the paradise of fools before the fall.

Three new boys within two weeks took my mind off such thoughts. They had the usual troubles, mostly caused by problems not of their own making. Typically brief notes accompanied the new placements, lives summarized in a few brutal facts. Ethan, 12, from Queens, his father in a psych ward, his mother deceased. A foster home had not worked out for him. Garret, from Brooklyn, 14, father in jail, mother an addict, now a sick uncle no longer could care for him. Nat, 16, from Staten Island, mother couldn't control him, took out a PINS petition, hanging out with gangs in Mariners Harbor. Garret and Ethan were scared and confused but friendly. Nat told me his being there in the boarding home was only temporary. He had better places to go. When I asked him, "then why aren't you there?" he smiled and said, "Ok, ok. You got me. You got me." Nat was too close to home, to the gang he had started to hang with.

Thankfully, I hired more good staff. Herman came on board at Sheila's recommendation to replace Al. A new weekend counselor Jamie also was hired, the first woman I had hired to do weekends with sleepovers. She was a tall attractive woman with long red hair, little round eye- glasses, and a look that said do not even think about it. Three years out of college, she was applying for graduate school, determined to get a doctorate in sociology.

"If you need a case study, this is it. The non-familial family or something," I told her.

"Really. Talk about non-traditional."

"Yeah, and a diversity of races too. Their running connection? Poverty. It's really what it comes down to. Most of the boys appreciate what we give them here, not just the clothes and the food – they eat well. It's a sense of order. They know what they're coming home to."

"I'll be sure to have dinner on the table same time. I cook pretty well."

"That's great, Jamie. How did you know I was just going to ask that?"

"Ten boys? I can't imagine the grocery bill the way my three brothers eat. I can't believe the size of your pots!"

That's how Jamie was, intuitive always, one step ahead of the boys and of me as she'd prove.

Hired for part-time weekday coverage, Herman was a different story, an older man, married, very laid back, short and less than fit, only a high school degree. He had a jolliness about him, a way of smiling and speaking that made people relax. His large green eyes would light up when he wanted to make a point as he lifted his head and laughed a bit. He himself had been raised in a Catholic so-called protectory in the Bronx.

"You want to know crazy? Well, I grew up in a reform school. Fifty boys. Some good, some mean. Same thing with the staff. I know how to handle these guys here. Believe me. It's chore, dinner, homework, TV, shower, bed. Let'em have some fun along the way. But not too much."

"You got it, Herman. Yeah, fun helps. Lord knows there's plenty of silliness. Endless pranks. Sometimes I join in or provoke it. But things can get out of hand quickly so you have to know when to cool things down. As long as we all get done what we have to, it's all good."

"Pranks. O, man. I got some stories I can tell you. I won't tell the guys. Don't want to give them any ideas, know what I'm saying?"

"Yes, silly can get crazy quickly here so we don't allow rough-housing. No jabbing, poking, wrestling. Also no cursing at each other."

"That's all pecking order stuff. Believe me. I know the score. I lived it."

So the new hires, one book smart, one street wise, or so they appeared at first. Herman sometimes referenced Karl Marx and Malcolm X in his logs and got some of the guys to talk about politics. Jamie gave me a hard handshake at the end of her interview and told me, "Don't worry. I can be tough. I have three brothers all younger than me. I'm the one who really raised them after my mom died of cancer. My dad was never really around. I also have a brown belt in karate."

So I was lucky to have such help. We needed it.

Herman told me at the end of his third day, "That Nat, gotta watch out for him. He thinks he's supreme. Found out he's paying Garret to do his chore. When I told him he's got to do it, he said 'Ain't nobody's nigger. I can buy that. It's the way the world works.'"

"What did you say to him?"

"I told him not to give me any of his chilly-wop bull. We all equal here. We all pitch in. And we don't talk that way here. I told him he can do Garret's chore too when I get back next week. I talked to Garret too. I saw him sweeping the basement. That's how I found out. I stopped him and made him give me the two dollars Nat gave him. I told Nat I'd give it to you for safe keeping. And you know what he said?"

"What?"

"He goes, 'people take my money they be sorry. No way. That ain't going down.' I put all this in the log too. No telling what that kid has in mind."

I spoke to Nat and Garret together after I spoke to them alone. Garret looked down and seemed ashamed. I told him he can do extra chores to earn some more pocket money if it's ok with a counselor, but he can't do someone else's. He apologized. Nat one on one with me kept saying "Yes sir," and saluted me, but when I brought Garret into our talk, Nat smirked and said under his breath, "Ain't gonna be no next time for him." I said, "No next time for anybody," and he said, 'Yo, that's what I said. No next time. No need to repeat it. I got you the first time." I knew I had to arrange for him to talk to a therapist as soon as possible. His seething anger was dangerous to ignore.

Jamie's first weekend went well except for Nat's not coming home Saturday night. He showed up just in time for Sunday's dinner. She spoke to him and explained he had lost privileges for next weekend, with a curfew restricted to dinner time. He told her "Yeah, Missy J, sure, ok," but at the dinner table he kept mumbling curses under his breath. When she told him to stop, he said, "Like a damn prison here," and left the table to finish his plate of food in his room. I had a long private talk with him, pulling no punches. We weren't running a prison but if he wanted a more secure place, we could arrange for it. But why not give our house a chance? He could finish up high school the next two years, work part-time if his grades were passing, save some money for himself and help his mom out too. Make her be proud of him. Why all the anger?

"You don't know what's it like out where I live, sir. There's plenty of money there. Just got to know how to get to it, sir."

"But if you get it the wrong way, what happens?"

"So you do some time. More connections in jail than outside."

"Yeah, the wrong ones. I hope you don't have to find that out the hard way, Nat. Give yourself a chance to do the right thing for yourself and for your mom."

"Yes, sir," he said and saluted me.

"Cut the saluting act. This is not the military. I'm not your boss man. I live here myself. I'm the guide and caretaker. So stop the routine."

"Ok, captain," he said, rolling his eyes.

"Captain? You want me to treat you like a soldier? A private, private Nathan Holmes?"

"Ha, that's my government name. Yeah, might as well be in the army. America's one big boot camp if you ain't rich and white. Just like you, living here for free, watching the kiddies with a price on their heads. Ain't that the truth, master D?" He raised a fist Black-Panther style.

"O I'm the master now? Please. Well, well. You got me shaking my own head, trying to lose the price tag on it. Didn't Mr. Herman tell you Malcolm X says capitalism is legal theft? Sure, ok, I have to work so I can support my family. Your bill's paid by the same people who pay me. We're all in it."

"Some more than others."

"But legal does not mean illegal, Nat. There's a steep risk for crossing that line. What's this talk of your government name? Tell that to your mom. What would she say?"

"She's the great grandchild of slaves. I got other plans than to walk that line, captain. I'm my own man, standing tall."

"Yes, responsible for the choices you make. We all have to own our choices. Can't stand tall on the wrong ones. And cut the captain stuff. I'm just Mr. D. What's the name you'd give yourself?"

"BB."

"Meaning what?"

"My boys call me that."

"You have children?"

"O come on, man. I got home boys, real home boys, not these dish wipers here."

"So what's BB stand for?"

"Berry Blade. You know I cut sweet and bury it."

"Well we'll stick to the name your mom gave you, Nat. And the only thing you'll cut here is the mustard. None of that gang stuff in this house or you're back to Family Court."

"Yessum, Master D. Yessum. I hears you loud and clear," he bowed his head and backed out into the hallway.

One weekday night Lisa brought a dinner of shredded pork for the boys. José, Bobby and Jimmy had been asking about her, and she wanted to do something for them. She brought Ariana along too. Sheila was happy to see her and so were the boys with whom she had lived in the house.

When I introduced her to Nat, he bowed his head a bit, reached for her hand and said, "O now, I'm meeting the real boss." Lisa said, "I like this boy." We all laughed.

Nat pulled the same routine the next weekend Jamie worked, disappearing Saturday night and returning for Sunday supper. A call to his mother received no answer just as it hadn't since after his placement. This time Jamie told him he could eat alone at the table after everyone else ate. "I eat when I want," he said, made his plate and went off to his room. When she followed him to his room, he told her, "Look. I don't want no trouble from you and you don't want to get none from me, Missy. So that's it. Just stay out of my room and I'll stay out of your face."

"Is that a threat? You're in no position to make it. Why you're making all this trouble is beyond me. We've got a few simple rules here. Follow them or you'll be transferred like Mr. D told you."

Under his breath, he said, "Bitch, keep talking. Keep talking. You'll see, you'll see."

She wisely left the room and closed the door. When I got back Sunday from my all-day stay with Ariana, I spoke to Nat who started with the "Yes, sir" routine again. I warned him never to threaten anyone again. He denied he did.

"Threat? She'll know when I do that. So will your wife. She might like it. Just saying."

"What did you say? How dare you."

"Dare nothing. Just saying what it is."

I put my finger in his chest and warned him he was on thin ice.

"Don't put your hands on me."

"Don't threaten," and I fingered his chest again.

"Who the fuck think you are? You don't know how you dealing with. Put your hands on me? I got backup. You better watch out. Like I said. You got family."

"You little punk," I said and pushed him with my hand on his chest, pinning him to the wall. "You hurt anyone of my family or my staff and you're arrested."

He kneed me in the groin and began slapping at me. I grabbed him and we scuffled in the room, falling on and off the bed. Jamie burst in the room and quickly put Nat in a full Nelson and pinned him on the floor.

"Stop it now. Stop, Nat," she said.

He stopped struggling, and she let him go.

"Ain't gonna forget this. You'll see." He gathered his stuff in a garbage bag, including all the clothes we had bought him, and walked out the door. We just let him go.

"I thought you had left," I told Jamie.

"No, no. I stuck around a while. I figured there'd be trouble between you. Better it ends this way then some big explosion from him. Are you ok?"

"He threatened you and my wife."

"I heard him. He told Jorge yesterday we didn't know who we were messing with. He could have the whole house robbed and anyone he wanted beat up."

"That gang he's in or thinks he's in. Not good."

"There was another murder in Mariners Harbor last week. The papers said it was gang related."

"Yeah, I saw that. Drugs involved of course, a turf war."

"I think you should call the police. What if he comes back with backup like he said?"

"I'll keep on eye out tonight. Tomorrow I'll call in a missing person's and call BCW. I doubt he'll come back. Why would he? He took all the clothes we bought him. There's nothing for him here."

"We showed him up. That's a big deal with gang members. Their code of honor. I was reading about it, you know, how status is the core of a gang member's identity and any threat to it has to be answered."

It was an uneasy night for me. I told Bobby, Luis and Jorge to keep an eye out. Jorge told me he didn't believe what Nat said about sending his "crack crew" back to rob us. He had also told Jorge he had a .38 caliber, but none of it rang true.

Jorge said, "Mr. D, he's just ain't screwed on right. He lies a lot. Trying to impress how bad he is, wearing his pants backwards and stuff."

When Sheila came in the next day, she wasn't surprised. "That boy, he think who the hell he is. He lucky I wasn't here, ah huh. I'd sit on his sorry self and he be crying like a baby. Threaten your family like that. Good God almighty. He think he Wu-Tang or something. Get real. His gang gonna come round here and rob us? What he smoking?"

His BCW social worker called me back. Nat had walked into their office to report me and Jamie for abuse. He had black and blue marks over his neck and arms. My agency was called too, warning them of our impending investigation. An investigator would visit my house tomorrow and wanted to interview me, Jamie, staff and some of the boys. Nat in the meantime was placed in a group home in Queens. I told Jamie not to worry about a possible impact on her career. My staff and I had a good record, with just one prior accusation in many years of work and that was dismissed. The investigator came and talked to a few of us. She shook my hand on the way out, told me the boys talked highly of the house, and left. That was the end of that.

We had barely caught our breath from all of this when two days later, another boy, Gerald, an eleven-year-old from Brooklyn, was placed in the house to fill Nat's bed. Adam found himself sharing his room again with a stranger and was worried, seeing how Jason and Nat had caused so much trouble for everyone. Short of rearranging all the room assignments and moving the boys who had been in the house the longest, I had no choice. Adam understood and said he'd keep an eye out for all of us.

"I mean this is our house. We don't need some asshole coming in and messing everything up."

I reminded him of when he first came to the house, how he tried to rob from my apartment while I was sleeping.

"I was stupid then, Mr. D. You know I've done better now. That was like last year."

"Yes, you've come around. Maybe it's time to move back in with your aunt? She said she would consider it if you turned things around."

"Mr. D. I don't want to go back to live there. I mean I like my aunt and all. But that building she lives in, that neighborhood? No, man, I like this place and made a lot of friends. Plus I like the school here."

"I'll make sure the new kid respects that he's sharing a room. You keep it tight, and so he has to too. You're a good example, Adam. He's only eleven years old. You could be like a big brother to him. In fact, why don't I bump your allowance up a bit? For all the trouble we've put you through. In return, I expect you will help the new kid feel at home and respect the rules."

The new boy had an unusual situation, coming from a well-to-do home. His father was a psychiatrist who had suddenly left his second wife and family and could not be located. Apparently, he had run off with one of his patients, a much younger man. His mother began having seizures probably triggered by stress and was in and out of the hospital. She had called the downtown agency to put the child in a home nearest to her until she was well enough to care for him. Gerald was the youngest of three boys who were his half-brothers and were both away in college. There was no extended family who came forward to take the boy. Arriving with two suitcases packed with expensive clothes, he was in disbelief at the room he was moving into.

"I have to share a room? And sleep in that bed? There must be a mistake. What about upstairs? Can I stay in your apartment?"

"I just interviewed you at my kitchen table. That's my private apartment where I live. The boys live in their own rooms. Don't worry. We'll take good care of you."

"The bathroom down there is gross. I have to share that too? Can't I use the one in your apartment?"

"Why do you say it's gross? It's cleaned each day. You'll have to pitch in and help keep it that way. We all work together here."

"I have to clean a bathroom other people use too? There's no maid? O my God. I got to speak with my mother. I can't stay here."

"She knows all about it. Until she gets back on her feet, you'll have to make do with what we have. I think you'll have a lot of fun here once you get to know the guys and counselors. Give it a chance. You really don't have much of a choice, Gerald."

"Can I talk to my mom in private?"

"Sure," I said.

I brought him upstairs to my kitchen again and he made his call from my wall phone. I stood in the hall and heard him begging her to let him come home. The house was dirty and full of street kids. He was scared he'd get an infection and could never sleep in the room we gave him. She asked to speak with me.

"Please, please, don't let him run away. I just can't take him back right now the way I am. I feel so ashamed."

"We can arrange for visits home for him and you are certainly welcome to visit him here once you feel up to it. Please feel assured we'll take care of him here. It's a good place. I'll take him under my wing and so will my staff. I'm here all the time with the boys."

"Please don't let him run away, please. I'm so worried. I will let you know about the visits when I am a little better. Right now, I can barely take care of myself."

A week later, the mother was institutionalized with a complete nervous breakdown. At first, Gerald sat in the basement TV room almost round the clock, pouting on the couch, not talking to anyone. He refused to do chores or take a shower. The agency social worker had a long talk with him, and we arranged for psychotherapy. All he told her was that he wanted to go home. Since he was the only child at home all day, the other boys all working their summer jobs, I took him everywhere with me except for my visits to Ariana and Lisa. He was amazed at how much food I bought in the supermarket, filling two carts as usual and asking him to push one around for me. I let him pick out a couple of dinners he would like, even buying the shrimp and porterhouse steaks he picked out.

"I'll tell the guys you picked out special dinners for them. You'll get some brownie points with them."

"Why not eat this way all the time? It's not your money. What do you care?"

"We eat pretty well. But I have a budget I have to stay within. We'll eat hamburgers, chicken and fish sticks, once in a while London Broil and flounder. The guys love pork with rice and beans, and my spaghetti and meatballs and my chicken parmigiana.

Special occasions like birthdays and holidays, though, I splurge. You came to our house now, so that counts as a special time to help make you feel more at home."

For the first time, he smiled a bit and then soured, saying, "It will take a lot more than that." When we got home, he finally took a shower. Adam got him to erase the chalk line he had drawn on the carpet in the room to divide his half of the room from Adam's. Things were looking up. He was beginning to fit in as the new boys Garret and Ethan had more readily, seeing the place as an improvement in comfort over what they had left behind. Marcos was the one, though, to reel Gerald down from his Brooklyn Heights. When Ms. Sheila set the porterhouse steaks out for dinner, Jimmy had asked if it was somebody's birthday or something. Adam said that was because Gerald had picked it out when he went shopping with Mr. D.

José said, "Well, excuse me. Lucky he don't like something weird like chocolate bugs or something."

Luis added, "Next time I get rich, it's lobster just for me."

Ms. Sheila spoke out loud and clear, "'Nuff of that talk. Be happy it's on your plate. It's there by the good work of the Lord being spent on you. Nobody rich or poor at this supper table and in this house. We all the same."

Then Marcos quipped, "Yeah this is the Hotel Hooker. It's free for all."

All the boys busted out laughing, including Gerald who banged the table a bit, adding to the outbreak of jolliness when the boys saw him drop his sullen reserve. Marcos's eyes lit up when he had cracked his joke, raising himself tall in the seat to do it. It was a victory moment for him. He had made a pun everyone laughed at. Hooker Place was the cross-street for the house. Ms. Sheila pretended to fume, "'Nuff of that talk or you gonna get a hook and be sent to bed early." That only made them laugh more. Then they feasted. The steak dinner had sealed Gerald's place. He was a home boy now. José christened him with a nickname that stuck, "Goldie."

At last - at least for the time being – there was some peace and quiet on the front line. It was this down time, however, that was hardest for me to face alone in my empty apartment. I was very much on the rebound from having lost both my lover and my wife. I also felt I had been unfaithful to myself, by having married too young with little experience in love, not really knowing who I was or which direction to go in. Hard-wired to be a husband, I had just gone through the paces, neither here nor there. Now my marriage had failed. A riptide of self-hatred and self-pity set in. The dissertation I had finished so I had some free time, but it was the last thing I wanted to face. Free time felt empty, but no time felt free. I lived where I worked so that had a lot to do with it, someone always knocking on my door, looking for Mr. D. But most of all, having lost Karrin was unbearable.

By the end of summer, Lisa's affair with the doctor had blossomed. I had agreed to take Ariana every other weekend, never letting her out of my sight although Lisa was not pleased with this idea of her staying at the group home again. Ariana did not understand why I wasn't sleeping at home anymore. I kept telling her the boys needed me more than ever. With Lisa in agreement, I arranged with my mother to take her for a week before school started. I told my mother on the phone what was going on. She was shocked by Lisa's behavior. I explained to her what had happened on my side of things with Karrin. When I arrived at the house in the Bronx, my mother cried and hugged me. She repeated what she had said to me when I first told her I was getting engaged. "I never thought you two were well matched. She doesn't have that artistic drive you have." She told me we should not say a word of our separation to my father. Two of my sister's marriages were also on the rocks, and he had not handled that news well, accusing them of having married the wrong guy to begin with. His generation did not divorce, and Catholics weren't supposed to at all. Work things out. That was his attitude. I left before he came home from work. I didn't like the idea of shielding him from things but out of respect for my mom, I did. He did tell my mother that he was looking forward to seeing his granddaughter, just didn't know why she had to stay a week.

The free time I both needed and dreaded did not materialize. Sheila gave me notice. Her newly married daughter had invited her to come live in her new house in North Carolina. We gave her a going-away party. José found himself a bit embarrassed when he stood up at the supper table and protested he wouldn't let her leave. Marcos out and out cried. She ended up consoling the boys who had had her as a counselor for three years. A supervisor at one of the homes I administered also left but without giving anyone advance notice. I had to arrange round-the-clock coverage of his group home of eight boys, two of whom had just been placed. I was frantically trying to hire his replacement and Sheila's. Vetting potential staff, especially a live-in supervisor, was a crucial and time-consuming task that one must do under the gun, so pressed for help as we were. But the burden and fear of such entrustment - with the lives of children at stake - were without end. Who can be deemed worthy? Who has the right to deem worthy? Whatever the emotional and moral quandary I felt, crisis did not allow for the time needed to vet fully. Again, I complained to the agency director that the administrative part of my job really should be a full-time one. I could not both supervise my home and administer seven others. The same reply was made, that "when things calm down" my proposal to leave the supervising position and be made full-time Borough Administrator would be considered. But they never calmed down in our line of work and were only made worse by skimping on the staff needed to do the job. My request met with deaf ears and platitudinous tongue again. My new hire to replace Sheila was fired his third day when I came home earlier than expected to find the house reeking of pot. The guy told me he had come in early that day to make a special supper and all the kids were in school, so why couldn't he smoke up a little in the basement? I wasn't having much success finding a new group home supervisor either.

I was shuffling back and forth between group homes.

Finally off duty for the weekend, I went out to a bar and got wasted, wandering around the woods in the Greenbelt on Staten Island like a werewolf after the bar closed. I didn't want any of the boys to see me that way so I waited until the middle of the night to return when everyone would be asleep. I tried to slip up the stairs quietly but fell. The stairwell light came on and I was discovered. It was Jamie. "You, ok?" she asked me. I weakly smiled and tried to get up but didn't quite make it. I put my fingers to my lips and whispered "shhhhh." She sprang into action, putting an arm around me and helping me to my feet. She guided me up the stairs to my apartment, taking the keys from my hands when I fumbled trying to open the door. She helped me to a seat and I plopped down. She closed the door and made some coffee. It took me a while to come round. I kept apologizing and she kept saying no need to. I thanked her and told her I was ok to get up and go to bed. "Don't tell Mr. D," I whispered. She laughed, patted me on the shoulder, and left.

I woke up to a quiet Saturday afternoon. I had to get away and seized on a plan to do some solo hiking for a few days if I could find some coverage for my house. Herman said he could do some sleepovers. Frank could come in too if need be. I got all my gear together but before I put it in the car, I had to talk to Jamie to let her know my plans and who'd be relieving her tour. I found her in the counselor's room and immediately apologized. I felt embarrassed.

"Please, no need. Been there, done that. Glad to have given a helping hand."

"Of course, be sure to write up that in the log for Mr. D to read it."

"Yes, hoisted by his own petard."

"You can say tippled by my own tankard but don't spill any ink on it. Sorry about that. Where is everybody? The house is so quiet."

"Some of the boys are away on a visit, some are working or gone off to the movies with friends."

"Yes, that's right, Adam, Ethan and Jorge at their aunts and Marcos at his mom's for the weekend. And José and Jimmy..."

"Tony, you're off duty, remember? You wrote it all down for me. Everything's going as planned."

"Where's Garret?"

"He went with Luis and his girlfriend to the movies."

"O that's nice of Luis."

"Yeah, otherwise Garret would have been home alone with me the whole day."

"Could be worse," I teased. "I feel bad for the kid. We're trying to locate an older sister but the social worker..."

"Tony, I read the log. You're off duty. Relax."

"Guess you heard what happened at the house on Tilden?"

"Yes, I read what Herman wrote. What, the supervisor just took off?"

"Yeah, Keith just left. Been there for three years and then gone. I found out from the boys there he had been moving furniture out of the apartment for a while and then just didn't come back. He just burned out, I guess. I could tell he was pretty down last time I saw him when I did a home inspection. Some personal issues going on. Kind of sad. Anyway, he left the weekend counselor hanging. So I got the call. Can you do some hours there?"

"Sorry but I'm really booked with grad school starting. Yes, burn out is a real thing. I know you must need a break."

"Well, you've read my mind. I'm taking off a few days. Don't worry. I won't pull a Keith on you. Herman will be relieving you Sunday and will sleep over."

"Spending some time with Ariana?"

"She's at her grandmother's for a while. I'm doing a solo hike probably up in New Hampshire."

"Everything ok with you?"

"O you mean last night? Yeah, I'm just fried myself a bit. Lots of changes I'm going through. I need some down time."

"How down are we talking?"

"I'm ok. Finished the dissertation so it's like a let-down from that stress and it's time to celebrate."

"You were celebrating last night, that's true."

"Yes, I was a little too successful at it, I guess."

"That's easy to do when you're doing it solo. Know the feeling pretty well myself."

"Are *you* ok?"

"Sure, now I am. I'm loving grad school. Takes my mind off the ex- and the one before that."

"That's what this place does for me, and the dissertation did for me too although I've had a little too much of both distractions. I am surprised you've had no luck. You're so intelligent and, well, you're in great shape, you know, attractive. So what's up with these guys?"

"There's no telling. Some people need to figure themselves out first before getting involved with someone else."

"I wish I had known that a while back myself. Now I've figured myself out and don't know what to do with myself."

"O come on. You just finished a diss. You must be on the job market now, yes?"

"Have been for a while but now with the manuscript completed, I've got a better chance in a very tight market for a tenure-track position."

"So then what's the problem? I know I'll be on cloud nine if and when I get my Ph. D."

"Yeah, that part of my life is fine. It's all the other stuff."

"Yes, I heard about your wife leaving the house here. I guess it's more than that."

"It's failed marriage time. Her fault. My fault first. Nobody's fault, I guess."

"Yes, fault is probably not the best way to think about it. I know in my first long term relationship I wanted the relationship more than I wanted the guy. So maybe it's more about finding yourself. Blaming I find beside the point, having done it to myself for years."

I felt the tears beginning to well up.

"I feel so stupid. Sorry."

"Again no need."

"Heh, how did you get so much smarter than me? And you're the one beginning grad school."

"Just some pain earlier in my life than yours, perhaps. In some ways, it's good to have your heart broken at some point and preferably early on. Then it's about how to put it back together. I'm still learning. I do know I'm not like a friend of mine who seems to want her heart broken again and again. It's like she's her own sadist, pursuing married guy after married guy. I think she enjoys jealousy, feeling it and making others jealous. She'll ask me, 'Do you think he'll leave his wife?' The first affair, I commiserated with her. Now

– what? – the fifth cheating husband? - I just answer her question, 'Tune in next week to find out. Will he or won't he?'"

"Sounds like she loves the drama of a love triangle. Yeah, jealousy. I'm still growing up in that regard too. How to forget someone, how not to think about who's she seeing now, how to drown feelings in the ocean. How even an ocean may not be deep enough."

"Hmm. I hear you. How is Lisa doing with all of this? Is it a friendly breakup if you don't mind my asking? At least for Ariana's sake?"

"Don't mind, not at all. I don't really talk to anyone about it. But to tell you the truth, it feels like failure and release for both Lisa and me. I do think she'll be happier without me."

"Well, you two accomplished a lot together living here for so long. No failure there. I can't imagine being married for ten years. Not sure if I could achieve that. And then all the stress here. Sounds like you both need a good break."

"Yes, we do. But that's not what I need to forget." I was surprised I was starting to bleed on her, not really wanting to go there.

"Someone else then? Was that the first fault as you called it?"

"You listen carefully, don't you?" I was choking up a bit.

"Don't mean to pry. Just can help talking about it sometimes. I'm certainly willing to listen."

"Let's just say sometimes people teach you more about yourself than you ever knew, sometimes more than you wanted to know. It just can't fit into your life without much change."

"But if it's true what you're finding out about yourself, then you have to accept it, I guess. It takes time."

She was looking into my eyes, into me, deeper than anyone had since Karrin. I touched her hand. For a moment, it felt like we were going to kiss. Then she touched my hand back and said, "Tony, you're a good man doing a difficult job pretty well and dealing with a lot of personal change to boot. Take some time for yourself. Let's not complicate things. Just not a good time for you and for me. We're both on the rebound."

"Yes, circumstances not good. I'm just pretty vulnerable right now. Thanks for listening."

"Anytime you want to talk. I know a good psychotherapist who does family and individual counseling. He was mine for a while and really helped me get things together."

"Yeah, I could use a paid ear."

"You can talk to me anytime. No charge. It's just..." she trailed off.

"I understand."

I went off to the mountains for a few days, to a secluded spot in the Pemigewasset wilderness in the White Mountains. I had done a solo there right after I met Karrin, trying to come to terms with the feelings I had for her. Now I went there to bury the feelings, to tell them to a river again and let it wash them out of me. On the way to the site I planned at the foot of Mount Garfield, I wandered off the trail and ended up in a marsh. I sloshed through deeper and deeper for no reason when I should have turned round and traced the way back. Again without thinking, I walked over a massive beaver's dam to reach the further side of the marsh where I could see a rise above it. My foot broke through the cut branches of the dam, one spike impaling my leg. When I finally reached the end of the marsh, I found the trail again. Thankfully, all the blood made the wound look worse than it was. I took it as a metaphor for the despondent mood I had been in. I marveled at my error in judgment. The wound brought me to my senses. It dawned on me where I was, in the wilderness, its spirit all about, teaching me to be carefree, a will of the wisp and at the same time be fully aware that anything can happen. Loneliness crossed over into solitude. I reached my intended tent site near where a stream comes pouring off the mountain in a wide reach of rock forming a u-shaped canyon. I stayed put for two days there, waiting for the sun to rise above the ridge, bathing in the slides and waterfalls a few hundred feet away. Besides the birds, the only creature I saw was a dead moose calf who had fallen in a steep crevice. Cold water streamed over it, stretching its front legs forward as if it were swimming. How hard its mother must have tried to reach it, how long she must have waited, watching the legs move that way. The difference between life and death is always a step away. City life tends to obscure it. The woods make it most evident.

Somehow this wild place gave me strength to walk my path come what may. Before I left, I knelt next to a stream to thank it. I cried tears of grief and joy. I knew I would need its courage.

Chapter 15

The Calling

I came back to good news for me personally but horrible news for the boys at the Tilden home and in my own. The University of New Haven left a message saying they wanted to interview me. Great. But there had been a stabbing at Tilden. A boy was in the hospital in critical condition. In my house, Gerald's psychiatrist father had shown up out of nowhere and taken the boy. Also, Garret had gone missing overnight. I rushed over to Tilden house and spoke to the counselor on duty there. He told me the sorry story of how one of the new boys Dion was found going through Enrique's drawers. A fight broke out and Dion drew a knife. Enrique ended up with the knife and stabbed Dion. Enrique then fled and hadn't returned. Dion was brought to the hospital where he was admitted. He had lost a lot of blood from a stomach wound but should be ok. The counselor was supposed to get off duty the day before but his relief never showed up. I thanked him for his loyalty to the boys. He left, and I ended up taking charge of the house for the next two days, conducting interviews for counselor and supervisor positions. The boys at Tilden were understandably anxious about the whole situation so I made huge dinners for them to settle things down. I also had to make sure all the reports were made regarding Gerald and

Garret as well as for the incident at Tilden. Dion who was stabbed was now in stable condition. In the confusion at Tilden, no one had called his mother. On the phone with me, she cried and then was angry we hadn't told her right away. She was going to visit him that day in the hospital. On the plus side, the downtown agency finally pulled through, sending counselors who wanted extra-time from the Bronx, one of whom was interested in the supervisor position at Tilden.

Back at my home, I relieved Herman who had called Gerald's mother just out of the hospital. I made another phone call to her, my second that day to a grieving mom. She was frantic at the thought his father had taken him. I had to tell her there was not much our agency could do. The father had not lost custody of the child nor had a court ordered the boy's placement. We had called the police to file a missing person's report and told them that the father had taken him without agency consent. I put her in touch with an agency social worker. A report for Garret was also filed. I suspected he had gone back to his sickly uncle's apartment in Brooklyn to hang out with his friends in Prospect Park. Or had he gone in search of his older sister? With us, he had been a quiet kid who was grateful to live in what he called a nice house. He got along with Ethan, with whom he shared a room and kept his side neat as Ethan did not. He never complained and was a bit of a loner. When I spoke to Luis about the night at the movies, he told me Garret took the bus with him and his girl but then stayed on it when they got off to go to the movie. He said he just wanted to ride around. Maybe he felt like a third wheel. We had registered him for his freshmen year at the high school down the block, and he seemed to look forward to starting. Other than accepting a bribe from Nat, he had gone under the radar, as Ronnie Byars used to say, where he himself wanted to be. I talked to Ethan who said Garret had gotten a phone call that really upset him but he wouldn't say why or whom he spoke to. In the morning when Ethan woke up, Garret was already gone.

I was unusually worried about this boy who had been with us only for a short while. Fact is, I had grown increasingly numb over the years of work as a supervisor. I think if a couch had really been set on fire, and not just in jest as the boys had done with Mr. Al, nicknamed Easy Al by them ever since that prank, I probably would just tell one of the boys to fill a bucket and put it out as I got up to reheat my coffee in a kind of functioning shellshock. But there was an innocence still about Garret along with a quiet acceptance of what had happened to him.

I hired for my own house one of the counselors sent from the Bronx to do weekday sleepovers at Tilden. Just in time. I had to pick up my daughter in the Bronx and also wanted to stop on the way in Brooklyn to visit Garret's uncle's apartment. No one had answered the phone number we had for the uncle, but we had an address. His apartment was in an old rundown tenement house generously festooned with graffiti on a block with much newer apartment buildings. When I arrived, a group of guys hanging out a couple of doors down across the street took too much of an interest in me. I watched two of them stand and cross their arms, glaring at me as I entered the building where the uncle lived. I knocked and knocked on the door but no one answered. I went outside and saw Garret talking to the group that went back to the stoop where they had been sitting. When I called to him, he flashed me the peace sign and took off. I risked crossing the street to talk to the group and told them I was Garret's group home supervisor. I asked if anyone knew Garret's uncle and would they tell Garret to come back to the group home. He's not in trouble. There was a long moment of astonishment that I had approached them and then ridicule from two guys who had gotten up to stand behind me.

"What the fuck would we know where that old man's at?"

"You coming here asking your questions. Should know better, supervisor man."

An older man in the group raised his hand to them and took me aside. He told me not to worry about the kid. They had him covered, and the uncle was down with that.

"Thanks for looking out for G. Now best to leave. Know what I'm saying?"

I took his advice. In the car, I wondered if the older man was the uncle. I knew I'd probably never see Garret again. Another kid lost to the street. I thought I could not be sadder than I already was.

I had a long talk with my mom when I picked up Ariana.

"I always thought you married too young, Tony. Lisa was ready but you weren't. With the way you think, maybe you'll never be."

We laughed because she knew it was one of my pet peeves, my Woodstock-generation mindset in which marriage is property ruled by the state whereas love is "an ever-fixed mark."

"That's ok too, my son. Just be open. You never know whom you might meet. The biggest accident is love. Who plots that out?"

I told her about my accident with Karrin.

"Sounds like the time wasn't right for you or her. That's what I mean about planning things out. Some people can. Your father had a check list. Others can't even though they might try hard. I think you're a go-with-the-flow type. Be who you need to be. I just want to see you happy with your own choices."

Out of compassion, I did not ask her what type she was. She was very glad to hear about my forthcoming interview with the university.

As I drove back to Staten Island, Ariana had a lot of questions for me, mostly about when I was going to stay at the house again. She told me Lisa had told her I had work to do and that I loved her very much and would always be there for her like her mom. I told Ariana my love for her will never change, and yes, both Lisa and I would always be there for her. I did not stay long at Lisa's apartment. It felt very awkward to ask her how her affair was going, though it was the burning issue in her life. I also did not want to risk showing the hypocritical anger I felt. Nor did I mention the interview. I wanted her to feel free of my future. It was increasingly clear to me also that I could not see a future with Lisa beyond friendship although it felt too soon to realize that. She was still my wife, and for many years, we felt we were right for one another.

Over the next few weeks, things quieted down. Tilden got a new supervisor, a single lad just out of college, idealistic, enrolled in a doctoral program in psychology and eager to start work. My new counselor Jim proved a welcome addition. He was still doing sleepovers at Tilden and would take Sheila's daytime position with our house. He was an older man who, like Herman, had survived a difficult childhood, in and out of foster homes. After finally finishing high school, he joined the army, going overseas to Germany. Unlike Sheila, he was soft-spoken and laid back but like her, he had a way with the boys that convinced them it was not just another job for him. He also could put on his "boot-camp boots" when needed, he told me. In the initial interview, he had bluntly revealed that he had been pretty down and out, getting and losing a string of part-time and full-time jobs, all in retail, all lost due to the alcoholism he was recovering from. He not only needed a job he could believe in but a place to stay until he could put some funds together and get an apartment. After checking his background, I gave him a chance. He turned out to be what he said he would be, a good counselor and cook. He had shown up at the right time. A most welcome serendipity!

We certainly could use all the help we could get when two new boys eventually arrived to replace Garret and Gerald, the latter apparently swept off to California by the father. One of the new boys, Sean, had been freed for adoption but it never worked out. He had run away from his last foster home, lived on the street for a while, and ended up in a Queens hospital with pneumonia. At sixteen, he had seen more than enough of tough times. He was only too happy to come to our house, and he stayed that way, thankfully, working hard to catch up in school and getting along with the other boys who looked up to his hard-won street smarts, although he told them over dinner one night there was no such thing as street smart. "If you that smart, why you in the street in the first place?" The other boy Mike, 15 years old, was a different story. He was bitter over being placed by his father who, after Mike's mother died, had remarried a woman with three young children. Up until then, Mike had been an only child. After moving with his father into their new house and family in Howard Beach, Mike soon stopped attending high school, hanging out with a bad crowd. His stepmother found a stolen stereo-system and a switch-blade in his room. He threatened her when she went to confiscate it. The father felt he had to take action and had him placed. We worked hard to get him to laugh. His eyes were always elsewhere when we tried. During my interview with him, when I told him to give our home a chance to help him, he smirked and said cryptically, "I'm working on it. Got my own stuff going down. Don't worry. No problem." He wouldn't explain.

Meanwhile, with things seemingly quiet for the time being, I was spending more and more time with Ariana, greatly appreciating her. The way she greeted me lit me up like nothing else. This was always true, and now more than ever. She still asked me questions about the boys in the home. "Where's Nando?" as she called Fernando. "How's John?" I had to explain how they both had gone to live with family.

"Why did they leave now? And they never said good-bye to me."

"They told me to tell you they would miss you and your mom. Maybe when things settle down, we can have they come back for a farewell party. In the meantime, let's make them a good luck card, and we can mail it to them at their new home."

She also questioned why people put their children in a group home in the first place. Why send them away if they are your family? When I told her how families sometimes go through hard times, she looked deeply worried.

"Is that what is happening to us, daddy? Are you and mommy going away?"

I reassured her nothing of the sort, but her fear burned in me the way it burned in her. I gave her a long hug, hiding the tears in my eyes. Lisa and I agreed to have more dinners together. The awkwardness we felt toward each other counted for little in the face of what Ariana was feeling. What sense can a child make of one's essential aloneness? It takes a lifetime to come to terms with it. A path divides or changes course. One horizon blots out; another opens up. One says flippantly "move on," but the question is what to keep, what to let go? For the time being, all Ariana needed to feel was that we both would be there for her.

The interview at the university went well. The chair asked me what was my favorite Renaissance poem and was impressed that I knew Latin so well, reciting some lines from Milton's poem written for his drowned friend, "*Epitaphium Damonis*." I had memorized parts of it to help me deal with my own grief. A few weeks later, the Dean called to offer me the job. The length of time indicated I wasn't their first or even second choice although the pace at which such things occur going up the academic ladder is often slower than it takes orange peel to rot. The Dean did say he admired the work I had been doing in the group home. "That kind of experience will come in handy with some of our own students here." The pay for this full-time, tenure-track gig as an assistant professor of English was just a little more than I was getting in the group home. I mulled over the offer about in my mind for a day. There had been few requests for my portfolio, but this had been the one interview. I'd probably have to wait another six months or so for the next hiring cycle. Overall, it was a dismal job market in the humanities. I took the job. I had very mixed feelings about leaving the group home though I knew it was time. The new boy Mike accelerated my need to get out.

One weekend, two of his older friends from Queens showed up at the house in a Fleetwood Cadillac. Jamie on duty told me they were well dressed and polite, wearing gold chains and sunglasses they didn't take off. Mike asked permission if he could go for a drive with them. Jamie uneasily granted it but told him to be home no later than 10. Before allowing him to go off, she had also asked one of the friends to show her a driver's license. "You know, it's like when you try to buy cigarettes, they ask for ID. That's all, guys" Jamie joked with them, and the driver complied. "Here you go, lady, no problem, No problem." She copied down his information, one Salvatore Salerno with a Bronx address. When she asked him how he met Mike, he said he had moved to Queens since getting that license and he knew Mike through his aunt who lived in Howard Beach. "Yeah, we're almost cousins, heh Mikey?" Sal said. "No, Sal. Like a brother to me," Mike said. She also tried to call Mike's father but he didn't answer. Asked where they were going,

Mike said just a drive around, and they'd go for pizza somewhere for dinner. He promised to be home by 10. When Jamie made the check of rooms before retiring herself for the night, she found Mike asleep in bed at 11 so he probably came back at 10 although he had not told her he was back as he should have. The next day, when she took out the garbage from the counselor's room, she found a bloody shirt in the trash bin. When she brought it in the house, Sean, his roommate, said it was Mike's, but Mike denied it.

While Mike went to school that Monday, Herman and I searched his belongings. We found eight hundred in cash deftly hidden under one of his drawers which had to be totally pulled out to find it. He claimed the cash had been given him by his father. His father when he finally returned our call told us this wasn't true and that the friend Sal was bad news. He was a known thug in the neighborhood there. It became apparent that Mike had been paid to do some dirty work, and the bloodied shirt was evidence of what he had done or witnessed. When I spoke one on one with the boy, he laughed for the first time when I asked him whose blood was on the shirt.

"I don't know. I didn't catch his name."

"But it's your shirt. I know that because Mr. Jim bought it for you the first week you came here."

"Yeah, but I lent it to some guy to wear after he spilled pizza all over his shirt."

"So what, you gave him the shirt off your back?"

"No, I had it in my backpack in case I had to stay over."

"And the blood?"

"Yeah, his. Heh, he got wise with Sal. I tried to break it up. His nose was bleeding. That's all. You know, guys acting stupid. We made up, we made up, ok? Nothing to worry about."

"And what about the money?"

"Brought it with me. I did some jobs round the neighborhood before I got here. I didn't tell my dad because he would have taken it. Now you got it. See what I mean?"

"What kind of work did you do?"

"I was helping the butcher, you know, cleaning up. Heh, I can give you his number if you want."

When I called and introduced myself, one Lou Rossi, owner of the pork store, told me he knew Mikey, "a good kid," who did some odd jobs around the store. "Is there a problem?" he asked. "Just verifying where he got the money. Thank you."

At least, that part of the story apparently cleared up. I felt like turning the bloodied shirt over to the police, and when I asked Jim, he agreed. "No telling what that kid's up to. Howard Beach? Mobster land. Maybe he's being recruited. Maybe stabbed someone. Who knows what they asked this kid to do for that money? May never find out but got to try. Just my two cents."

I called the police. I also told Mike he could not have any contact with Sal from now on, that his father called Sal a thug, "*mafioso*" the actual word his father used. Mike just shrugged his shoulders.

"Ok, Mr. D. If that's what I gotta do. You boss here. But big dots about Sal. And that money, that money's mine."

"It still is. I'm only holding it for you."

A detective came to the house, and we gave him the shirt and Sal's address and license number. He interviewed Mike, who was angry with me at first for calling the police and then cooperated, repeating the same story he had told me. The detective told me he'd get back to me about the blood on the shirt and whatever information he could give me on Mr. Salerno. He never did, and my own phone calls went unreturned. My whole staff now felt very uneasy about Mike. We never found out the truth. A week later, in the middle of the night, as his roommate Sean told us, Mike left with all his stuff. He saw him get into a big car parked right outside the house. He never said where he was going. We filed a missing person's report and told his father. I also left a message for the detective. That was the last we ever heard about the boy. He left a chill in all of us.

I told Lisa about my job offer. She congratulated me and then worried about my living arrangements. Would I continue at the group home? How often would I see Ariana? I told her I had requested a two-day schedule from the Dean as I planned to commute the hundred miles by car from Staten Island to New Haven at least for the first semester.

"And then what? Even if it's for two days, the traffic will be horrendous on 95."

"Two days a week, I can deal with it. I'll leave the group home but first I have to make arrangements with the agency to replace me. I can't just give two weeks' notice or something. It's not fair to the boys and my staff. Then maybe I'll get a studio apartment in the north Bronx. That'll cut a third off the trip. I'll make it work. Every second I can get I'll be there for our daughter."

Neither one of us knew what to say next. We looked at each other and then looked away. The silence was painful. I had to ask.

"What are your plans?"

"My plans? No change."

"How is it with Bill? You're still..."

"I've been wanting to tell you but I have to make up my own mind first."

"What?"

"Well, he's talking about living together."

"And?"

"I'm not sure."

"Too soon?"

"Hello, we're still married."

"That hasn't been true for, how many months now? How long have you been seeing him?"

"Not as long as you were seeing what's her name."

More silence.

"I was trying to forgive you, Tony. I really was. Then I got emotional at work one day. I had just gotten off the phone with my mother who asked me how we were doing. I told her we were trying to work things out. I didn't tell her how you still had this other woman in your heart. Bill saw me crying and asked what was wrong. I ended up telling him the whole story. He told me how his wife had cheated on him and things never worked out."

"So he caught you at a weak moment. Forgiveness went out the window. I understand."

"But you had her in your heart. You probably still do. How can I live with that? How can you?"

"We broke it off. Imagine breaking off with Bill. There'd be spillover. Pain."

"And a lot of denial, self-denial and faking it."

"Self-sacrifice. Doesn't sacrifice mean to make things holy?"

"What are you talking about?"

"Marriage is like joining a religious order."

"Gee, and I thought it was a celebration of love."

"Love needs no law. It's its own law."

"That's something you must have read. Let's focus on where we are now. Save the philosophy for your students."

"We used to talk about these things. You did say you have to make up your mind. You're doing your own philosophy there. But whatever. You're right. What do we do? You want to answer your boyfriend. He's pressuring you."

"No, he's not for your information. It's more from me. I want to get on with my life. I feel half-married."

"Yes, my father told my mom we should make a clean cut. That we're a disgrace."

"Easy for him to say. I remember how he greeted you with a slap in the face when your family came over for Easter dinner."

"Well, that was just after you told my mom I was cheating on you. Besides, it was more a performance from him, an honor thing. He certainly sat down to eat the dinner we cooked."

"Your father could eat in a tornado."

"Yeah, he'd be sure to save the leftover tortellini before he ducked in the basement."

We laughed, happy for a moment's distraction, a ghost of what we once felt.

"Yes, but all that doesn't help us now, Tony. No matter what others say, it's our decision."

"Well then, let's say it outright. Let's officially separate. But please don't let the guy move in or move into his big house for a while, I guess. For Ariana's sake."

"I won't. But you know this is not only about my feelings for him. It's about us, about my feelings towards us."

"And about your own life too outside of us."

"And that's what's hardest to see."

"Agreed. I feel the same way. But then again, can one see oneself alone, outside of all relationships, as if one were piloting a boat?"

"Well, there's a lot of fish in the sea."

"Maybe we found that out too late."

"Too late for us now. Yes. It feels that way."

With my job beginning in the spring semester, I made my announcement downtown of my intent to leave in January, giving the agency ample time to find a replacement for me. I also told my staff, holding off telling the boys until after the holidays. As I thought he would, Herman said he was interested in the job, and I said I would fully recommend him for the job after he had his own brain examined. He laughed.

"My wife does that for me, Tony. And I am a little crazy. Just like you."

Jamie gave me a big hug and wished me well, saying she'd like to stay in touch once things settle down. I said I'd like to also once my head stopped spinning from all the change ahead.

"In a way, the most important thing about you is not changing. It's the work you're doing, another extension of it, just much less stressful, like the one I'm doing by getting a sociology degree."

"And what work is that? Jamie, are you accusing me of idealism?"

"Me? I'd never do such a thing. It's more like a commitment to what's going on now, not some idea or ideal. It's a calling, a calling to help out."

"O that's what that rash is on my legs."

"Yes, it's telling you to move on but keep to the path. You'll always be a homie."

We laughed and hugged.

I showered all the boys with gifts that Christmas. Ariana and Lisa came to the house for Christmas day dinner with the meal she had helped make. She wanted to do something for the boys, at least for the four boys who had nowhere else to go for the holidays, Luis, Marcos, Sean and Ethan. Luis chose not to stay at his aunt's so he could see his girlfriend. Marcos's mother was away but made sure to have a long call with him Christmas morning. Sean and Ethan had no one. The one family member Ethan had contact with, his aunt, had died, and Sean was long since a ward of the state. Our social workers had tried in vain to locate extended family for both of them. In vain. Hard to imagine at 16 and 13 years old to have no family in one's life. But that was the sad case. On the surface, they both took it in stride, doing ok in the home and school. The last thing they wanted to do was talk about it. I would wait for them to say something or show some emotion, but they would never bring the subject up. I'd reassure them many times if they needed to talk, I'd listen. Ethan would just say he's ok and weakly smile though I know he was close to his aunt whose sudden death from stroke we found out about a month after she died. Sean would just say, "What's the point? I got to live my own life. No choice." My leaving would just be another change they had come to expect as their lot in their young life. But I could not help but feel the sorrow they must have hidden deep inside. A sadness beyond coming to terms with though one must not give up trying, its denial or dismissal leading to a kind of emotional suicide or apathy or outright violence against others.

Herman was approved as my replacement. I knew he would be both because of the welcome my recommendation received by Leo, the director, who was loath to conduct interviews with strangers seeking to work with children in our care, especially for a live-in position. That was the usual case as my own experience hiring showed.

After the holidays, when all the boys returned, I announced I would be leaving to teach in a university and replaced by Mr. Herman, there at the dinner table with his wife Vicky whom in the weeks before I had hired as a part-time counselor so she could get to know the boys. A chorus of "no way" from some of the boys greeted my announcement. Bobby immediately stood up to shake my hand across the table, congratulating me. He would be leaving soon himself, graduating high school that year and returning to his mother's new apartment near Arthur Avenue to live with her and his brother Lennie. Sitting right next to me, José threw up his hands and sighed, shaking his head. Marcos didn't seem to understand, asking "when will you be back, Mr. D?" The other boys, a bit stunned at first, had little further reaction except for Adam who to my surprise took it the hardest, leaving the table immediately while shouting "That's just great, great." I followed him out into the hallway and coaxed him back to the table. "You gonna miss out on my spaghetti and meatballs? Come back. Sit down." He turned, wiping tears from his eyes, saying, "This sucks, Mr. D. Really sucks." I realized he left the table as much out of anger and disappointment as the need to hide his hurt feelings, any display of which was taboo among most of the boys. I told him I would be back to visit and would definitely miss him too. When I went to give him a little hug, he shrunk back. "I'm ok, Mr. D." He did return to eat. I explained to all the boys that it would be another month or so before I actually moved out, and Mr. Herman and I would make sure everything would work out.

Over the next few weeks, I made sure to speak one on one with the boys as well as in a group at the supper table. José, who with Bobby and Jimmy had lived the longest with me, proved the most despondent, and I spoke to him the most. He had visited a couple of weekends Fernando and his mother in the Bronx. The possibility of his moving in there was looking up, with the mother having gotten a much better job and Fernando's working part-time helping out while attending community college full-time. The father had also contributed though he was not told about the prospect of José's moving to the Bronx. That would have to be smoothed out, seeing how José had not too long ago tried to stab him. I reminded José that the success his brother was meeting was also within his grasp if he stayed focused on his school. He told me how he liked Anita, Fernando's mother, who was treating him like a stepmom would, asking him to think about if he'd like to come live with her and his brother. After a few talks concentrating on the positives ahead of him, José appeared to forgive me for planning to leave. He told me he would miss me but was glad I got the job I always wanted. With his head down, he told me, "I wish you were my dad, Mr. D." A startling expression of love from the boy who had called himself "Dr. Drop" for years. I told him if I were, I'd be proud to have him as a son. He cried a bit, looking down. "Give me a hug," I told him. He hesitated a moment and then did. I cried too.

Jimmy's reaction was to laugh it off when I spoke to him one on one.

"I know that, Mr. D. Why you telling me again? I know. You'll miss me a lot. That's ok. I'll be ok. You too. Don't worry."

I had to chuckle how he was consoling me, sensing perhaps how I felt I was abandoning him. And yet, he had been one of the boys to yell "no way" at my announcement. His own family situation was not promising, to say the least. His sister Gena had decided to have her mother's boyfriend Rocky's baby, and the four of them lived together off and on, depending when Rocky would show up from one of his disappearances. His father, the urban cowboy who had once ridden around our neighborhood flashing a pistol, had disappeared. His brother Sammie remained in Pennsylvania with a maternal aunt. Jimmy wanted to stay on the island where, to his credit, he had a large network of friends and work connections from holding part-time jobs. He had also been a good kid to have in the group home, mostly respectful of others, following the rules, doing his chores, keeping a clean room, eager to share a laugh. His stay with me of nearly six years outlasted more than a score of other boys who had come and gone. Jimmy was a tried and true "homie," and some of the boys would greet him with that term as a tease, "heh, here's my homie." Jimmy would smile at the taunt because he knew it was a term of affection and acceptance. The one rage he had shown against Miguel during a baseball feud proved anomalous, thankfully. It was doubtful, however, if he would graduate from high school, his grades always borderline failing or failing though he would work diligently with a tutor. Despite his family's lack of support beyond his sister Gena, who would call him regularly, he showed no bitterness, accepting it blankly as a matter of fact. He was essentially on his own, and with that knowledge in his eyes, he looked at me after my announcement as just someone else he loved who would leave him on his own. I had also felt my leave taking as a betrayal of the children I cared for, and that too must have shown in my face when I tried vainly to console Jimmy.

Marcos when I spoke to him just told me he was thinking of leaving soon too. His mother Titi had moved in with a man in a big Brooklyn apartment, and they offered him a spare bedroom at school year's end in June. A recent home visit had gone well according to the social worker who was impressed, having visited the place before and after Marcos's visit and meeting both times with Titi and her lover Cesar, who was a lawyer. Marcos had his doubts, however, as confided in me: "Not sure if I want to move out, Mr. D. Had some good times here. My mom, yeah, she's always worried." I guess Marcos didn't recall the attempt on his life by Ricardo or his drug-induced psychosis when he thought his mother had been kidnapped by the Nixon. The good times he thought of were probably the free-for-alls with Willie. There were certainly enough reasons for Titi to worry about his safety and sanity.

"You know how much your mom loves you, and you love her too. I think the move to her new home would work out for both of you."

"She worries too much. And that guy now."

"You mean Cesar? Do you get along with him?"

"Yeah but...he's...you know...like strict."

"Well, you let some good times roll here, Marcos. Maybe it's time to get strict with yourself. More effort in school. That's probably what Cesar wants, no? I know your mom would love that."

"Yeah, she loves him, I guess."

"I was saying she'd love it if you did better in school."

"O that. Yeah. Guess so."

"And how about Cesar. Does he make you laugh?"

"I dunno. Wait. What do you mean?"

"You know does Cesar have a sense of humor?"

"Yeah, he laughs. I've seen it."

"So that's good. He's not only strict. Overall, it sounds like it's worth a shot."

"A shot? What?"

"Moving in with your mom and Cesar. A few more weekend visits will help you make up your mind. Give it some time. No pressure on you."

"O, ok."

The other boys did not have much of a reaction or at least did not show it to me if they did. Jorge just shook my hand and said, "Good luck to you, sir." He was probably bound to live sooner or later with his aunt who was in the process of obtaining a bigger apartment. I spoke to the newest boys Ethan and Sean together in the room they shared. They would probably stay in placement at the house at least until after they were eighteen. Both at first smiled a bit awkwardly when I asked them how they felt about the coming change. Ethan shrugged his shoulders and said, "I'm good. Hope things work out for you." Sean said, "Yeah, we good. Good luck with that, Mr. D. Don't worry about us. Mr. Herman's cool. He'll do the job." That he said "us" and thought I'd worry indicated Sean had made connections to the home in just a few months. I told him he was like a big brother for Ethan, had to set a good example and give him good advice. "Yeah, he could keep his stuff on his side," Ethan piped up, making Sean chuckle. "Sorry yo. Just folding my laundry. But I know what you're saying, Mr. D. No problem. He's my homie. We cool, right E?" Ethan lit up a little and smiled.

Their evident camaraderie was encouraging to see. Together they could make a stand. So far they had put up a brave front against a world that had not been kind to them. Sean was more practiced at it. I saw that as mostly a positive thing, even an admirable strength given their previous trauma. On the other hand, I knew such a front often not just hides but denies one's deeper, sorer feelings, leading to callousness. This was a tendency I saw with many of the boys who tried to deaden themselves as a form of self-protection. It also appeared to me a widespread danger and much more so among men than women. I struggled against it too. My awareness of the problems with being cool, so close to cold, did not always prevent me from not having enough compassion for the suffering of others. This would lead to remorse, self-hatred, and a simmering resentment, a "whatever" attitude, a vain, cynical attempt to convince oneself and others that one does not "give a shit." It is a vile expression, implying giving a shit is what we do when we do express empathy though one never hears someone say, "I give a shit." I found myself saying it to myself often, waving the red flag of self-deception, and I knew it. In this case, risking embarrassment and the perception of insincerity, I told Ethan and Sean I'd miss them, asking for a group hug. Sean smirked a bit at Ethan and then looked at me and said, "sure." "I need it," I told them. As we hugged, Sean repeated to me, "We'll be ok. Don't worry."

All the change coming my way privately unnerved me although I would not tell anyone I was afraid. What right did I have to feel that way when the boys were facing so much more uncertainty?

But my anxiety was real. Success and failure were hard on the heels of each other, a completed Ph. D., new job and place to live, a failed marriage and looming divorce, happy to get out of the group home but feeling sad and guilty in leaving the kids. Most of all, worry about the impact of all this on Ariana, and, to my daily surprise, the deepening grief I felt over having said goodbye to Karrin.

I secured a furnished studio apartment in New Rochelle, about an hour's drive to the university, and would move there in a month, a couple of weeks after I had begun teaching. Mr. Herman and his wife Vicky threw me a farewell party. All the boys and staff were there as were Ariana and Lisa, more for our daughter's sake than anything else. She wanted to say good-bye to the boys, and we wanted to give her a sense of closure. Herman had also invited Sheila who showed up just in time with an apple pie she had cooked. The guys were happy to see her again, and when she revealed the pie she had baked, a favorite with the boys, Jimmy cried out, "Now I'm really happy to see you." "O so you're that way, huh? Sure enough," Sheila said. "Come and get it. Enough for all of you but Mr. D gets first cut." "He always did," said José, and Lisa confirmed, "I know the feeling." The double tease made everyone laugh. I thanked Herman, Vicky, and Sheila and made a little farewell speech to the boys about how much it meant to me to have lived with them. "Be strong and be good to yourself. Promise me. That's how I want to think of you." I cut my speech short to avoid another round of tears on my part.

I left that weekend, leaving the furniture that Lisa had not taken to Herman. The new job kept me focused for a while, a relief from the way my head spun living alone in the new small apartment which afforded a tiny though most welcome view of Long Island sound. For a while, I lost myself in teaching, overpreparing courses, as I quickly realized, the students scaling back my expectations of them when I received their first round of papers. I told them how teaching in a prison and living in a group home had helped prepare me to teach at the university. "Now I said, teaching in a prison, not living in one." They found that amusing, not the kind of background they expected from a professor, I guess. I shared quite a few anecdotes about the group home, about how I was still trying to absorb all the insights into people's lives that such work afforded. After class, one student hung back to ask me, "Why didn't you become a social worker, professor? Seems like that's where your heart is at." I thanked her for the question and told her my greatest drive was to share joy with people and that literature almost more than anything else was a source of delight and insight into life. "If I can share that, what bigger reward?" She told me she was an artist and sharing the joy was what her painting was all about. When I asked, she hesitantly showed me her sketch book filled with portraits of animals, homeless people and abandoned houses. It was evident she was very gifted, and I told her that. She beamed.

Despite some early success at teaching, the future seemed like blurred type on a page. A deep depression came over me as the weeks went by. I had thought freedom from the stress of living in a group home would be a great relief. It wasn't. To unwind, at first I drank and smoked even more than I usually did, but then forced myself to go on long walks around a sound-side park, trying to stay one step ahead of the complete sense of let-down I was feeling like a balloon losing air. I'd find a secluded place to sob and then couldn't get the tears out. I felt more dumbfounded than anything else as if I were shell shocked. Ariana stayed with me every other weekend, helping us both get used to the new situation. I asked her about her mom's friend Dr. Bill, and she said he was a nice man but she missed me and wanted her mom and me to live together again so we would be a family. I told her we would always be her parents and her mom and I were best of friends. Just the husband-wife part had not worked out as we had hoped. She cried a little and said she felt like a group home kid. "Why don't families stay together? Why can't you and mommy get along like you used to?" How to answer such questions to an twelve-year-old when the parents too are baffled for some ultimate explanation? "The cause may be too deep ever to find," as the poet Anthony Hecht puts it, although on the surface, reasons are commonly evident enough. I would stop searching although that would take years. All I could do now was reassure our daughter we would always be there for her, always be her parents who loved her dearly.

One Sunday in May, when I dropped Ariana off, Lisa told me she was planning to move in with Bill in a few months and wanted a divorce. "Let's make a clean break," she told me. I sighed and agreed, seeing little point in delaying what appeared inevitable.

Summer rolled in. It was amazing and alarming not to have any work responsibilities. I kept expecting a knock on my door or a phone call from the agency looking for a headcount for my house. I was solo now. I poured myself into reading and writing that would hopefully lead to the publishing I had to do to obtain tenure. I tried to take up writing poetry again but every time I did, my feelings for Karrin emerged, mackling every line. Music helped emotions come out that I wanted otherwise to drown. One weekend when Ariana wasn't visiting, I decided to call the group home to speak to Jamie. I had spoken to Herman during weekdays a few times as well as some of the boys on the phone. Herman told me all was going well at the house, saying he would spare me the details when I asked for some. I wasn't sure why I wanted to speak to Jamie other than say hello and chat. She answered the phone and said, "Well hello, Tony. I was just thinking about you. Sorry I missed the farewell party. How are you?" We had a long talk. We agreed to get together, meeting at the Metropolitan Museum of Art the following Saturday when she wasn't working.

When we met on the front steps, we hugged in delight and then both felt a little awkward. This was no longer employer and employee. We were there to see if friendship and something more were in the wings for us. But it was more awkward for me than I had imagined. Friendship, hopefully, something more, very doubtful. Some emotions were welling up, holding me back, making me feel a little ashamed and uneasy. It did not take Jamie long to sense that something in me was elsewhere. As we strolled around the museum, she said she was glad we were keeping in touch but, given how her other friends acted, she had low expectations.

"Everyone's so busy, it's hard to give friends, even close friends, the time needed to keep a friendship going."

"I hope we will," I told her. "I need a friend, a friend just like you. You're a hard person not to keep in touch with."

"I think that's a compliment," she replied.

"It is," I said. We laughed.

We found ourselves in front of a small painting by Millet, "Retreat from the Storm." It depicts a mother and child fleeing through a dark ominous landscape, their clothes whipped by the wind. She appears frantic and the child gray and sickly. With one hand, she clutches to her chest a bundle of faggots swaddled in a blue cloth, trying to keep it dry. With the other, she leads the child along by the arm.

"A beautiful rendering of a terrible moment," Jamie said.

"Yes, one must take care saying that. Suffering isn't beautiful."

"Tell that to De Palma or Stone. I just saw *Platoon* last week for a class."

"Never saw that one. Did see *Scarface*. I thought that one glorified violence."

"Yes, say hello to my little friend."

"*Platoon* glorifies?"

"Hmm. Not sure. More purposely, I guess, more like a criticism than an endorsement of violence than *Scarface*. Stone felt he had to show explicit scenes to make an impact. It's a very disturbing film."

"Well, the war changed my mind about everything. That certainly made our own violence explicit. And I think of all the gung-ho war films I saw growing up. *Platoon* from a review I read sounds like it de-glorifies."

"See it for yourself and let me know what you think. It sickened me in a way *Scarface* didn't. It's as if America plays the role of Tony Montana in *Platoon*."

"That's a chilling way to put that. Wow. You know I was almost drafted? Yes, I sat in a cafeteria in college with a couple of hundred other guys listening over the loudspeaker as random birthdates were assigned a number in the coming draft order. I had two hundred something, but the guy next to me got ninth. He was in Vietnam a few weeks later. Next time I saw him he had only one leg."

"Christ, how horrible. But lucky for you. Would you have gone?"

"Not sure. Probably not. A terrible decision I didn't have to face. Fate didn't unwind its thread that way."

"More like Uncle Sam."

"O that guy. Just as imaginary as Lady Luck, I guess."

"Funny how luck's a lady when she's more like a bitch."

"Let's not go there."

"Sounds like you already were there."

"I'm still there. A toy in the hands of Madame Fate."

"Better than Sir Fuck." That had us howling. The guard looked our way. Then Jamie asked me, "Divorcing? I'm sorry to ask."

"No, no, that's fine. Yes, it's been a long slide toward that, but Lisa and I aren't bitter with each other, thankfully, for our sake and Ariana's. It's more along the lines of big disappointment, you know, when a marriage fails compared to the high expectations once had."

"Kind of like the digestive system."

"Yes, yes, funny, Jamie. Fruit going out looks nothing like it was going in. No, it's more along the lines of heartache."

"O, I see. *Amor. Amor fati.*"

"You're too clever. But no, not love of fate. More like love as fate."

"It need not end in hurt, Tony."

"True. But right person at the wrong time? That's not a good deal."

"Sorry but I'm hearing Dr. John's voice go off in my head."

"Oh that song. No, that's the right place at the wrong time. But that would be a one-off situation. Mine's everyday."

"Oh well. I've been there or thought I was at the time. Not sure if time healed me. More like you make yourself forget with practice. Maybe it will work out for you? Better yet – make it work out either way. Just my two cents earned the hard way."

"Doubt it. Whatever. I'll let you know. So, so what about this painting?"

"Oh, ok, back to that. Harrowing the longer one looks at it. But a woman like the one in the painting wouldn't even get a chance to see it, much less hang it in her hovel. She couldn't afford it and wouldn't want to be reminded anyway."

"Yes, arm-chair pity now for us in a museum, I guess. What to do with such feelings? Speaking of which, how are your studies going?"

"Love it so far though much more reading than I thought. So time-consuming. Reading Marcel Mauss right now. *The Gift.*"

"There you go. I'll give a dollar to that homeless dude we saw outside the museum, a gift to him in honor of the mother and child in this Millet."

"Oh you've given more than that, I think. Yes? Heh, how's the teaching going?"

"Well, I'm learning to take small steps with most of my students. They're certainly not as privileged as the Yale students across the river so there's some envy there as if they were second or third class. But still a lot to offer the world."

"And still more privileged than most. I guess we're both fated in different ways to serve the less than privileged."

"Serve? Partly that, I guess. The group home also helped me get through the dissertation. There were benefits to not paying rent as I'm finding with a salary now a little more than I was making. You said the boys are doing ok?"

"Yes, Herman and Vicky are both understated but they have a good way with the boys so far. I'm sure they will be tested soon."

"Adam? Luis?"

"Herman told you? Yeah, those two are running a little wild since you left but we're roping them in. You are missed by some, José and Bobby especially. I get them to reminisce."

"I've spoken to them a few times. The whole place is on my mind constantly."

"I bet."

"How's next door doing?"

"Oh they're always complaining to us. Miguel was telling me how he hates all the behavior charts. They all do. And Linda, David's wife, has nothing to do with the boys at all. Miguel thinks she hates them. It's probably more than she bargained for."

"Why am I not surprised? I tried to tell minister David to lighten up. A kid like Miguel doesn't need a chart. Some of the boys would benefit, but even then, a light touch, make it fun in some way if that's possible. I learned that the hard way."

"Didn't you use charts at one time?"

"I did at downtown's insistence. Some of the kids had so many x's it didn't have an impact after a while. Every time they'd curse, they'd get x-ed. You gonna x me up, Mr. D?"

"You'd get some too on that score too, Tony."

"Fuck yes. But seriously, I found the charting too impersonal. More like an institution than a home feel to it."

"Well, if you can make that happen, great. And you mostly did, Tony. That feeling's still there with Herman. Not sure if David next door can pull it off."

"I did with some of the boys. It took a lot of learning from mistakes, and the learning is endless."

"For sure."

"I'm just kind of empty now. All that stress is gone, but the feelings for the boys remain. I have mixed feelings about the success of my own work there. Too many mistakes."

"Nat? That boy who almost killed Marcos? Willie? What can one do honestly? So traumatized by the time they get to us. Sad but seemingly incorrigible."

"Apparently some are, yes, I admit that. But still at that young age? I don't know. I was living there. Too often a part of the scene and not a director of it. Hard to strike a balance, turn one role on and the other off. I don't know what the answer is."

"Well, it was rarely a horror show. More like a family melodrama but without the family. There was as much if not more uproar in my own childhood house with my crazed brothers and stressed-out parents, for God's sake. You really tried. You cared. Still do. Go easy on yourself. You're enjoying teaching now, yes? Same kind of service but in a different way."

"Yeah, I don't have to get my students to brush before they go to sleep. They just sleep. A different kind of captive audience." We laughed.

"You know in a way teaching literature is a lot like the group-home work. You offer this intense interaction with strangers, you get to know them a little, reading their essays, talking with them about serious life-issues raised by the stories and poems, and then they're gone, out of your life, with the vast percentage never heard from again."

"But you never know what impact you've made later on in their life."

"That's more from reading Kafka or Sappho than anything they get from me."

"Well, just keep refilling the pitcher, Tony. Keep giving it all you've got, professor. What else can we do?"

"You're like a refresher course in life, Jamie. That's why the boys listen to you. They know it when they feel it like I always did with you."

"Thanks. I really hope things work out for you."

"And for you too, my dear. Let me know how your studies go. We will keep in touch, yes?"

"I'd like that. Let's."

We hugged and kissed on the steps of the museum, reluctantly letting go of our hands. We would phone each other once in a while until even that petered out. It was the last time I saw her.

The summer whizzed by. Before I knew it, I was back teaching. I finally realized I had carried around intransigent feelings long enough and took action. Come what may, I resolved to call Karrin.

Epilogue

She proved more than anxious for my call - we were married two years later. A year after that our son was born. Ariana not long after moved in to join us with Karrin's two children, a hybrid family living in the house we had bought from her ex-husband who proved generous. In some ways, this felt like another group home or a group family, a perspective my work with the boys brought into my life, a view from outside or beyond the traditional family as if I had been living in a tribe or camp the last decade. The six of us for a while lived in relative harmony. Lisa moved in with her doctor but hasn't remarried. To the relief of Ariana and all involved, Karrin and I have spent many holidays with Lisa and Bill. Lisa and I occasionally reminisce about life in the group home with a mixture of astonishment and sadness.

I kept in contact with the group home now and then, but outside of Fernando and Bobby with whom I stayed in touch, I mostly lost sight of the boys. Fernando has become a contractor with a small family of his own in New Jersey, Bobby a bus driver for the city of New York. We have happy memories of having lived together for so long at such a crucial period of their lives. José eventually moved in with Fernando and his mother but then moved away to the west coast with his girlfriend, had two children with her, and then apparently disappeared. He has not spoken to Fernando in years. At 20 years old, Jimmy left the group home for Tennessee where his father had some family. Juan out of nowhere called me to tell me he had graduated from the Fashion Institute of Design and was living with his boyfriend in upper Manhattan. He thanked me for putting up with his confusions and for encouraging him to be what he needed to be. It was a happy phone call though our only one. Word came in dribs and drabs about some of the other boys. Tony, famous for his "tee hee, tee hee" laughter, owns his own construction company on Staten Island. Marcos moved in with his mother, and Luis, after graduating, with his girlfriend. Ethan at sixteen disappeared out of the group home for parts unknown shortly after Sean, upon graduation, had moved to Queens for a job as a gas station mechanic. Jorge also graduated and moved in with his aunt. Adam too finished high school and moved into an apartment with a couple of friends.

Willie stands at the head of a long list of boys I wonder about. I often find myself dreaming that the boys and I are making mischief in my own childhood home, planning an adventure to get lost somewhere, free from all worry, taking any means possible to get there, dancing over electrical wires like fey people or finding a hole in a wall that opens to a river.

The last time I saw any of the boys was many years later. While shopping for groceries, I thought I recognized someone. I followed the person around a crowded aisle and came eye to eye with him. "Jorge? Jorge!" I exclaimed. He looked at me with a blank expression. "Yes, I'm Mr. D. Remember? The group home?" He nodded his head in recognition, shrugged his shoulders as if he didn't know what to say, and walked away.

About the Author

Anthony DiMatteo's memoir *Home Boys* draws on 10 years of living in a group home as a supervisor of ten boys. His published works include poetry collections, essays, reviews and a translation. His recent collection of poems *Secret Offices* regards a lifelong search for beauty and grace. Each search—each poem—begins accidentally, a secret from the seeker, a prerequisite for discovery. A previous collection *In Defense of Puppets* explores the way we imagine things when we speak for others or they for us. Though his essays and reviews have appeared in dozens of scholarly and literary journals, he considers *Home Boys* the most important work of his life. A professor of English, he has defended the mysteries of writing, literature and art at the New York Institute of Technology for nearly 40 years. He lives on the Outer Banks of North Carolina with his wife Kathleen O'Sullivan, an artist and musician. Please feel free to leave a trace at his e-tent: https://anthonydimatteo.wordpress.com

Apprentice House is the country's only campus-based, student-staffed book publishing company. Directed by professors and industry professionals, it is a nonprofit activity of the Communication Department at Loyola University Maryland.

Using state-of-the-art technology and an experiential learning model of education, Apprentice House publishes books in untraditional ways. This dual responsibility as publishers and educators creates an unprecedented collaborative environment among faculty and students, while teaching tomorrow's editors, designers, and marketers.

Eclectic and provocative, Apprentice House titles intend to entertain as well as spark dialogue on a variety of topics. Financial contributions to sustain the press's work are welcomed. Contributions are tax deductible to the fullest extent allowed by the IRS.

To learn more about Apprentice House books or to obtain submission guidelines, please visit www.apprenticehouse.com.

Apprentice House Press
Communication Department
Loyola University Maryland
4501 N. Charles Street
Baltimore, MD 21210
Ph: 410-617-5265
info@apprenticehouse.com • www.apprenticehouse.com

www.ingramcontent.com/pod-product-compliance
Lightning Source LLC
LaVergne TN
LVHW010558100826
845148LV00014B/2763

* 9 7 8 1 6 2 7 2 0 6 3 0 3 *